Black Women's Christian Activism

Seeking Social Justice in a Northern Suburb

Betty Livingston Adams

NEW YORK UNIVERSITY PRESS

New York and London

NEW YORK UNIVERSITY PRESS
New York and London
www.nyupress.org

References to Internet websites (URLs) were accurate at the time of writing. Neither the author nor New York University Press is responsible for URLs that may have expired or changed since the manuscript was prepared.

ISBN: 978-0-8147-4546-5

ISBN: 978-1-4798-1481-7

For Library of Congress Cataloging-in-Publication data, please contact the Library of Congress.

New York University Press books are printed on acid-free paper, and their binding materials are chosen for strength and durability. We strive to use environmentally responsible suppliers and materials to the greatest extent possible in publishing our books.

Manufactured in the United States of America

10 9 8 7 6 5 4 3 2 1

Also available as an ebook

BLACK WOMEN'S CHRISTIAN ACTIVISM

To Tirzah and Bethlehem

CONTENTS

ACKNOWLEDGMENTS

When I relocated to Summit, New Jersey, many years ago for what was to be an eighteen-month corporate transfer, I could not imagine the place this New York City suburb and its history would assume in my life. As my tenure came to be counted in years rather than months and the incongruity between the physical and imagined geography of the suburb became increasingly apparent, my curiosity turned into intellectual inquiry and my weekends into uncovering shards of the extraordinary story of African American church women concealed in the faded pages of the suburb's newspaper and the fragmented histories of the faith communities they had built and nurtured. A record of faith and courage against seemingly insuperable odds began to emerge, a record that introduced me to a tradition of African American women's engagement with religion and society.

In writing this book I have received many gifts and incurred debts far too numerous to recount in this small space. However, I would not have been able to complete this book save for a serendipitous—dare I say, providential—encounter with Glenda Elizabeth Gilmore. Her genuine warmth and interest transformed intellectual curiosity into the narrative of Christian activism I have tried to tell in these pages. She inspired me with her rigorous scholarship, challenged me with her insightful questions, and encouraged me with astute and usable feedback. I am eternally grateful for her mentorship and friendship so generously shared along this improbable journey.

I am also grateful for the support and collegiality of the Rutgers University History Department that made Seminary Place a "home away from home" for this corporate expat. I had the good fortune to receive the postdoctoral fellowship in Race and Gender History and spend a year as a Global Scholar in the Institute for Research on Women (IRW) and subsequently as an Associate Fellow in the Rutgers Center for Historical Analysis (RCHA). I am particularly grateful to Jennifer Hammer and Constance Grady at NYU Press for their unfailing advice, assistance, and guidance throughout this process.

The book is dedicated to my granddaughters, Tirzah Howard and Bethlehem Livingston Adams, my hope for the future.

Introduction

In 1897 twenty-seven-year-old Violet Johnson moved from Brooklyn, New York, to Summit, New Jersey, a place in the process of transforming from a country village into a New York City suburb. Within a year, the domestic servant had organized a Baptist church. Others would later extol her "genius for organization, religious, civic, social and industrial[:] institutions flourish at her touch."[1] The decision to create a sacred space for African American domestic workers thrust Johnson into public space and onto the path of Christian activism. For as the North Carolina native discovered, religious choices are rarely just about religion.

This book tells the story of the complicated intersections of politics and religion, race and gender, and place, space, and black women's quest for social justice in the early twentieth century. Black women like Violet Johnson, living and working in the northern suburbs, entered public spaces, shaped religious practices, and influenced the twentieth-century struggle for civil rights. Their faith and willingness to assume responsibility mattered in the churches they established, the institutions they built, and the communities they sustained. Their organizing made a difference.

This book interweaves the narratives of American religious space, women's space, and white middle-class space from the end of the nineteenth century to World War II, roughly 1898 to 1945. In examining the public presence of black women and making them visible in spaces generally considered masculine and white, this volume documents the contingent strategies and organizational models church women employed in the fight for social justice while also revising the chronology and trajectory of northern racial oppression and civil rights protest. Both religion and the suburbs emerge as discursive sites for the negotiation of meaning and power. By locating women's Christian activism in this historic moment, a departure from traditional emphases on race relations in the South or the post–World War II North, this book privileges the agency of ordinary, non-elite black women who were integral to the process of American suburbanization and the expansion of American Protestantism. It traces the development of their institutions and documents their struggle for social justice and civil rights, locally and nationally, over nearly five decades. It reperiodizes the history of the civil rights movement by showing how racial segregation worked in the North in the first half of the twentieth century.

This volume also documents the trajectory of Christian influence in an increasingly secular society. Missionary and temperance women turned to the woman suffrage movement and partisan politics to address housing, health, and employment in northern communities. However, they wielded less power in these secular institutions than in their autonomous religious organizations or the interracial church women's movement.

The book tells a story of national significance and amplifies the strategies Christian women used in their struggle for social justice. It offers a broad history anchored in the religious narratives of two women who emerged as leaders in New Jersey and the nation, one a domestic servant and Baptist lay leader, the other a seamstress and ordained Methodist minister. Violet Johnson (1870–1939) arrived in suburban New Jersey in 1897 with her white employers; in 1925 Reverend Florence Spearing Randolph (1866–1951) accepted an interim appointment to a fledgling African Methodist Episcopal (AME) Zion congregation in the same suburb and during the Great Depression built an institutional church that served the entire community. Among the first generation of free-born citizens of color, they came of age in the optimism of the post–Civil War era and shaped their worldview in the egalitarian message of Protestant evangelicalism and the Reconstruction Amendments. They expected to assume their place in a multiracial, Christian nation. However, confronted with increasing evidence of political and social retrenchment on the question of equality, these ordinary working women entered public space and challenged hegemonic assumptions of gender and race.

As women of the Victorian era, Johnson and Randolph participated in the discourse of true womanhood and separate spheres, a discourse often at odds with the gendered and color-coded society in which black women confronted both the *Woman Question* and the *Race Problem*, as Anna Julia Cooper eloquently phrased it in 1892.[2] Discriminated against because of their gender and race and having to wage discursive and material battles for physical and moral space, they experimented with various organizational models, yet retained "a vision of the potential strength and influence of a union of Christian women and faith in their willingness to assume responsibility."[3] This vision impelled them to transgress boundaries in their quest for just laws and an ethical transformation of the religious and political order—at times in concert with, but often in opposition to, black and white men and middle-class white women. Sometimes that meant simply standing up for the right to speak in church or to build a church on a street demarcated as *white* space. Other times it meant engaging in direct political action through the Woman's Christian Temperance Union (WCTU), the woman suffrage movement, the National Association for the Advancement of Colored People (NAACP), or the Republican Party. Often it meant sustaining autonomous organizations with meager earnings, while supporting male-led denominations and interracial women's organizations.

Initially, Johnson and Randolph translated their missionary and temperance activism into an instrument for reform. They gained national stature and achieved modest local improvements. In the 1920s, with the ballot in hand, they changed their language and their tactics and entered the political arena, adding politics to their Christian service. In contrast to women in the South, they were heard by Republican politicians. However, the religious and social conservatism of the interwar years and the devastation of the Great Depression brought a halt to their progress. The New Deal compounded their problems as relief proved illusory and elusive for black women and children.

This book develops several key themes. First, religion made a difference in women's organizational order. Viewing religion as an institution and a system of meaning, African American women advocated a *politics of civic righteousness*; that is, reforming civic institutions by placing morality and justice in the realm of public policy, laws, and institutions. They organized missionary societies and temperance unions to extend the work of the church in society. Later they turned to the women's club movement, the Republican Party, and the state to address deteriorating housing, health, and economic conditions in their northern communities. Second, black women's organizing in the North differed from that in the South. They made repeated attempts at interracial alliances as suffragists, ecumenical Protestants, and partisan Republicans. Third, the course of segregation differed in the North. Unlike the South, which forcefully settled the question of race relations in the 1890s, the northern pattern of segregation moved incrementally but steadily during the early decades of the twentieth century through the New Deal, tightening the color line and expanding demarcated white space. Fourth, the arc of justice bent differently in the North compared to the South. New Deal policies and practices spurred a suburban land grab and hardened a hierarchical and color-coded economic structure that compounded problems of housing, health, and employment for already beleaguered black communities.

Finally, suburban segregation in the twentieth century was no accident. The institutionalization of race and class differences was as much a part of the suburbs as the single-family detached home and lush lawn. Elite white suburbanites demarcated "white" space and attempted to remove black citizens whose presence, they feared, would lower the value of real estate—and undermine the status of an anxious white middle class. New Deal funds subsidized the recovery of the housing sector and fueled racial cleansing as a suburban strategy. The dilemma for suburban segregationists, however, was that they required a black presence to confirm their valorization of white space. As white northerners resorted to violence, intimidation, and legally sanctioned tactics to reify an imagined community and expand the color line, black church women maintained their vision of social justice based upon Christian principles and just laws. Eventually their vision found voice in the civil rights movement. Ultimately, this book argues that religion made a difference in the lives of ordinary black women who lived, worked, and worshiped on the margins. Their way of being religious inflected race and gender discourses and influenced economic and social issues in the first half of the twentieth century.

This analysis complicates our understanding of African American leadership and class status. While not the professional elite who are traditionally the subject of historical studies, these ordinary working women were unquestionably leaders in their communities and institutions. They took pride in their work as cooks, laundresses, and housekeepers and sought respect for themselves and their work. Yet, these women who earned their living as domestic servants and providers of domestic service were far more than their work. They created a forum in which they could be heard, a redoubt that contrasted with the increasingly oppressive local sites that sought to silence and erase the presence of working-class black and white citizens. E. P. Thompson would have recognized them as actors in an economic and social matrix whose experiences need to be understood in both cultural and economic terms.[4] Capturing the intersecting subjectivities in their *being* and *becoming* over decades adds to our understanding of gendered agency across class and racial boundaries.

The "Ideal Suburb" and Working Women

Between 1870 and 1910 developers and speculators transformed pasture land along railroad tracks in northern New Jersey into residential space, beginning the process of suburbanization in the quintessential suburban state. In the last years of the nineteenth century Summit, New Jersey, transformed itself from a bucolic village and summer retreat into the "ideal suburb."[5] Sitting more than five hundred feet atop the third Orange Mountain, and only twenty-five miles west of New York City, the six-square-mile town was an attractive stop on the Delaware, Lackawanna and Western Railroad. As technology changed business interactions and southern European immigrants changed urban geography, white middle-class entrepreneurs and corporate managers moved their families from the teeming city to the suburbs. Thus middle-class men could participate in the nation's industrial growth while ensconcing the family hearth in a homogeneous space, safely removed from urban heterogeneity.

Among the amenities awaiting prospective residents to the "ideal suburb" were a ladies' literary club, men's field club, several bustling retail businesses, a bank, weekly newspaper, and New York City entertainment. A public school, a private boarding and day school for boys, and a "French and English School for Young Girls and Ladies" added to the suburb's appeal. Residents also had their choice of religious institutions, including five local churches, a Young Men's Christian Association (YMCA), and the WCTU.[6] The suburb seemed ideal indeed.

Although the local newspaper editor and resident booster boasted, "We have no noisy, dirty manufactories that fill the town with a class of people, who, in themselves, are not very much desired in a strictly home village, such as ours," Summit was not the homogeneous suburb of middle-class imaginings.[7] East of the train station stood tenements that were home to the Polish, Italian, and German immigrants hired to construct the suburb's infrastructure. On the northern edge of town, beyond the macadamized roads, were more tenements that housed the families of the Assyrian and Armenian silk factory workers in an area mockingly dubbed "Weavers Court."[8]

Adding to the suburban diversity were African Americans who found seasonal employment at one of the three resort hotels. Primarily single men and women without familial or social ties, few remained in Summit beyond the summer season. Those who did most often worked as housekeepers, gardeners, or coachmen in the country homes of the Newark and New York business and managerial class who sought refuge in an area noted for its salubrious air and artesian wells. In the 1890s, Summit's African American population barely exceeded one hundred in a total population of nearly six thousand. Only three nuclear families could be counted among the suburb's black residents, and none owned real property.[9]

Yet in the interconnected web of race, gender, and class, white middle-class migration to the suburbs also expanded the geography of black women's presence. In June 1904 Leslie Pinckney Hill, an African American student at Harvard University and future NAACP executive, wrote to Booker T. Washington, principal of Tuskegee (Alabama) Institute, seeking about thirty persons to fill domestic positions in New Jersey's expanding suburbs. Opposed to the idea, Washington responded, "I rather feel that we should do everything we can to persuade our people to keep out of the large cities of the North, and in every way, it seems more satisfactory to suggest that the wisest thing would seem to be the training of the colored people who may be in the Oranges, rather than to import large numbers of others."[10]

Washington's disapproval notwithstanding, by the end of World War I southern-born African Americans constituted the majority of domestic service employees in the New York City suburbs. The demand for maids, cooks, gardeners, and chauffeurs continued through the interwar years, the golden age of suburbanization. From 1920 to 1930, Summit, New Jersey's population increased from 10,174 to 14,457. The black population remained relatively stable, though the rate of increase outpaced that of white residents, nearly doubling from 4.8 percent to 8.7 percent. By the mid-1930s, Summit's white population increased to over fifteen thousand and the black population peaked at about fifteen hundred, nearly 10 percent.[11]

* * *

Though often invisible in contemporary accounts and silenced by historians, black women were integral to the suburbanization process. In many respects, they made the suburban lifestyle possible. Swedish and Irish immigrants could not satisfy the demand for domestic servants, a perquisite of white middle-class status. As suburban historian Andrew Wiese notes, premier suburbs "often housed bustling communities of shopkeepers, mechanics, industrial workers and servants," including black women and men.[12]

At its root, the white, middle-class suburban ethos was contradictory and contingent. The maintenance of suburban space necessitated continual surveillance and patrolling of borders, for the race, class, and gender assumptions of the "ideal suburb" did not go uncontested. By the end of World War II, white suburbanites had had decades to work out strategies and to devise means to discriminate against African Americans in housing and labor and to decree areas as white spaces. The determination of black women in Summit to claim moral, civic, and physical space alerts us to the need to examine more closely these sites of contestation and race relations in a northern context.

Working Women and Religion in the Suburbs

Black working women played a crucial role in the Protestant missionary campaigns of the late nineteenth and early twentieth centuries. Following the Civil War, African American Baptists in the North organized separate congregations initiated and led by black ministers with the support of white clergy. Educated and trained in American Baptist Home Missionary Schools and seminaries like their white northern counterparts, black Baptists saw themselves as part of a reconstructed and multiracial Christian America.

Before long, black ministers began to chafe under the proscription of Northern Baptists and to resent being treated as "wards." Desiring more control over their ecclesiastical affairs, especially the ordination of ministers, in 1874 black Baptists in the Northeast organized the New England Baptist Missionary Convention (NEBMC) as an independent association with a territorial reach from Maine to Virginia.[13] By ordaining ministers and establishing churches, NEBMC created a religious space in which African Americans could control their ecclesial institutions and practices removed from the oversight and gaze of white Protestants. Black congregations led by trained men were envisioned as schools for teaching the principles of Christian citizenship suitable for a multiracial Christian nation.

Following Southern disenfranchisement in the 1890s, northern black Baptists adopted an explicitly political program that positioned their churches as a bulwark against the southern forces of white supremacy and Jim Crow. Cognizant of the public revisioning of the meaning of citizenship and the reformulations of race theory that informed that discourse, black Baptists sought to break the linkage between citizenship and whiteness. They challenged assumptions on race, critiqued government policies, and worked to create a shared racial and political consciousness among black men and women.[14]

While Northern Baptists shared an evangelical worldview and believed that theirs was the age of missions, black Baptists viewed the suburbs as a fertile mission field and another site for realizing the denomination's religious and political mission. Further, the predominance of African American working women made the suburbs important in the struggle for racial and political equality. For African Americans in the Northeast, the black church was the embodiment of an oppositional discourse; for middle-class white suburbanites it was, quite often, merely the source of a reliable workforce.

Working Women and "Woman's Work"

The world in which black women lived, worked, and worshiped at the turn of the twentieth century was gendered and highly sexualized. Even as urbanization and industrialization increased the demand for women in the workforce, working women suffered economically and socially in a sex-segregated labor market that relegated them to the lowest paying jobs and in a class-based society that regarded as morally suspect any woman who worked for wages. Single working women bore the brunt of the attacks from those who policed the boundaries of respectable behavior, especially middle-class reformers who disseminated and reinforced the image of "women adrift," who, as historian Joanne Meyerowitz notes, "became a symbol of the threats that industrialization and urbanization posed to womanhood and the family."[15]

In 1898 white sociologist Frances Kellor characterized single women as more immoral than their married sisters due to their less developed maternal sentiment, "the crowning honor of womanhood." Unlike the married woman who had the "protection" of a man to bridle her innate criminality, the single woman's "low morality" remained unchecked. The problem was compounded for black women, who, like black men, Kellor added parenthetically, were ruled by sexual passion.[16] Commenting further on the black working woman, married or single, Kellor attributed problems of labor exploitation to "her increasing inefficiency and desire to avoid hard work."[17] Ironically, Kellor, who helped found the National Urban League, advocated for better employment conditions for black women and worked closely with Sarah Willie Layten, future president of the black Baptist Woman's Convention and Kellor's successor as general secretary of the National League for the Protection of Colored Women.

Practitioners of the new social sciences were not the only ones who promoted images of black working women as "pathological." Mary White Ovington, a white founding member of the NAACP, wrote disparagingly in 1911 that "numbers" of them were "slow to recognize the sanctity of home and the importance of feminine virtue."[18]

Despite the centrality of working women to the growth of the denomination, black ministers were ambivalent about their presence in the church as well as their position in society, both of which mattered in the creation of a denomination and construction of a race. The numerical predominance of single working women raised questions of ecclesiastical viability and threatened to subvert the church's patriarchal agenda. Black working women continuously had to negotiate space and place across boundaries of gender, race, and class, whether earning a living or constructing a Christian womanhood consistent with their understanding of the role of religion in society. Through their "woman's work," they presented their own view of the church, womanhood, and citizenship.

No one articulated more clearly the perspective of black working women than the young, energetic, and often controversial corresponding secretary of the National Baptist Woman's Convention, Nannie Helen Burroughs, whose parsing of the problems confronting domestic servants stood in radical opposition to the pervasive conflation of class and morality that dominated late-nineteenth and early-twentieth century discourses.[19] Burroughs consistently called for proper respect for working women "whose salvation must be attained before the so-called race problem can be solved." In an inversion of masculine and middle-class formulations of morality and respectability, Burroughs stated that working women deserved respect *because* they worked outside the home and frequently traversed public space. Those guilty of "pulling aside of our silken skirts at the approach of the servant woman," Burroughs charged, had a more detrimental effect on the morals of black women than servants with character and honesty enough to work.[20] Careful to separate black women's morality from structural and economic problems, Burroughs asserted that the conditions, not the women, needed reforming. Burroughs explicated the woman question and the race problem in a voice that reflected the experiences and Christian ethics of domestic workers in suburban New Jersey, women who began their organized woman's work in this sexually and racially charged milieu.

Concerned about the effects of industrialization and urbanization on the sanctity of the home and the impact of the economic depression of the 1890s on the dislocation of women and children, white and black women undertook rescue work. Historian Sarah Deutsch argues that rescue work for elite white women was a prescriptive for controlling moral disorder by imposing their superior moral vision on the sexual and material lives of working-class women. Black women, she added, acted out of the impulse of mutual protection. With an understanding of the class differences among African Americans, historian Wanda Hendricks concludes that middle-class black women were activated by their commitment to Victorian mores and to elevating the image of African American women.[21]

As this book argues, for non-elite black women, the reasons were less complicated but more urgent. Northern black working women drew upon shared experiences to provide for the moral and material conditions of their migrating sisters in a society that had little regard for working women and their children. In founding street missions and organizing churches, these women responded to the Christian mandate to save souls; they also formulated their own understanding of the church and its mission. In the process, they created a discursive space for constructing their own image of black womanhood.[22] Later, they would seek a place in the biracial temperance and interracial church women's movements, the secular women's club movement, and electoral politics.

This book offers a narrative of ordinary, non-elite, working women's leadership and public activism told from the margins; women of little status and even less power who resisted and cooperated, subverted and partnered with more powerful black men and white women. It tells of a vision and faith that sustained Christian women's activism. At its core, it argues that black women's Christian activism made a difference over the first half of the twentieth century. Their understanding of the intertwining of race and gender, religion and politics can be found in the bedrock of the civil rights struggle.

* * *

Summit, New Jersey, was a typical New York City suburb. From similar sites, working women like Violet Johnson and Florence Randolph moved into public space, mobilized communities, and influenced the development of black womanhood and public discourse in the state and the region. Locating this study in that site allows us to hear the voices of ordinary women, trace the development of their organized activism, and witness their day-to-day struggle for just laws and moral institutions. This book adds another dimension to understanding African American women's role in the long civil rights movement.[23]

This book traces the Christian activism of black working women in a northern suburb over a fifty-year period. Chapter 1 locates the emerging suburbs and American Protestantism as sites of contestation for the meaning of race, gender, and class in the late-nineteenth and early-twentieth century North. American industrialization and urban decentralization stimulated the movement of middle-class whites to the suburbs. African American working women were at the center of that movement. They founded churches, sustained communities, and formed a network of Christian women throughout the Northeast. Although they constituted the public presence of the independent black Baptist denomination and the race, their religious activities often conflicted with the ecclesial institutions black clergymen were constructing.

When faith and gender conflicted, church women had to negotiate space within the church for their model of Christian womanhood. When race and space collided in pre–World War I Summit over the location of the church, Violet Johnson had to defend her church against a hardening color line and a northern version of Jim Crow. Black church women lived at the intersection of religion and society.

The number of black women in New York City suburbs increased with the increase in the number of white middle-class families. However, their presence remained problematic. For black ministers, their predominance raised questions of institutional viability and racial leadership. For white middle-class men and women, their proximity generated anxieties over black women's pathology in intimate spaces of the Anglo-Saxon preserve. Their inclusion in the black church and the white WCTU was as much an attempt at social control as of sincere Christian outreach, since black women were often viewed as the ones in need of reform. Chapter 2 examines the arguments church women advanced as they fought for a place for *woman's work* in the church and for their race work within the major woman's reform movement. Throughout the 1890s and into the 1910s, they advanced intertwined gender and race arguments as they mobilized to form missionary societies, WCTU units, and the New Jersey State Federation of Colored Women's Clubs. Their activities add a heretofore unexamined dimension to women's interracial coalitions. As black Protestant churches struggled with the question of gender and biracial sisterhoods foundered on issues of race and class, black women erected an organizational framework that created discursive and public space for both their racial and gender identities. They offered an alternative understanding of the intersection of religion and society.

Chapter 3 analyzes black women's activism in the World War I period. Having been schooled in the science of organizational management and the art of political negotiation in their denominations, Johnson and Randolph entered New Jersey's suffrage battle and expanded their Christian activism amid war, migration, and increasing segregation. Their public presence disrupted elite white women's hegemonic discourse. After 1920, armed with the ballot and a vision of an ethical community based upon *civic righteousness*, the practice of morality and justice in civic institutions and laws, they claimed full-fledged citizenship in the midst of invidious—and at times violent—opposition. They concatenated personal behavior, mutual responsibility, and state intervention, and placed moral behavior within the purview of civic responsibility, thus expanding the politics of respectability. Throughout the 1920s they pursued the goal of a transformed society at the polls, in legislative halls, and across civic platforms.

Chapter 4 explores the contingent strategies these working women deployed in the post–World War I years. Based upon their experience in biracial suffrage coalitions, black church women expected to stand side by side with their white sisters in an expanded democracy. Their language changed and became more demanding as they sought to maintain social and political gains against the rising tide of white supremacy. Despite their best efforts, however, these Christian activists were unable to staunch the rise of the Ku Klux Klan or Jim Crow segregation in the North in the 1920s and 1930s. In Summit, class and color politics, a color-coded economic structure, increasing valuation of suburban property, and the devastation of the Great Depression eroded the gains they had made. Nonetheless, they remained committed to an activism based upon moral principles, just laws, and the intertwining of race, gender, and class. They worked for social justice and against an ever-widening color line through the NAACP's Anti-Lynching Crusade, the Federal Council of Churches Church Women's Committee, and the Republican Party.

Chapter 5 discusses working women's experiences with electoral politics. Viewing the ballot as a sacred instrument, New Jersey's black church women added politics to their service. They saw themselves as agents of moral redemption and as leaders of a modern Christian citizenship. Cooperating with white and black Republican politicians, they took to the hustings, explained the electoral process to new voters, critiqued candidates' platforms, and encouraged black women and men to vote. Meeting in churches and homes, the New Jersey State Colored Women's Republican Club coordinated successful get-out-the-vote campaigns and helped to change the political landscape. Considered political partisans because of their fervor, Randolph and Johnson had few illusions about the American political process. Their relationship with the Republican Party was complex and, as the Great Depression deepened, they would revisit their allegiance.

The Great Depression and the New Deal profoundly affected African American women's Christian activism. The Great Depression eroded the economic position of Summit's black residents and concomitantly increased race and class tensions. New Deal recovery programs disproportionately benefited a growing white middle class and increased the economic marginalization of African Americans. As middle-class whites used federal funds to solidify the suburb as a white preserve, African American women's bodies and homes came under increased assault. Black women had to combat the studied indifference of the Republican-Protestant elite and to defend themselves against an aggressive white middle class anxious to consolidate its hold on the American dream reified as the single-family detached home. Fueled with taxpayer dollars and stripped of its complexity and morality, suburban housing became a new battle site and the instrument of erasure of both the black middle class and the white and black working class. Chapter 6 analyzes the Christian women's fight against the structural and economic inequality exacerbated by New Deal policies, especially the attempt at *racial cleansing*, the removal of Summit's black citizens under the New Deal *slum clearance* program.

The Conclusion extends the arc of Johnson's and Randolph's activism and vision of a just society into the 1940s. The language of resistance changed from civic righteousness to civil rights. After a lifetime of work, Randolph and other church women found themselves in a new world. In sum, Christian activism had been their vehicle for social change for more than half a century; yet, by some measures, they had made little progress. Mainline Protestant denominations had done little to forestall racial discrimination in employment, housing, and education. Over the next three decades, federal action pushed by a southern-led civil rights movement would seek to fill the void—to take the action that religious men and women of mainline Protestant denominations had failed to take.

The issues Johnson and Randolph raised—the relationship between social justice and government, the efficacy of large institutional response and community action, the intersection of religion and society, and the empowerment of marginalized citizens—continue to reverberate into the twenty-first century.

* * *

While there is a rich literature on southern African American women's Christian activism, along with less geographically focused national work, this book is one of the first to take a long view in a localized northern venue. It provides one of the few close looks at how segregation and oppression worked in the North. The book revises the timeline of northern segregation and civil rights. In the process, it contributes to the ongoing documentation of the diversity of voices and leadership styles in the civil rights movement. Further, by asking what difference black women's Christian activism made over the first half of the twentieth century in a northern suburb and on the state level, this work complicates our understanding of the relationship between religion and politics, women's private and public spaces, and women's changing roles within religious communities and the public sphere.

Chronologically, the book follows Glenda Elizabeth Gilmore's *Gender and Jim Crow* and Evelyn Brooks Higginbotham's *Righteous Discontent*, works that problematized women's public presence and agency. By foregrounding the Christian activism of ordinary African American women living and working within a white, middle-class suburb, this book approaches American Christianity and women in ecumenical settings from a different perspective. It complements Judith Weisenfeld's *African American Women and Christian Activism*, Nancy Marie Robertson's *Christian Sisterhood*, and Bettye Collier-Thomas's *Jesus, Jobs, and Justice* as it illustrates the contingent nature of religious women's leadership.[24] A microcosm of the history of a region and nation, this local story extends our knowledge of women's Christian activism.

At its core, this volume tells a complex story of American religion and politics. Although the working women fell short of injecting civic righteousness into the public sphere, they expanded the religious discourse beyond personal salvation and offered an alternative model of religious and political interaction. The women's religious faith, mediated through race, gender, and class, shaped their political activism and sustained their commitment to social justice. By locating women's Christian activism in this historic moment, this book examines the religious thought and practices that sustained their community-based activism. It also makes a contribution to the historical understanding of the intertwining of religion, gender, and politics in an increasingly secular society.

This book addresses the constellation of race, class, and gender in the suburbs and, like Thomas Sugrue's *The Origins of the Urban Crisis*, extends the study to the grassroots activism that coalesced in opposition to racial injustice in the urban North. The suburbanization experience of African Americans prior to World War II was as much a part of urban decentralization as the movement of middle-class whites out of urban centers. Classic works on the suburbs, like Kenneth T. Jackson's *Crabgrass Frontier*, Robert Fishman's *Bourgeois Utopias*, John R. Stilgoe's *Borderland*, and Margaret Marsh's *Suburban Lives*, have linked the historical and cultural meaning of suburbia to industrialization and urban decentralization. More recent studies, for example, Andrew Wiese in *Places of Their Own* and Becky M. Nicolaides in *My Blue Heaven*, have expanded the discussion beyond the trope of the white, middle-class suburb to include questions of race and class.[25] As this volume demonstrates, the economic inequality that surfaced *within* the spatial and cultural setting of the suburban enclave prior to World War II is historically significant. Reclaiming the voice and public presence of working-class African American women alerts us to the complexities and diverse geographies of the long civil rights struggle and reminds us that the conditions that give rise to injustice and oppression and the ordinary people who struggle against them cannot be reduced to myths, representations, or tropes.

1

"Please Allow Me Space"

Race and Faith in the Suburbs

When twenty-seven-year-old Violet Johnson arrived in Summit, New Jersey, in 1897 it was an area in transition, undergoing a redefinition of space and place. In some respects, the same could be said of Johnson herself. Among the first generation of freeborn African Americans, Johnson had witnessed many transformations and re-creations. Born in 1870 in Wilmington, North Carolina, she moved North and found employment as a domestic servant in Brooklyn, New York, with the John Eggers family. When the Eggers joined other white middle-class families moving to New Jersey's emerging suburbs, Johnson moved with them and shared household space and duties with two other servants, an African American woman from Virginia and an immigrant man from Sweden.[1]

In the 1890s Summit's African American population numbered a little over one hundred out of a total population of over five thousand. Only three nuclear families could be counted among the black residents, and none owned real property.[2] Predominantly single women and men employed at the residential hotels and without familial or social ties, few remained in Summit beyond the summer season. Those who did worked as maids, housekeepers, gardeners, or coachmen in private residences.

Life among a white middle class in the process of solidifying its economic and cultural space offered employment but few amenities for those in the service sector. Domestic workers shared intimate space with white employers who expected them to remain virtually invisible. The YMCA, woman's literary society, Town Improvement Association, churches, and other organizations existed for the pleasure of the white elite, not the hired help. For black suburban workers, most of whom had lived in urban centers in the South or North, the New Jersey suburbs seemed stark and isolated compared to the communities they had left behind. African Americans had either to create their own community or spend precious leisure hours traveling by train and ferry to Newark, Brooklyn, or Manhattan.

Shortly after her arrival in Summit, Violet Johnson organized a Christian Endeavour Society Bible study group. The international, interracial, and intergender evangelical Protestant organization, begun in Maine in 1881 with the motto "For Christ and the Church," emphasized fellowship and service. Members prayed and read the Bible daily, committed to a time of private devotion and Christian service, and attended regular consecration meetings that reinforced spiritual commitment and fellowship.[3] In contrast to the Endeavor Society organized in 1881 at Summit's white Methodist Episcopal Church, Johnson's nondenominational group appealed to the young African American women and men on the social and economic margins with no public or private space of their own. Johnson paid the first month's rent on a meeting place and converted a commercial laundry into temporary sacred space.[4]

Evidently the Endeavor Society met a need among the suburb's black workers, for within six months they organized a mission "where all Christians regardless of denomination might gather and worship." They engaged a local cook and ordained Baptist minister as their spiritual advisor and affiliated with Mount Zion Baptist Church, an African American congregation in Newark, nearly an hour's ride on the Sunday train.[5]

Despite the challenge of finding space and the financial strain of rent and the minister's salary, within a year Johnson's interdenominational mission was "set apart as a regular Baptist Church," a public declaration that African Americans were committed to sustaining an independent institution in suburban space. In June 1898 Reverend William Thomas Dixon of Brooklyn, Violet Johnson's former pastor and Corresponding Secretary of the New England Baptist Missionary Convention (NEBMC), headed a church council that formally recognized Fountain Baptist Church and its eight members, all domestic servants. The church's organization preceded the suburb's incorporation by a year.[6]

Establishing an official Baptist church signaled a change in expectations. Previously black domestic workers had been scattered about the suburb in boarding houses, rented rooms, or staff quarters, often invisible in public space. Now within a year of Violet Johnson's arrival, they had become a visible community, sharing a commitment to institutional independence and to each other.

The newly formed congregation joined other religious groups, including German Lutherans, Episcopalians, Presbyterians, and Northern Baptists as well as a recently organized Swedish Evangelical Lutheran mission of "about thirty Swedes, Danes, and Scandinavians," and a Roman Catholic Church with separate services for Italian, Irish, and English parishioners.[7] Within the first few months the newly organized Baptist congregation established a building fund for a permanent house of worship.

Organizing an independent congregation was a commitment; erecting a permanent church building would be a sacrifice. A pastor's salary, rent for worship space, and contributions to a building fund amounted to a considerable undertaking for workers whose long hours and endless tasks were rewarded with meager pay.[8] Moreover, a building fund represented faith in the long-term presence of African Americans in the suburb. For as many recognized, given their tenuous ties to Summit the odds were against their remaining long enough to see a completed building. The suburb was not the first stop on the journey from their native Virginia or North Carolina; for many, it would not be the last. Gardeners, cooks, chauffeurs, and maids followed the work—from Saratoga in upstate New York to the Jersey shore.[9] They were subject to dismissal at will, or, like Violet Johnson, could relocate with their employer. Still others found the isolation from family and friends unbearable and moved to more congenial places.

The decision by a young black woman on the suburban frontier to organize an independent church was as much a political as a religious one.[10] The same year that Violet Johnson arrived in Summit, for example, domestic workers Edward and Ana Schuyler moved from New York City with their daughters and son. Ana, a member of a prominent black church in the city, was "unanimously received into the fellowship" of Summit's First Baptist Church, organized in 1867 along denominational rather than racial, national, or linguistic lines. In 1902 the white congregation accepted as candidates for baptism Ana's daughter and a black laborer who had moved to Summit three years earlier. Another Schuyler daughter was baptized at First Baptist in 1906.[11] In the late nineteenth century African American Protestants in the North had options.

Although First Baptist welcomed all Baptists regardless of color, Johnson chose to participate in the programmatic plan of African Americans to create a denomination and construct a race suited to the demands of industrialized and urbanized America. In the wake of Southern dis-enfranchisement in the 1890s, black northern Baptists positioned the church as a bulwark against the forces of white supremacy and Jim Crow segregation. Thus, northern African Americans saw themselves as fighting a "southern problem," and their remedies varied from those of southern blacks. They appealed to the common sense of white northern-ers and their longstanding relations and pointed to pious church women who were abused in public space. They viewed local congregations led by seminary-trained men as a Christian training ground and a school for American citizenship. Independent churches would provide material evidence of black men's ability to manage their own institutions and af-firm their fitness for the franchise.

Independent churches also positioned African American women as active agents in that religious and political process. Despite their cen-trality to the expansion of northern churches, Baptist ministers viewed black working women's presence with ambivalence, even as their num-ber increased with the migration of middle-class white families to the suburbs. Violet Johnson would have to fight for a woman's place in the church she had founded and that church's space in the suburb.

Creating a Denomination, Constructing a Race

Following the Civil War, African American Baptists in the North began to organize separate congregations led by black ministers.[12] With a the-ology grounded in New Testament scripture and the optimism born of the Civil War and Emancipation, black ministers envisioned a multira-cial, egalitarian society and themselves as equal agents with their white brothers, with "one ... Master ... and all ... brethren."[13] America could become the reified New Testament church with neither slave nor free, but all equal before God and under the Constitution. They had only to provide the leadership and thereby prove themselves and the race wor-thy of God's blessing and American citizenship.

Educated and trained in American Baptist Home Missionary Society (ABHMS) colleges and seminaries, northern black clergy soon chafed under the "proscription" of "Anglo-Saxon auspices" and resented being treated as "wards."[14] In 1874 black Baptists organized the New England Baptist Missionary Convention (NEBMC) as an independent association with a territorial reach from Maine to Virginia. With the objective to "propagate the Gospel of Christ, and to advance the interest of his kingdom, by supplying vacant churches . . . sending ministers into destitute regions . . . and by planting and building up churches," black Baptists announced their readiness to control their own ecclesiastical affairs, especially the ordination of ministers.[15]

Based upon the theory of natural and divine rights and a linear reading of church and American history, NEBMC ministers claimed dual citizenship as "American citizens" and "citizens of the Kingdom of God" and designated the church as the primary institution for teaching both Christian principles and ideals of citizenship.[16] Pastors were to use "their high and God-given privilege and right to train the church along all practical lines, how to . . . vote intelligently . . . and be powerful and effective in the national life, for the good and well-being of our race."[17]

In an era when *Christianized* was synonymous with *civilized*, NEBMC annual sessions were part spiritual revival and part political forum. Aware of the imperial gaze of Anglo-Saxons who deigned to evaluate their development and rule on their fitness for citizenship, convention leaders believed it was their Christian duty to provide direction on political matters. "[W]hile this is an ecclesiastical, rather than a political, a religious, and not a secular body," NEBMC declared, "it is nevertheless in the line of duty for us to take cognizance of and give timely expression in relations to matters that effect [*sic*] us as a class of citizens, in our social and political relation, to our great body politic."[18] Religion and politics were intertwined.

In the wake of the evisceration of the Fourteenth and Fifteenth Amendments and the racial violence in the South in the 1880s, NEBMC ministers critiqued American politics in their sermons. They lauded the Constitution with the War Amendments as the highest achievement in human government and denounced white supremacy as the "demon of caste prejudice" that sanctioned the robbery and assassination of African Americans "without effectual protest of either church or state."[19] Yet, because most of the segregation in the North was customary and flexible to a greater degree than in the South, they believed that these racial proscriptions would wither.

Thus, northern black Baptists denounced the 1896 *Plessy v. Ferguson* U. S. Supreme Court ruling as a "mischievous law." In a statement that reflected their past hopes more than their coming experience, NEBMC clergymen argued that *Plessy*, though promulgated as a ruling against a race, was a class-based ruling on individual and group advancement. In language that appears mild in light of *Plessy's* pernicious effect, the denomination disavowed any desire for preferential treatment and sought only to "warn the common people" of the "seriously injurious" discriminatory laws "perpetrated upon it by a pampered aristocracy . . . raised to positions of trust and honor by the franchise of the masses."[20]

As *Plessy* became established law, northern black Baptists drew a direct line between the "lawless factions" in the South and American imperialism. The great "sociological problem" threatening the republic and civilization was not "the Negro," but the "imperialism" of Republican President William McKinley's administration.[21] From efforts to nullify the Fifteenth Amendment in the South, to the war in the Philippines, the Boer War in South Africa, and the Boxer Rebellion in China, the tidal wave of white supremacy fueled violence and transgressed divine law. In a resolution distributed to the press black Baptists declared, "God made of one blood all nations . . . . We do recognize *individual* superiority, but we do not recognize *race* superiority."[22]

As "enemies" of the race "Southernize[d] the North" and the federal government acquiesced in the "nationalism of Jim Crow," black ministers noted "with alarm the increasing and wide-spread encroachment upon the civil and political rights of our people in this country."[23] The bill of indictment included the drift of northern capital south, Jim Crow cars in interstate travel, disenfranchisement in the South, and the "strange and studied silence" of white northern ministers.[24] By 1905 northern black Baptists felt compelled to address the white supremacy sexual charge of social equality. "As it is commonly asserted that we are seeking social equality, thus placing us in a false light before the people of races in this country," the convention declared, "we emphasize the fact that it is not social equality we seek, but that we demand the rights of equal opportunity to pursue every occupation that will make life desirable."[25] Men and women carried the message to cities and suburbs in sermons and convention reports.

Cognizant of the public redefinition of citizenship begun in the latter half of the nineteenth century and the race theories that informed that discourse, black Baptists made a distinction between "caste," a reference to physical traits like skin color, and "race," a mark of character. Physical traits were immutable and, at best, misleading; character, on the other hand, was amenable to cultivation. The Ethiopian could not change his color, but character traits required for citizenship responded to the civilizing influence of the Christian church.[26]

NEBMC clergy developed a three-pronged argument for full citizenship rights and male suffrage. First, they posited the right of citizenship for all African Americans in divine law. Second, they claimed the right to equal treatment based upon the character of *representative* men and women of the race. Finally, they postulated that by establishing and maintaining their own religious and civic institutions, namely, churches and denominational schools, men of the race earned the right to the franchise for themselves and full citizenship for a race that demonstrated the requisite degree of self-help. Independent black churches would provide visual and material evidence of a citizenship based not on the color of one's skin but on the content of one's character, a formulation that foreshadowed Martin Luther King's famous dictum by over a half century.[27] NEBMC's masculine discourse combined biblical principles, self-help philosophy, and American sacralization of institutions as a countervailing force against white supremacy and its intimations of interracial sex.

Constructing a race with character traits suitable for exercising the franchise received as much clerical attention as creating a denomination. While the latter required exposition of church polity, the former necessitated the regulation of behavior. "[T]he highest duty of every Christian citizen [was] to give the church and state a pure manhood and womanhood."[28] Late nineteenth-century discourses conflated Christian principles and Victorian conventions to invest character and respectability with great worth. As historian Evelyn Brooks Higginbotham argues, the *politics of respectability* positioned individual behavior and attitudes, manners and morals, as a strategy for reforming the system of American race relations.[29] By focusing on public behavior as a marker of good Christians and the best citizens, black Baptists elevated the discourse of respectability and character—its formula for middle-class success— into a religious practice. By their behavior church members would prove that African Americans had reached a state that supported black men in the free exercise of the ballot and mandated equal treatment for black women and children. The burden of proof fell disproportionately on black women.

Regulating public behavior was a challenge. New forms of working-class leisure competed with the middle-class Victorian behavior the denomination sought to inculcate. Urban working-class congregations, Protestant and Catholic, black and white, frequently sponsored picnics and boat or train rides to beaches or amusement parks to relieve the discomfort and drudgery of urban life and work. Yet as one NEBMC minister warned, the "future success of the Baptist cause" and, by implication, that of the race depended upon disassociation from Sunday excursions that desecrated the Sabbath.[30] Ministers inveighed against giving and attending concerts, patronizing skating rinks, and dancing, even though fledging congregations frequently used these as fund-raisers. Black clergy reserved their strongest condemnation for the cakewalk, a popular dance denounced as a perpetuation of slave-quarter behavior.[31] According to NEBMC's seminary trained ministers, such activities imperiled the civil rights of the race and fueled the northern expansion of Jim Crow segregation; an assessment not necessarily shared by the denomination's working women.

Motivated in the late nineteenth and early twentieth centuries by the Protestant watchword "North America for Christ," white Protestants established mission stations at New York City's Convent Garden and later at Ellis Island to convert European immigrants. NEBMC took as its mission field northern cities and suburbs. The "cause of Christ" suffered especially in New Jersey where southern migrants found "no church of their own denomination, and none to look after them." They risked mingling with "loose members" at the Lord's Table, having their children educated in Roman Catholic schools, and, most troublesome, being deprived of the church's socializing influence.[32]

Denominational statistics confirmed New Jersey's dearth of Baptist churches. In 1890 out of more than forty-seven thousand African Americans, only about 10 percent claimed a denominational affiliation and a mere two thousand identified as Baptist. Deeply disturbed, the white state Baptist convention appointed a missionary to work among migrating black Southerners.[33] Determined to assume responsibility "for the advancement of God's Kingdom among these destitute places," NEBMC appointed its own field missionary "to watch out for favorable opportunities to extend . . . denominational work" by meeting in private homes, conducting revivals in open tents, and establishing missions.[34] Unfortunately, perennial financial deficits limited NEBMC's effectiveness.

For founding member and Corresponding Secretary Reverend William Thomas Dixon, Violet Johnson's former pastor whom she had asked to help build the Baptist church in Summit, the work was too important to be constrained by a lack of funds. "We are more and more convinced," he wrote, "the fields of our operation demand missionaries, who are more willing to do pioneer work and trust God, than we have yet found."[35] Dixon often functioned as a field missionary, establishing missions, sitting on recognition councils, and serving as interim pastor at struggling churches, adding church expansion to his duties as pastor of Brooklyn's Concord Baptist Church. For nearly thirty years, Dixon left his theological and political imprint on the black Baptist denomination in the Northeast. The missions and churches that he organized stood as "silent monuments of his generalship and service."[36]

Thus, Dixon's presence in Summit in June 1898 was neither coincidental nor insignificant. Rather, it signified denominational support for the suburban church founded by a domestic servant and the importance of such congregations to the ecclesial and political aims of African Americans in the North.

Forming a Congregation, Constructing Gender

Fountain Baptist Church was a *woman's* church. As one minister conceded, it was the "good ladies" who sustained the church.[37] Forming an independent black denomination and constructing the race depended on black working women, especially in the northern suburbs. In the interconnected web of race, gender, and class, white middle-class migration to the suburbs expanded the geography of black women's labor and, concomitantly, the ecclesiastical reach of black Protestants. Black women who filled positions as cooks, laundresses, chambermaids, nurses, and waitresses in private homes and in public hotels and restaurants, also filled church pews. Their leadership and personal connections sustained the "small and constantly changing" congregations in overwhelmingly white suburbs.[38] To NEBMC's dismay, its churches depended on working women.

Often the success or failure of a struggling congregation hinged on the timely appearance of a preaching woman. For example, when Nora Taylor, a Methodist evangelist from Lexington, Kentucky, preached in Summit in 1904, she revived the membership during a period when the church was without a pastor.[39] Young men weighed carefully a call to a fledging suburban congregation barely able to support a minister. In 1891 NEBMC leaders chided "the men who claim they are called to preach, and yet sit around the pulpits and churches at home, waiting for their pastor to resign or die" rather than "enter the field . . . and prove their call to the work."[40] Nonetheless, NEMBC vetted and endorsed women as evangelists but denied them ordination or pastoral appointments, despite their importance to the denomination.

Still, working women like Violet Johnson sustained churches and maintained the public presence of the race in northern suburbs. In their limited leisure hours, they organized fund-raisers to pay the pastor's salary and to rent worship space. In the process, they built relationships and inflected suburban culture with their own idiom. As historian Kathy Peiss argues, leisure provided working-class women with social space to experiment with their identity and to try on new images and roles as they pushed the boundaries of working-class life.[41]

A leading fund-raiser, Violet Johnson collected individual subscriptions from white donors and organized cultural events open to all, even the unchurched. African American classical musicians, many trained at conservatories in Boston and Rhode Island, supplemented their income by organizing traveling shows and musical ensembles of ballads and popular tunes interspersed with operatic and classical specialties and performed in suburban opera houses and music halls for church fund-raisers.[42] In 1901 Johnson sponsored an evening concert featuring a violin trio and ending with the cakewalk, notwithstanding Baptist ministers' strong opposition to dancing in general, and the cakewalk in particular. For an evening of entertainment that included "plantation melodies," or spirituals, and tableaux at Beechwood Hall, Johnson issued a special invitation to white residents in 1903, "since the object is a good one."[43] With a similar appeal in 1906 she invited all residents to a Friday evening performance of the Baston Millar concert with *prima donna* Flora Batson, the "Double-Voiced Queen of Song" famous for her soprano to baritone vocal range.[44] Such performances contributed to the development of American popular culture and highlighted the public presence of African American women in the suburbs.

Of all the fund-raisers, the annual Christmas bazaar was the most popular. Typical was the 1912 event that featured a fishing pond and fortune telling booth in addition to the apron and fancy goods stalls filled with items crafted by black women. Over three evenings, local residents provided entertainment and attendees purchased cake, ice cream, and supper. Since the entertainment supported the church's building fund, white and black neighbors attended along with friends from as far away as suburban Westchester County, New York, more than an hour's ride by train.[45]

These church-sponsored activities enabled domestic workers and recent southern migrants throughout the Northeast to create a space separate from their work. At the same time, the cultural productions provided an alternative to suburban isolation and connected black working women to the southern life they had left behind and the suburban places they were helping to shape.[46] Moreover, the ritual enactment of popular American culture conflated sacred and secular representations of community life and provided black women—and their white employers—with an identity that was simultaneously different and familiar, oppositional yet inclusive. They showcased models of race, gender, and class in the making.

Implementing a program of Christian citizenship from the economic and social margins required faith—and perseverance. The Summit congregation witnessed transiency in the pew and itinerancy in the pulpit. As one church member explained following the precipitous departure of yet another pastor, "In passing judgment on Fountain Baptist Church . . . the history and background should be kept in mind. . . . It was, of course, unable to pay a sufficient salary to care for a minister."[47] The lack of suitable housing presented an additional hurdle. Nonetheless, before long the congregation outgrew its original site in a public laundry and moved to rented space in Temperance Hall on Springfield Avenue, the main thoroughfare, where it would remain for nearly eight years.[48]

Yet as all Protestants understood, demonstration of the capacity for self-government required material evidence, namely, a proper church building. In 1905 NEBMC boasted, "[O]ur people are bidding farewell to halls and are building . . . beautiful houses in which to worship God."[49]

The reality was far less glorious. While a few congregations completed new buildings or purchased older ones from white congregations moving into modern facilities, others remained in rented rooms, private homes, unfinished basements, warehouses, or, weather permitting, tents. Annually, NEBMC received appeals for assistance to purchase property, complete a building, or pay a mortgage. Generally the convention could offer little more than congratulations to ministers who completed buildings and prayers for the others.[50] However, in a nation in transition, space—sacred and civic—mattered.

The herculean task of building a church in Summit exceeded the financial resources of the Baptist congregation that, like many struggling immigrant congregations, sought assistance from wealthy residents, especially the "staunch friends" of the white Methodist and Baptist churches.[51] When Fountain Baptist Church's fifth pastor, Edward N. Mc-Daniels, an NEBMC veteran and consummate "race" man, announced his intention in 1905 to purchase two lots and build a church, he appealed "To the Citizens of Summit" for "moral and financial support in the work."[52]

In language that stoked the race, gender, and class anxieties of white middle-class women, McDaniels warned, "[U]nless the white people of Summit take hold of the work for the colored people . . . as the white people in other cities and towns of the North have done there will never be a colored church in Summit within a generation." Further, he noted, "[T]here are too many servant girls in Summit . . . to be without a good colored church. . . . Male members are scarce and that in itself is a drawback to the work.[53] Late nineteenth-century social reformers blamed urban vice on single working men and women. By 1900 as the "moral geography" for women changed, historian Sarah Deutsch concludes, the "image of the sexualized working girl" stood in contrast to the desexualized middle-class home as a site of class and gender moralizing.[54] The correlation between domestic service and low morals that had characterized European immigrant women was transferred to black women as they entered domestic service in the North.

Moreover, the discourse of civilization intersected with ideologies of race and gender to position male power and racial whiteness as the evolutionary ideal. Race and gender theorists presented white women as central to civilization's advance and portrayed black women as the loose radical in the alchemy of race.[55] With her moral laxity and procreative fecundity, the "black woman" had the potential to degrade two races; she could upset racial whiteness and undermine the character of cultural blackness by producing mixed-race children.

Apparently, McDaniels's rhetoric had the desired effect. Within a year the congregation purchased two lots on Chestnut Avenue that conformed to NEBMC's counsel to "purchase eligible property and . . . select building lots elsewhere than in the rear of main streets, or too far from the residences of those whom they would benefit."[56] Intersecting two major streets, Springfield and Park Avenues, Chestnut was bound on the northern and southern sides by the Roman Catholic and Methodist churches.[57]

A vacant lot could not shelter a congregation. McDaniels continued to stress the "need for a colored church" with imagery that linked religion, politics, and black women's sexuality. "Negroes are coming from the [S]outh in large numbers," he stressed, "and they bring their conditions with them, and unless these conditions are rightly considered and dealt with prudently, problems will arise here as well." Those who disregarded the church as God's method "to regulate the family circle" would "find themselves in utter darkness."[58] With a proper church building, the male pastor would save democratic institutions and protect white middle-class suburban homes from the southern barbarity transmitted by black women.

An able theologian and skilled politician, McDaniels intermingled fear and flattery. "Shall it be said that I have to go outside of Summit to seek aid to build a church for the colored people . . . [w]hen the very word 'Summit' means wealth. . . . The white people of [neighboring] Morristown and Madison are helping the colored churches of those towns."[59] To allay any concern that the church building, unlike unchurched black women, would not blend with a suburban aesthetic, McDaniels noted that the white Summit resident and New York City architect who designed many of the suburb's expansive homes and the white Baptist Church had drawn the church's plans.[60]

In August 1908, three years after McDaniels's arrival, the congregation celebrated the laying of the cornerstone, a gift from a group of live-in domestics and their employers, and invited white and black residents to "Come and See what the Lord has done for us!"[61] The celebration was a watershed moment. Those who spent their days serving others led the public event that was both civic ritual and religious service. More than a dozen black congregations and ministers from suburban New Jersey and New York's Westchester County participated, along with Summit's white Protestant ministers and their congregations. Revered white Methodist minister and Summit resident William I. Haven delivered the major address, symbolically bestowing the imprimatur of white Protestantism on the black congregation. The African American head waiter and his staff of waiters and waitresses at the prestigious Beechwood Hotel, along with the staff of the nearby Blackburn House, managed the grand collation that capped the ceremony.[62]

White generosity had its limits. The congregation completed only the basement, and marched into it on Christmas Eve 1908. The indefatigable William T. Dixon preached in the roofed-over stone basement the following month.[63] Despite its unfinished state, black working women believed they had created a site of respectability and autonomy.

However, as McDaniels's interactions with white middle-class suburbanites and black working-class women illustrate, race and gender relations were unstable and complicated. The "race" man exploited the trope of morally suspect black women to further a program based on black men's fitness to lead.

Sacred Place, Demarcated Space

Over the next five years Violet Johnson and members of the fledgling congregation faced the daunting tasks of completing a church and retaining a pastor. Unable to find suitable housing for his family, McDaniels's successor left after nearly two years; the seventh pastor, "not [finding] things altogether genial, and not likely to be congenial for sometime," resigned before his first anniversary.[64] Faced with a flooding basement too wet even for Baptists, by 1912 the congregation was once again in rented space.

In March 1915 under the leadership of the eighth pastor, Reverend E. Elias Jackson, the congregation offered $7,500 to purchase Old City Hall.[65] Located on Summit Avenue and designed in 1892 by Summit's leading architect at a cost of $12,000, the two-story brick building housed city offices until the city relocated municipal functions in 1909 to Springfield Avenue, the main thoroughfare. Amid growing taxpayer dissatisfaction with the property's failure to generate any revenue, city officials placed the building on the market in 1912, only to refuse the lone offer of $7,000.[66] Thus things remained until Fountain Baptist Church tendered its bid.

Within days white Summit responded. "Sale to Negro Church Fought/Summit Property Owners to Urge Council Not to Sell Old City Building," read the *Newark Star* headline. White property owners and residents, many of whom rented commercial or residential space to African Americans, "use[d] every effort to prevail on the members of the Common Council" not to sell "to the congregation, which is composed of negroes [*sic*]." Business and realty interests along Summit Avenue claimed the sale would "result in the colonization of negroes . . . with alleged resultant ruin of property and business." Using a term that labeled European immigrants as the unassimilable "other," the white coalition contended that African Americans had "established a colony" on Chestnut Avenue and were "therefore in no urgent need of a church in the central part of the city." The *Newark Star* doubted that the "city fathers" "seriously considered" selling "to the negroes," though "[they] have long been desirous of disposing of the property."[67]

Violet Johnson recognized what was at stake. White residents were declaring certain sections of town *white* space and off-limits to black *ownership*. Such a construction could not go uncontested. Johnson's public defense of the church she had founded and the sacred place she had labored to make permanent began politely, "Please allow me space in your paper to refute a statement." Regarding the "so-called colored colony," she retorted, "[N]ot a house has opened to colored tenants other than those which were open five years ago when we first began to worship there." Further, she stated, "[T]here are more colored people living on Summit avenue, Beechwood road, and Franklin place than there are on Chestnut avenue. There is no colony of negroes."[68]

Enclaves of black and white domestic servants who lived-in or rented rooms on residential streets bordering the business district were a necessary but erasable feature that middle-class residents rendered invisible with quotidian activities.[69] By seeking to own one of the leading symbols of suburban identity, even one no longer in use, the African American congregation had become all too visible.

Johnson next rebutted the specious correlation between property valuation and race and revealed the disjuncture between ideational and physical geography. "And as for lowering property values, the places in the very section where [Old City Hall] is located . . . are such decent white people would hesitate to go into them. Such property is no doubt valuable," she caustically added.[70] According to the strategy of alterity, the subjective designation of space as *white* was intended to make racial exclusion of the "other" appear natural.[71] Space mattered in the ideal suburb, an *imagined community* where not even sacred space, if inflected black, could be allowed to transgress space encoded white.[72]

Johnson lobbed an assault on that chimera of white supremacy, the phobia of interracial sex. "A decent church would raise rather than lower the moral tone. . . . We have no desire to push ourselves where we are not wanted."[73] The paradox of a domestic servant who worked in intimate space—the home—having to address sexual relations when discussing a sacred place—the church—could appear natural only when viewed through the lens of American racism. Black and white residents read different moral maps.

Johnson's appeal to "His Honor, the Mayor, [to] do his duty by us as citizens, irrespective of race or color" fell on deaf ears. Within weeks the city council announced its refusal to sell Old City Hall to the black congregation, purportedly because the city would soon require the building.[74] In truth, city officials had concluded that although renting space to black people was permissible, selling space implied equal status. Differing ideations of space became the site of a power struggle.[75]

Johnson was devastated. She had not expected her Christian and Republican "friends" to privilege race over religion. Yet, race and faith collided over a building no longer in use. Prominently located on a main thoroughfare and visible from the train station, Old City Hall, the quintessential suburban icon, retained its cultural valence for those creating an imagined community based on class and race.[76] The attempt to overwrite the inscription of *white* space had provoked an immediate response from those who controlled the suburb's civic and material culture, demonstrating that northern discursive power could be as authoritarian as any southern state's police power, even in the absence of Jim Crow laws or physical violence. Inscription is also about erasure.

Moreover, as the struggle over a permanent site for the church revealed, religious issues are rarely just about religion. Rather, they are about self-identity, public presentation, inclusion and exclusion, and power. While black Baptists envisioned a multiracial society that resembled the New Testament community, Summit's white Protestants imagined another.

In the years since Johnson's arrival in Summit, the position of African Americans in the North had deteriorated. Now a forty-five-year-old woman, she found her choices constrained to a degree that would have been unimaginable when she was twenty-seven. Proscription had hardened into racialized space encircled by a widening color line.

Drawing the Color Line

As 1915 drew to a close, Violet Johnson could not deny that the church's progress had been thwarted by Jim Crow with a northern accent. Racial boundaries had not always been so rigid. For example, in August 1911 after Fountain Baptist Church member Fred Roy refused to leave his seat on the theater's lower level and move to the balcony during an afternoon vaudeville performance, managers of the Summit Opera House physically ejected him and charged him with disorderly conduct. Many expected Roy to sue over the violation of his civil rights. A month later in Paterson, New Jersey, Minerva Miller, president of the local African Methodist Episcopal (AME) Zion Woman's Home and Foreign Missionary Society and future member of the State Federation of Colored Women's Clubs, successfully sued the Paterson Movie House for charging her and two companions a quarter for admission when white patrons paid a nickel.[77] Though there is no evidence that Roy took legal action, the knowledge that he could and the fact that Miller did suggest a color line still in flux. By 1915, however, some twenty years later than in the South, northern proscription had hardened into racial exclusion.

In February 1915, a month before Fountain Baptist Church made its unsuccessful bid to purchase Old City Hall, Violet Johnson welcomed over three hundred and fifty white and black "friends and citizens" to an Emancipation Celebration and fund-raiser at the Summit Opera House. The evening included addresses by the mayor, leading black political and religious leaders from New York City and the state, and a "strong plea" from the pastor for help building a church. After singing "We've Fought Every Race's Battles But Our Own," the guests enjoyed a banquet in the church's roofed-over basement.[78]

Evidently, the celebration disturbed some white residents. The next edition of the local paper carried a public apology from Reverend Jackson, disclaiming any intent to "speculate on the name and honor of our Emancipator, Abraham Lincoln." Rather, he said, the purpose was "to show our appreciation for that day which marked the greatest epoch in the history of America's civilization . . . and to show the real status of the colored people of Summit."[79] Within nine months Jackson resigned his position, leaving the Summit congregation immersed in a flooding basement and a rising tide of white opposition. By 1915 presenting their real status had become perilous.

Throughout the 1910s, African Americans watched with alarm as once opened doors slammed tightly. In the nation's capital in 1913, the "Year of Jubilee" commemorating the Emancipation Proclamation, Democratic President Woodrow Wilson sanctioned Jim Crow segregation in the White House, notwithstanding his reputation as New Jersey's progressive governor and African American support during his presidential campaign. The following year, to the dismay of NEMBC seminary-trained clergy, Boston's Newton Theological Seminary closed its doors to black men.[80] Thus events in Summit reflected national choices expressly designed to reorder the civic and political landscape and reify white supremacy claims by demarcating public space as white space. Though not as bloody as in the South, Jim Crow segregation in the North was virulent and morally violent.

Upon his departure, Reverend Jackson recommended former NEBMC president Daniel W. Wisher as interim pastor. Wisher epitomized the radical Baptist and "race" man who linked the discourses of race and American citizenship to organizational independence. At an 1888 meeting to foster unity among black and white Baptists, Wisher proposed the creation of an autonomous black denomination. "It will enable us to destroy all narrow-mindedness among ourselves," he argued, "and like a stream rushing from a mountain . . . break down all prejudice and race pride of them who acknowledge us not as their equals."[81] In a dramatic reversal of fortune, at sixty-one the inveterate race leader who had ordained a generation of Baptist ministers, built a church valued at $135,000 in the 1880s, and appeared in a *New York Times* article on "Wealthy Negro Citizens," found himself with a three-month appointment at $10 per Sunday at an embattled congregation on the suburban frontier.[82]

Nineteen-sixteen began with Fountain Baptist Church once again in the news. "Property Owners Disturbed—Rumors of Location of Colored Church in Springfield Avenue," headlined the local paper. A real estate deal between the church and a prominent businessman would be "consummated within a short time unless the unforseen [*sic*] happens." For $12,000, Charles B. Grant, a leading opponent only a year earlier in the Old City Hall controversy, would exchange his building, a portion of which the black congregation rented, for the church's Chestnut Avenue property. The congregation would use the first floor for the sanctuary and church offices and convert the upper portion into apartments.[83] Although "several leading citizens" pledged to secure the mortgage, the local paper reminded readers that "the colored church officials with their white advisers and prominent members of other local churches" had made a previous "futile attempt" to acquire property in the heart of the business district.[84] Grant's decision to transgress boundaries surprised many, including the local reporter who tried unsuccessfully to interview him. Whatever the source of Grant's conversion, Wisher accepted the offer "under the direction of the Holy Spirit."[85]

Divine intervention notwithstanding, white Summit rose in opposition. Asserting that the "colored congregation" could complete its building on Chestnut Avenue for half the cost of the Grant Building, the white Methodist church denounced the "Scheme of the Colored Folks."[86] Methodist opposition did not stem from an abhorrence of proximity, for the Chestnut Avenue property was within walking distance of both the Grant Building and the Methodist Church. Rather, the transgression was black ownership of property in an area designated as white. Other white Protestant churches remained silent.

Together Daniel Wisher, the public face of the church, and Violet Johnson, the keeper of institutional memory, tried to change the dynamic with a narrative of shared faith and community. Wisher included the white Protestant pastors in his formal installation and the following month invited the white Baptist pastor to cohost a meeting of leading white men, no doubt identified by Johnson.[87] Seated in the church's rented space, Wisher assured them that the congregation "did not want to make enemies" and would rescind its purchase offer. He challenged the men to "come together & put us up a house of worship or complete our house on Chestnut Ave[nue]."[88]

On the eve of the United States's entry into World War I, the "general committee" of elite white men met at the YMCA and finalized plans for a "plain but commodious" $9,000 church building on the Chestnut Avenue site. Linking "civic duty" and war preparedness, the white men agreed to raise $6,000 to fund the project and assign a $3,000 mortgage to the black congregation.[89]

They provided details in the circular "An Important Matter to the Citizens of Summit." Citing the suburb's black population of approximately two hundred and fifty, less than 3 percent of a total population of nine thousand, and the two hundred attending Fountain Baptist Church, the general committee noted that "most . . . are in service in the homes of the white people." Moreover, the men explained, "[T]he church and its leader appeal to the better class of colored people," making "it easier to keep them in Summit and to attract others of the kind." Wisher had engendered "a noticeable improvement in our colored population."[90] Swayed by the narrative that linked the war in Europe and "a much larger company of colored people from the South," the local editor endorsed the plan to build a "colored church" as a "civic necessity."[91]

Glaringly absent from the discussion were any references to Christian brotherhood or the Social Gospel. Evidently, these religious tenets would not have generated the requisite level of white support. Whereas northern Protestants had once claimed "North America for Christ" as their watchword, in 1916 Summit Protestants embraced "civic necessity" and "an investment bringing large returns."[92]

Summit's leading white men created a discursive space that erased the church's inception that preceded the suburb's incorporation and its members who were long-term residents. Instead, they presented a montage of war, decreased European immigration, increased black migration, and the overriding need for white control of space—physical and moral. By restricting black ownership of place, the white middle class intended to protect home, family, and property.[93]

* * *

Observed from one perspective, 1916 ended more auspiciously than it began. Summit's white elite had united in support of the black congregation's quest for a permanent building and designated the location. In late January 1917 the congregation and its white friends walked from the rented space on Springfield Avenue to lay a new cornerstone on Chestnut Avenue. Though the congregation attempted to reenact the 1908 ceremony, the invitation to "Come and see what the Lord has done for us" was more subdued.[94]

Finally, in February 1918 the congregation worshiped in a completed and furnished building the cost of which equaled the amount offered for worship and residential space in the Grant Building. In exchange for their support the elite white men had exacted certain concessions: white trustees would hold the church's deed and control the hiring of pastors.[95] The more costly yet unspoken concession was the remapping of suburban space. Springfield and Summit Avenues became the "Anglo-Saxon preserve" and Chestnut Avenue the designated "negro colony."

In the waning years of the nineteenth century, northern blacks saw themselves as fighting a "southern problem." Consequently, their remedies varied from that of southern blacks. They appealed to the common sense of white northerners and their long-standing religious and political relations. The effect of southern propaganda with the chimera of miscegenation in a hierarchical society obsessed with the discourse of civilization and middle-class trappings added urgency to black church expansion as proof of the race's fitness for manhood suffrage in the North as well as the South. However, belief in American institutions and a Christian ethic had not been enough to prevent Jim Crow's migration north.

By the 1910s Jim Crow segregation had gained more than a foothold. World War I, anxieties about the future of the white races, and the rise in suburbanization continued the decline in race relations into the interwar years. The "good ladies" of the church, working women like Violet Johnson who helped create a denomination and a race, would have to contend with white and black men and white women to defend their Christian womanhood and their place in the church and society.

2

"A Great Work for God and Humanity"

African American Christian Women and Organized Social Reform

Violet Johnson no doubt mused on the disparate models of Christian womanhood as she led the 1902 organizational meeting of Fountain Baptist Church's Woman's Missionary Society in Temperance Hall, the expansive two-story building owned by the Woman's Christian Temperance Union (WCTU) of Summit and a portion of which the church rented. From its inception in 1874 the New England Baptist Missionary Convention (NEBMC) promoted its objective to give the church and state a pure manhood and womanhood and intertwined Victorian notions of separate spheres and middle-class domesticity with teachings on natural rights and the egalitarian principles of ecclesiastical and political citizenship. NEBMC clergy apotheosized the white Woman's Home Mission of the American Baptist Home Mission Society (ABHMS) as the model of Christian womanhood and lauded its middle-class members for carrying "Christian and womanly sympathy to the fireside and home" of black women.[1] Yet, for working women like Johnson the difference between their reality and the church's expectations could be stark.

Working in overwhelmingly white places and often living in their employers' homes, Johnson and her sisters recognized that they would have to fashion their own model of Christian womanhood, one born of their experiences and grounded in their religious beliefs. Black domestic workers built churches, led congregations, and sustained communities out of their meager earnings and during their limited leisure hours. Defying the church's teachings, they walked the piers of New York and New Jersey to rescue women and families and admitted unchurched men and women into their Missionary Bible Bands. They provided more than scripture, prayer, and song in their street missions. They distributed clothing, located temporary housing, and provided employment and educational assistance to migrating southerners.

Intent upon building a manly middle-class church as evidence of fitness for the franchise, black ministers ignored "woman's work" and the church women who claimed the streets as their parish. White Protestant women also dismissed this working-class representation of Christian womanhood. Nonetheless, women like Johnson expanded the church's mission and practices, and ultimately forced black men and white women to recognize them and their organized work.

During the prohibition battles of the 1880s and 1890s, the predominantly white New Jersey Woman's Christian Temperance Union (WCTU) saw black women as potential allies. Already advocates of temperance through their churches, many black church women took the pledge and joined the WCTU in the fight for prohibition and woman suffrage. Though their number remained small, black women temporarily transformed the white, middle-class New Jersey WCTU into a biracial, cross-class organization. However, they fared worse in this Christian sisterhood than in their hierarchically gendered churches. White temperance women proved to be fickle allies but constant gatekeepers unwilling to accept black women as equals.

Following defeat of New Jersey's suffrage referendum in 1915, black women could no more ignore the race problem in the temperance sisterhood than they could overlook the woman question in the black church. Constrained by spaces marked by white women and black men, African American working women created their own discursive space, the New Jersey State Federation of Colored Women's Clubs (NJSFCWC), a sisterhood of black women "doing work for God and humanity."[2]

Black working women's organizational strategies reflected their desire for full participation in their church and society, even as their activism critiqued both. As committed to the construction of a representative race as their Protestant brothers and as devoted to home protection as their white temperance sisters, they rejected the leadership of a church that consigned them to a marginal position because they were women and of a women's group that considered their color and class moral defects. The intersectionality of race and gender led black women to subscribe to a different understanding of religion and society and to respond differently to their singularity of issues. As members of an evangelical network of black women, their moral agency led them to transgress boundaries of race, class, and gender.[3]

Working Women and Woman's Work

Black working women in New Jersey's suburbs established and sustained Baptist congregations and thus expanded the denomination. They secured meeting places and funds to rent, heat, and erect church buildings. They filled key leadership positions in congregations, voted on church matters, and served as delegates to religious conventions. They provided leadership from the pew and mapped the suburban landscape for transient pastors. Church work fell largely to working women.

In 1898, for example, twenty-seven-year-old domestic servant Violet Johnson located and paid the first month's rent on a meeting place for the nascent Fountain Baptist Church and remained its major fund-raiser throughout the prolonged building program. Johnson served on the church's disciplinary committee that examined and ruled on the conduct of men and women.[4] She used her personal connections to gain local white support and to attract national speakers; as in 1909 when Booker T. Washington spoke to the black congregation after speaking at Summit's prestigious white Athenaeum Club.[5] Despite their organized work and crucial role in church growth, black ministers and white church women studied them warily.

As the black Baptist church followed domestic workers to New York City's emerging suburbs, black women's visibility increased. They organized Missionary Bible Bands to minister to migrating women and children disembarking on the piers of New York and New Jersey. In 1891 without clergy sanction, women of NEBMC, a multistate association that included churches from Maine to North Carolina, issued a call to local missionary groups to form a regional organization. The women elected Sarah Luckett of New York and a New Jersey pastor's wife as president and vice president of the Woman's Missionary Bible Band of the New England Baptist Missionary Convention. The following year they incorporated their organization in Brooklyn, the site of NEBMC's incorporation six years earlier. With the objective "to assist our beloved Churches and to do Home and Foreign Mission work as the Lord may, in His divine providence, direct," the Woman's Missionary Band tried to balance a spiritual call to missionary work with the denomination's call to assist pastors.[6]

Though the women added "auxiliary" to the name, the Woman's Missionary Bible Band had no official place in the male-led convention.

The women had to meet in private homes and during recess periods at annual sessions. Despite the lack of denominational recognition, they stimulated the formation of local missionary societies and increased NEBMC's membership and coffers. Convention officials welcomed church women as dues-paying members and appointed them to administrative committees. Unfortunately, their contributions did not translate into a positive valorization of their organization.

NEMBC's ecclesiastical accounting system differentiated between the work of individual church women and organized "woman's work." For example, in the absence of a pastor in 1907 "Mrs. M. J. Desverney" had charge of Ebenezer Baptist Church in Poughkeepsie, New York, for the entire year and reported eight conversions to NEBMC. That same year as a field worker in the Missionary Bible Band she reported bringing sixty-nine "souls to Christ."[7] Though women like Desverney held fledgling congregations together with their preaching and administrative skills, the church denied them the rite of ordination or the opportunity to speak at denominational meetings. When Sarah Luckett, a founder of the regional Bible Band who began by organizing the rescue of children and fallen women in New York City, reported her work to the convention in 1889 it was indeed a singular occasion.[8]

Church men and women viewed the relationship between church and society differently. As the *gathered church* of regenerated believers, Baptists deemed it important to safeguard members from intermingling with unbaptized persons or "loose members" not in good standing. In contrast, missionary women welcomed unchurched "gentlemen and ladies" as members, albeit without the right to hold office or vote. Furthermore, missionaries did their work on the streets, alleys, and piers where women and homeless families congregated. Some ministers complained that Missionary Bible Bands diverted critical resources—women's time and money—from the church's mission. Others deemed street missions, if undertaken at all, the province of men.[9] For a denomination intent on securing its proper place in Protestant America, the women's forays into public space subverted its class-bound objectives and masculine leadership.

As the economic downturn of the 1890s and the migration of women and families from the South provided daily reminders of the need for their woman's work, church women continued their quiet campaign for denominational recognition and the moral authority and respectability that conferred. More than three years after organizing, the Woman's Missionary Bible Band earned a nod of recognition when NEBMC leaders conceded that the "spirituality of the [annual] session was increased and over fifty added to [the] membership" as a result of the women's meeting during the recess period.[10]

Church women in New Jersey's suburbs fared no better. Following a period of intense revivals fanned by the watchword "New Jersey for Christ," Baptists organized the New Jersey Afro-American Baptist Association in 1892, and excluded Missionary Bible Bands. Like their sisters in NEMBC, New Jersey women maintained a public ministry with an open membership and provided shelter, clothing, and aid to women, children, and destitute families.

After four years of being ignored, representatives of nineteen missionary societies gathered in suburban Plainfield in 1896 and formed the Baptist Woman's Missionary Union Bible Band of New Jersey.[11] The following year, New Jersey's missionary women achieved a minor victory when the state association granted Bible Band president Phyllis Brown "a few minutes" to speak on the women's work. Apparently, the men had never before listened to Brown, though she was a member of the association's temperance committee and a devotional leader. Brown so impressed the assembly that the recording minister broke with precedent and wrote, "Our brethren would do well to have Sister Brown before them again."[12]

Brown's "glowing report" did not surprise the women who frequently heard her "grand, noble, and stirring lectures" on "the great need of missionary work among women." Following one lecture the missionary secretary rapturously noted, "Our souls having been stirred for a more earnest work, we departed with great joy and will run to bring our sisters word."[13]

Through a confluence of events, in 1899 NEBMC clergy finally acknowledged the women's regional organization. Lewis Jordan, the influential foreign missions secretary of the four-year-old National Baptist Convention (NBC), made a personal appeal to NEBMC for monetary support. In dire financial straits and having borrowed money to print the convention program, NEBMC clergy turned to the women. The ministers invited the missionary women to a special joint session and suggested that they could "do more effective work" if they changed the organization's name to the "Woman's Home and Foreign Missionary Society of the N.E.B.M. Convention" and become an official auxiliary.[14]

Though surprised by the proposal, the women immediately grasped its implication. A name change required subordinating their organization and treasury to the men and the foreign mission project in exchange for denominational recognition. Following a lengthy discussion, Sarah Willie Layten, future president of the National Baptist Woman's Convention, made a motion and the women unanimously voted to accept the name change. They also agreed to sponsor a male missionary to Africa.[15]

To seal the arrangement, one minister offered a resolution on behalf of his "Dear Brethren." "In consideration of the vast importance of the females of our great Baptist brotherhood and sisterhood, Whereas, There has been a total oversight or willful omission on our part in giving them the proper recognition or place on our programs; and Whereas, The greatest of our numerical strength lies in that sex," he recommended giving a half-day during each session "to the woman's work on Home *and* Foreign Missions."[16]

If the minister intended to mollify the women for past omissions, he misread "that sex." Two years earlier they had remained silent when the men peremptorily dismissed their request to meet for a few hours during the annual session. Now, having exchanged their organizational autonomy for denominational recognition, they talked back. Church women told of the "many obstacles" from benign neglect to overt opposition ministers put in their way. Most egregiously, pastors often refused to designate the fifth Sunday as Missionary Sunday when women would have charge of the service, enroll new members, and collect the offering to support their home mission work.[17]

Surprisingly, the women did not consider the new arrangement a defeat; rather, it reflected their mastery of the art of negotiation. Without directly challenging the patriarchal leadership, they had expanded the church's mission, destabilized the locus of denominational power, and forced public acknowledgment of "woman's work." Their coalition strategy, one often employed by those negotiating from the margins, did not diminish their commitment to their gendered work. They immediately appointed two additional field workers and earmarked funds for expanded missionary projects in New Jersey. After years of having to meet in separate locations on travel day, the following year the women met during the annual session.[18]

Apparently, the 1899 NEBMC meeting was a dress rehearsal for the formation a year later of the National Baptist Woman's Convention.

When black Baptists organized the National Baptist Convention in 1895, church women petitioned to form a separate woman's auxiliary. After initially granting approval, the men disbanded the women's unit the following year and assigned its leaders to positions on male-led boards. Having learned from their sisters in NEBMC, in 1900 the women deployed a different strategy. They met in a secret caucus, formed an autonomous organization, and then sought clergy recognition. With support from the ubiquitous Foreign Mission Board Secretary Lewis Jordan, the vision of a national black Baptist women's organization became a reality.[19]

* * *

The national Woman's Convention drew its spiritual and numerical strength from domestic workers like Violet Johnson. Through the network of missionary societies, ordinary working women in the North and South connected their local experiences to state and national discussions of religion, gender, and race. The Woman's Convention represented and shaped the perspective of non-elite church women and united them in the struggle for the dignity of black womanhood and, they believed, the salvation of the race. As historian Evelyn Brooks Higginbotham argues, it created a "new discursive realm in which women's voices were neither silent nor subordinate to men's." Nationally, it legitimated a new form of representative politics by constituting a black woman's congress that "thrust issues of race and gender into the broad discursive arena of American social reform."[20]

The Woman's Convention became black Baptist women's most important source of training on Christian womanhood. Nannie Helen Burroughs, Corresponding Secretary from 1900 until she succeeded Sarah Willie Layten as president in 1948, produced program materials and organizational aids designed to develop women's leadership skills and turned missionary societies into "great preparatory schools" and concomitantly "commanded greater authority and respect for women."[21] Burroughs disseminated record books and bookkeeping advice at conventions and filled mail orders for guides, buttons, leaflets, and training material. In addition to her own writings, Burroughs adapted material from white women's missionary societies to meet the literacy and time constraints of working women.[22]

Most important, Burroughs championed the respect and dignity of working women. "We are no less honorable if we are servants," Burroughs averred. In an inversion of the middle-class formulation of character, she insisted that "[f]idelity to duty, rather than the grade of one's occupation is the true measure of character." Unlike "parlor ornaments" or those who "flirt and loiter about the streets," self-supporting domestic servants were "too honest, industrious and independent" to be "debased by idleness." They "have character enough for queens." Taking direct aim at those who constructed a narrow, middle-class notion of true womanhood, Burroughs proclaimed the "servant girl" to be "the prime factor in the salvation of Negro womanhood, whose salvation must be attained before the so-called race problem can be solved."[23]

Burroughs and Johnson placed domestic workers at the center of their model of Christian womanhood. This formulation was not an imitation of a middle-class ideal of separate spheres; rather it reframed respectability to incorporate the experiential reality of most black women in Northeastern cities and suburbs, women who deserved respect *because* they worked outside their own homes and traversed public space. Working women reinforced this model in missionary meetings with topics such as "The Influence of a Good Woman in the Church," "Character," "The Woman of Today," and "What Influence Should Women Have on Temperance?"[24] Their papers on Christian duty generated lively discussions. As one suburbanite shared with her "Dear Sisters," "It is our duty to lift high the stained banner for Christ and never let it trail in the dust . . . and to labor for the highest development of Christian womanhood." "We do not have to go into the dark fields of Africa to do missionary work. There is work for us to do right here at home." Echoing the Woman's Era philosophy of middle-class black women she added, "It is conceded by all nations that woman is the greatest factor for civilizing and christianizing [*sic*] the world."[25] For domestic servants, dignifying black women and their labor was a Christian duty and a racial imperative.

Violet Johnson and Nannie Helen Burroughs formed an enduring personal and working relationship. They applied their organizational and leadership skills to promote the dignity of non-elite women, one nationally and the other in regional, state, and local venues. They worked closely on the key program of the Woman's Convention, the National Training School for Women and Girls that Burroughs founded in 1909 in Washington, D.C. Johnson was a member of the Board of Trustees and a Woman's Convention vice president.[26] As the president and founder of her local missionary society, she also served on key committees, presented papers, and facilitated discussions at state and regional sessions.

Burroughs frequently visited New Jersey and NEBMC meetings. On one visit to Summit she spoke to Johnson's missionary group on "The Development of Womanhood." The pastor extended an invitation to "the white people of Summit to hear ["a typical negress of extraordinary gifts as an orator"] who advocates the real principles of her people."[27] Many accepted the invitation. Burroughs's reputation as a speaker and the intense, almost prurient, interest in black women would have been difficult to resist. Women like Johnson and Burroughs imbricated Victorian ideology, Woman's Era philosophy, and Christian evangelicalism to position nonelite women as integral to the success of the denomination and the race.

Paradoxically, black church men appropriated the same discourse to offer women "hearty praise for their most liberal contribution to our work" rather than accede to requests for a more inclusive church polity. When Baptist women attempted to extend their Missionary Bible Band meeting to a full day in 1908, for instance, NEMBC officials responded with a mellifluous but insubstantial resolution to "these sainted women [who] are to our Convention what the beauty and fragrance are to the rose."[28] Such trivialization reminded women that their church subordinated them and their views to masculine understandings of religion and race. Nevertheless, through a program of social activism grounded in the egalitarian message of the gospel, working women like Johnson expanded the church's mission and its practices.

As the clergy correctly sensed, working women's Christian activism was inherently political and ultimately subversive. Their separate organization and treasury gestured toward gender equality, while their public ministry disrupted the hidebound class discourse that male clergy tried to construct.

Working Women and Temperance Work

The Woman's Christian Temperance Union (WCTU) increased black women's public presence and, in turn, black women transformed the WCTU into a biracial and cross-class sisterhood in the fight "For God and Home and Native Land." New Jersey White Ribboners formed the first Union in Newark in September 1873, the year of "The Crusades" in

Ohio and the Midwest. Three years later, they declared the entire state organized for temperance and formed the New Jersey Woman's Christian Temperance Union (NJWCTU).[29]

New Jersey provided fertile ground for agitating and organizing. With the question of a constitutional prohibition before the state legislature in the early 1880s, the white middle-class women's reform organization wooed black and foreign-born working women who could influence the votes of their male relatives with urgent appeals: "Wanted! Ten thousand Christian women to the rescue of the drunkards of New Jersey; drunken men and drunken women, ruined youth; homeless, starving children. Woman, queen of the home, the angel of the household, cast down from her throne of influence by this curse of rum."[30]

During the heat of the prohibition campaign, the NJWCTU organized the first black Union in Mount Holly, a Philadelphia suburb, and a second across from New York City in Newark.[31] Following the legislature's defeat of the referendum on constitutional prohibition in 1884, the NJWCTU endorsed woman suffrage and established a Department of Franchise.[32] Woman suffrage and prohibition were politically intertwined.

With the state Union's politicization, the campaign among black women intensified. White women visited black Baptist and Methodist churches where they shared the podium with black men and women at Sunday services and temperance rallies. In Montclair white women stimulated "a new and desirable movement" among black women with "cottage prayer meetings." In Plainfield they organized WCTU No. 2 with equal representation from the local black Baptist and Methodist churches.[33] Helen Crane, mother of novelist Stephen Crane and president of the Union in the shore towns of Asbury Park and Ocean Grove, attended a large evening meeting at the local African Methodist Episcopal church and, following the pastor's invitation to "take the pledge," organized a Union with the pastor's wife as president.[34] By mid-1885 the white state superintendent enthusiastically reported that "the work among the colored people is growing in importance."[35]

Nationally, the politicization of the WCTU was well under way. The national organization had endorsed woman suffrage in 1881. Pursuing a strategy to influence the political process at the state level, national president Frances Willard made her first southern tour to enlist white women and created the Department of Southern Work. Under Willard's leadership the WCTU also established separate departments for Work among Colored People in the North and evangelistic work among German, Chinese, and Scandinavian women.[36]

Apparently, the work among black women fell short, for in 1883 the WCTU replaced the white National Superintendent for Work among Colored People with Frances E. W. Harper, the first African American woman hired by the national organization.[37] A member of the African Methodist Episcopal (AME) church and a Philadelphia temperance organizer since 1875, the former abolitionist believed that the equitable treatment of black women was not only white women's Christian duty but also in their best political interest. In some northern states, she explained, "[T]here may be colored voters enough to hold the balance of power, either for us or against us." She urged her "Dear Sisters" to make every effort "to win the confidence, awaken the interest and enlist the co-operation of the colored women . . . not as an object of charity, but as helpers and auxiliaries in a great and glorious cause. . . . [I]nvite them . . . to unite with you, or, if they prefer it, to form auxiliaries."[38]

Harper frequently had to remind white women to behave "in the spirit of the all-inclusive Christ." Despite evidence of race and class prejudice, she believed that the reform organization was "one of the moral and spiritual levers that [would] help lift up women of [her] branch of the human race to higher planes of thought and action" and unify "an earnest womanhood" to work "for God, for home and native land."[39] Harper conceded that organizing black women had its challenges, not for reasons of race but of economics. "[T]he masses of the colored women have not had a generation since slavery to straighten their hands from the hoe . . . grasp the pen, and to have purchased leisure from the cares of maternity and bread-winning to have accomplished very much purely benevolent work outside the pressure of their own home and church work."[40]

In New Jersey a unified womanhood waxed and waned with the legislative calendar. When the legislature began its discussion of local option, a gradual prohibition strategy that allowed local jurisdictions to hold special elections on licensing drinking establishments, the NJWCTU revived efforts to include black women. Plainfield's white Unions joined the all-black WCTU No. 2 and local pastors in mass meetings to close saloons.[41] In New Brunswick, home of Rutgers College and a town said to be "under the thrall of the rumsellers," the white Superintendent of Work among Colored People invited women from three black churches to participate in afternoon meetings at Temperance Hall. At one meeting church choirs provided music and the AME Zion pastor's wife presented a paper on "Woman's Work among the Colored People." Subsequently, the church women organized a separate union that met in the AME Zion parsonage. On home visits to black residents, the women "found sixteen families where a prayer was never heard and whose children had never been to Sunday-school." With financial help from the white Union, the new "White Ribboners" appointed a missionary to work among the families. White generosity notwithstanding, black women were wary of the WCTU's sporadic outbursts of interracial sisterhood and agreed with the AME Zion pastor that "the colored people [were] being asked to help the white people fight."[42]

Facing the defeat of a local option amendment, the NJWCTU began a lobbying campaign for passage of a bill on scientific temperance instruction in public schools. In early 1890 WCTU national president Frances Willard and state president Sarah Downs presented legislators with a sixteen thousand-signature petition in support of the legislation. Though Downs spent three weeks in Trenton lobbying for the bill's passage, the Democratic-controlled legislature rejected the local option amendment and compulsory temperance instruction.[43]

When the state Union convened its annual session in the summer of 1890, the women displayed their white ribbons and their legislative bruises. Undaunted, they issued a political call to arms: "Whether temperance is in politics or not, we have found that the saloon is in politics. The only remedy for this is in legislation, and the only way that this can be secured is by the ballot."[44] Crossing race and class lines, the NJWCTU demanded the vote for all New Jersey women, African American and foreign-born, working and middle class. Temperance was a political problem and woman suffrage the solution.

As the prohibition strategy shifted from constitutional to local statutory prohibition, the national WCTU revived the Department for Work among Colored Women and appointed Lucy Thurman superintendent with national officer status. A former teacher and AME missionary from Jackson, Michigan, Thurman had been a White Ribboner since 1876 when she signed the temperance pledge after hearing black evangelist Amanda Berry Smith at a temperance crusade in Toledo, Ohio. Dubbed "the colored WCTU evangelist," Thurman initially focused on the southern states, leaving the northern work to local and state super-intendents "where there is less race prejudice."[45] However, like Frances Harper she soon realized that northern white women needed reminding of the all-inclusive Christ. The summer of 1898 found Thurman in New Jersey urging white state officers to reach out to black women.[46]

The WCTU played a role in black working women's politicization. De-spite black women's reservations and white women's distrust, the WCTU educated women on subjects ranging from preparing and presenting topics to promoting legislation. In her study of social movements, political sci-entist Ann-Marie Szymanski highlights the "modularized learning" of the WCTU, particularly the ability to educate women on the political process and to develop skills to influence political outcomes. By routinizing the fundamental activities of collective action, such as information sharing and recruiting and training new members, the WCTU rapidly diffused learning from one group to another.[47] Chalk-talks, ten-minute speeches, and parlia-mentary drills turned even timid women into Christian activists.

The WCTU's production of an autonomous woman's organizational culture appealed to black working women.[48] Consider domestic servant Emma Ray, an African Methodist Episcopal (AME) missionary and member of the Seattle, Washington Union. The WCTU allowed her to claim the public dimension of "woman's work" and to validate her "call" to a preaching vocation, something her church denied. Through the WCTU Ray interacted with a cross-section of black and white women. When the national WCTU met in Seattle in 1899, Emma Ray entertained national organizer Lucy Thurman in her modest home.[49]

While the WCTU's organizational culture acted as a centripetal force uniting women across class and color lines, racial and class prejudice ex-erted a powerful centrifugal force, leading many black women to choose separate, autonomous organizations. Although Violet Johnson's church rented worship space in Temperance Hall and the Woman's Missionary Society met there, black women in Summit chose to promote temperance through their independent missionary society and Sunday school.[50]

Temperance Women to Club Women

Woodrow Wilson's 1910 gubernatorial victory ushered in a progres-sive agenda that promised direct primary elections, an end to corrupt legislative practices, compensation laws to include women employed in factories, and state control of railroads and public utilities. Increasing racial segregation, the financial setback of 1910–1911, and the depression of 1913–1915 could not dampen the optimism.[51] Progressivism was at its apogee, and New Jersey women did not intend to be left behind.

By 1912 the WCTU was poised for action. Reporting from Trenton, the white legislative liaison was ebullient: "'Votes for Women!' This was the motto which was flashed before the eyes of the New Jersey Legislature . . . on orange pennants, and when Senator Fielder fastened one of these to the chair of the speaker of the House, the chamber rang with cheers."[52]

Though more subdued, African American women also viewed as propitious the convergence of temperance and suffrage. Winning the vote would further their ability to apply Christian principles to social problems—to do work for humanity and the race. The all-black Rahway Union No.2 exemplified the "promise of good, progressive work being carried on" by black women throughout the state.[53] Nationally, WCTU Superintendent of Colored Work Eliza E. Peterson assured her temperance sisters that "the Christians among the colored race are going to do their part in the future in the protection of the black boys and girls from the demon that is sapping the manhood and womanhood of the race."[54] By the time the national WCTU unfurled its prohibition campaign at the annual convention in Asbury Park in November 1913, the fight was on.[55] Uniting with antiliquor proponents under the banner "A Saloonless Nation in 1920," black and white temperance women vowed to alter the political map.[56]

When the Republican-controlled New Jersey assembly passed a joint resolution in favor of a suffrage referendum in February 1915, the entire state was mobilized for suffrage and, implicitly, prohibition—for or against.[57] Despite intensive campaigning by the WCTU, the antiliquor coalition, and suffragists, the suffrage referendum failed by forty-six thousand votes.[58] The all-male electorate rejected woman suffrage and temperance.

The suffrage campaign revealed fissures in New Jersey women's public activism. In the weeks before the special election black and white temperance women, "feverishly active" throughout the state, jointly hosted suffrage meetings, marched in suffrage parades, and conducted poll watchers' training. Black women addressed men's organizations and participated in street rallies and house-to-house canvassing.[59] Despite black women's visibility, white suffragists ignored them, with one notable exception. On the eve of the referendum vote, the Woman's Political Union invited National Association of Colored Women (NACW) leader Mary Church Terrell of Washington, D.C., to a mass meeting in Newark to urge black men to vote for woman suffrage.[60]

In the wake of the resounding defeat, suffragists searched for an explanation. Some blamed black women. "Negro Women as Watchers Lost Vote for Suffrage, Men Say in Atlantic City"; "responsible citizens . . . express[ed] disapproval of their presence" and voted against the amendment, reported the *New York Times*.[61] In New York and Pennsylvania, the WCTU charged the "large foreign population . . . for the delayed victory for suffrage."[62] Such recriminations highlighted white middle-class women's distrust of working women unable to educate their men.

In the aftermath of the highly polarized contest and the criticism of their erstwhile white allies, New Jersey's African American women tested their organizational capacity. Within weeks of the suffrage defeat, Reverend Florence Randolph, president of the Jersey City "colored" WCTU and the AME Zion New Jersey Conference Missionary Society, issued a statewide call to Methodist and Baptist missionary societies "to consider the advisability of forming ourselves into an organized body." In late October representatives of thirty missionary groups gathered at St. Paul's AME Zion Church in Trenton to "arouse interest in Temperance work among colored people."[63]

"The First Conference of the Women's [*sic*] Christian Temperance Union of the Colored Women of New Jersey" opened with the question, "What would National Prohibition do for us as a Race?" After the assemblage sang "The Fight Is On," eleven missionary presidents spoke on the necessity of organizing. The afternoon session began with the hymn "Stand Up for Jesus" followed by prayer, scripture, the duet "Saloonless Nation," and the reading of a paper titled "Why Every Christian Should Be a Total Abstainer." The youth of the Loyal Temperance Legion marched into the sanctuary singing "Onward Christian Soldiers."[64]

The first conference of the WCTU of the Colored Women of New Jersey was the last. In an unexpected turn, the Methodist and Baptist women voted unanimously to organize the New Jersey State Federation of Colored Women's Clubs.[65]

Why at this moment did these Christian women choose to identify themselves as secular club women rather than Christian temperance women? The historical record remains tantalizingly silent on the discussion preceding that signal decision. Meeting within ten days of the suffrage defeat, an "interest in Temperance" conveyed multiple, often conflicting, meanings in a state riven by class, race, and religious tensions. Perhaps like black women in other states, not all wanted to sign the temperance pledge. Possibly some felt deserted by their white allies and simply lost faith in the WCTU as an organization.

More likely, by 1915 black women recognized that the structural and social evils "sapping the manhood and womanhood of the race" went beyond prohibition and could be addressed only when women could vote. In the words of that redoubtable defender of black womanhood, Nannie Helen Burroughs, the ballot was nothing less than the black woman's "weapon of moral defence [sic]." Boldly stepping where others feared to tread, Burroughs lifted the veil on the sexual exploitation of black women, especially black domestic workers. "Had she not been the woman of unusual moral stamina . . . the black race would have been made a great deal whiter, and the white race a great deal blacker during the past fifty years. . . . The Negro woman is the white woman's as well as the white race's most needed ally in preserving an unmixed race. . . . The ballot wisely used will bring to her the respect and protection that she needs. . . . to reckon with men who place no value upon her virtue, and to mould healthy public sentiment in favor of her own protection." Compared to the white woman or the black man, the African American woman needed the ballot more, for she bore "the burden of the Church, and of the school and . . . a great deal more than her economic share of the home."[66]

The Christian women meeting in Trenton that cool October day apparently agreed with Burroughs. For white middle-class temperance women, the ballot meant home protection; for their suffrage counterparts, it symbolized equality with white men and a counterweight to the errant black and foreign male vote. For women who had to fight for respect from white women and black and white men, the ballot represented personal protection and social justice.

What better place than the state capital to demonstrate black women's agency? Though Randolph had added a third day to the previously scheduled AME Zion Missionary Society's annual session, the selection of Trenton no doubt impressed the women as more than mere geographic convenience. As Randolph later recalled, "[T]he success and enthusiasm of that meeting went beyond our most sanguine expectations."[67]

No matter how compelling, however, ideology alone seldom suffices to sustain independent action. Having assayed their social capital, these predominantly working women reified it in a bold organizational move. By 1915 the convergence of several factors, locally and nationally, augured well for a statewide organization led by black Christian women. Restrictions on foreign immigration and the economic uplift due to the war in Europe had expanded employment opportunities and increased black migration to New Jersey's cities and suburbs. Nationally, black women's experience with limited suffrage and the expansion of the National Association of Colored Women (NACW) beyond its upper middle-class boundaries had increased cross-class interactions and political aspirations. Begun as an organization of college educated, upper-middle-class women in 1896, the expanding color line and attendant changes in the political and economic fortunes of African Americans transformed the NACW into a middle- and working-class woman's organization with a broad social agenda.[68] Within these economic, social, and political shifts New Jersey women voted to affiliate with the NACW and "join hands with that galaxy of . . . noble women . . . determined to 'Lift as they climb.'"[69] They formed a statewide organization through which to address the *Negro problem* and the *woman question*.

By the time President Florence Randolph presided over the first "record-breaking convention" of the New Jersey State Federation Colored Women's Clubs (NJSFCWC) in 1916, not even the July heat could wither their enthusiasm. Representatives of thirty-three enrolled clubs "doing work for human betterment" met at the First Baptist Church in suburban Englewood and addressed the two most contentious political issues, prohibition and suffrage. In response to the question "What Will National Prohibition Mean to the Negro?" they enumerated tangible benefits: "better homes, larger bank accounts, and more real estate." On the question of suffrage, they created three new departments, Suffrage, Race History, and Education.[70]

The State Federation grew to forty-nine clubs by 1917 and reached eighty-five the next year. The number of departments peaked at twenty-one in 1920. Department heads researched relevant issues, outlined an action plan, and coordinated with local clubs on implementation. Within this discursive space, supported by a decentralized structure and centralized program of communication and education, non-elite Christian women increased their public activism and their civic engagement.

* * *

In many respects, the contours of this working women's narrative seem familiar. Like their white and black middle-class sisters, they participated in available discourses and accepted Victorian values and social conventions. However, by some significant measures their story is unique. As working women and southern migrants in the suburban North, they operated in liminal space and their personal lives were never private. Highly visible yet morally suspect, they were under the gaze of black male ministers and white middle-class women. Their inclusion in the church and the WCTU was as much a product of moral coercion and social control as sincere outreach, since they were the ones often viewed as most in need of reform.

As the women had learned in their churches, organization mattered. Their organizational choices not only illuminate their values and aspirations, but also reveal their consciousness of themselves as respectable agents with social capital. In the first instantiation their missionary organizations thrust them into a struggle with male pastors who embraced as normative the middle-class Victorian model of womanhood. In the WCTU, white middle-class women unable to accept them as equals damaged relations. Ultimately, without rejecting their gender, race, or class, they defined themselves and their model of Christian womanhood in the State Federation of Colored Women's Clubs.[71] Through war and suffrage, they would hold fast to the compelling "vision of the potential strength and influence of a union of Christian women and faith in their willingness to assume responsibility."[72]

Violet A. Johnson (1870–1939), circa 1900. Courtesy of the Fountain Baptist Church
Collection, Summit, NJ.

Reverend Florence Spearing Randolph (1866–1951), circa 1900. Courtesy of Ethel M. Washington, Plainfield, NJ.

3

"The Home Away from Home"

Suffrage, War, and Civic Righteousness

By the time Florence Randolph called the second annual session of the New Jersey State Federation of Colored Women's Clubs (NJSFCWC) to order in suburban Plainfield in July 1917, the war to make the world safe for democracy was in its third month and the East St. Louis, Illinois, riot only a few weeks past. Throughout the summer and fall, as African Americans tried to balance support for war abroad with denunciation of racial discrimination and violence at home, the predominantly working-class women of NJSFCWC waged their own battle on the home front.

Organizing in 1915 following defeat of the woman suffrage referendum, ordinary African American women entered public space determined "to solve the many problems confronting the race, to study the conditions in our own cities and counties and in the spirit of Christ by personal contact and sympathy, 'to Lift as We Climb.'" With the motto "To Work and Serve the Hour," Violet Johnson, Florence Randolph, and the women in the State Federation linked their missionary experience to the National Association of Colored Women (NACW) and modern social science in a program of civic righteousness, the Christian practice of infusing justice and morality into the public sphere. Initially comprised of only Baptist and Methodist missionary societies, within a year NJSFCWC opened its membership to any organization "doing work for human betterment," except purely leisure and social clubs.[1] For many women the State Federation was the first secular organization they had ever joined; it served as a bridge from church work to political activism.

World War I catalyzed black working women in New Jersey's cities and suburbs and provided a humanitarian reason to enter public life outside their denominations. As Violet Johnson and Florence Randolph confronted the economic and social dislocations of war and its aftermath, they crossed boundaries of race and class, negotiated the chasm between national rhetoric and local practice, and mobilized on the home front to demonstrate their patriotism as women and their ability as African Americans. Despite their best efforts, however, the leading white women's groups, the Woman's Committee on Defense Work and the Red Cross, bowed to racial prejudice and prevented their inclusion in the national mobilization program.

Eventually, it was sexual politics and not black women's patriotism or the desire for a united sisterhood that engendered interracial cooperation. Prompted by the War Department's fear of working women's sexuality and the susceptibility of men in khaki to sexual infection, the Commission on Training Camp Activities (CTCA) allied with the Young Women's Christian Association (YWCA) to create programs for African American women and girls. Though reacting to negative assumptions about black and working women's sexuality, the YWCA created employment opportunities for college-trained black women and enabled working women like Johnson to exchange domestic service for social work.

While State Federation women carefully mined the moment for opportunities to benefit their race and gender, economic inflation, discrimination in employment and housing, and the harsh winter of 1917–1918 exacerbated already intolerable conditions for the state's growing black population.[2] As Johnson and Randolph witnessed the social and economic dislocations of war and demobilization, winning the vote became pivotal. Thus, they joined middle-class white women in the New Jersey Woman Suffrage Association (NJWSA) and transformed the state's suffrage campaign into a biracial movement.

After 1920, ordinary black women pressed their claim as enfranchised citizens and attempted to renegotiate their relationship with the state, elite white women, and black men. As the postwar symbols of full citizenship tightened around a narrowly constructed vision of the Anglo-Saxon middle-class family and a detached home, Johnson, Randolph, and the women of NJSFCWC held fast to the alternative vision of civic righteousness, just laws, and moral institutions.

Black Club Women and White Suffragists

Reverend Florence Spearing Randolph's election as the first president of the State Federation of Colored Women's Clubs epitomized the geographic and social distance black women had traversed. Like many in the Federation, Randolph came of age in the post-Reconstruction South and migrated North as a young woman. Born in South Carolina in 1866, she attended Charleston's Avery Normal Institute where she learned the dressmaking trade. In 1885, nineteen-year-old Randolph followed her older sisters to the New York City area, settling in Jersey City, New Jersey. Northern life proved professionally and personally rewarding. Randolph earned three times more a day for the same work; married Virginia native Hugh Randolph, a cook on the dining car service of the Pullman Company; and gave birth to their daughter Leah Viola. Reflecting her skill and determination, Randolph's dressmaking business flourished.[3]

Confirmed in Charleston's segregated Methodist Episcopal Church, Randolph joined the independent African Methodist Episcopal (AME) Zion Church within a year of settling in Jersey City. Under the tutelage of Eli George Biddle, an AME Zion minister who attended Yale and served as a chaplain in the 54th Massachusetts Regiment during the Civil War, she began a systematic study of the Bible, Hebrew, and Greek and became a "helper" in Biddle's holiness class, responsible for strengthening the local congregation as a Sunday school teacher and Class Leader. Here she met two AME Zion luminaries, the Reverend Mrs. Julia Foote and Bishop Alexander Walters.[4]

Since the AME Zion Church competed with other Protestant denominations for converts in the Northeast, "all dedicated church members were missionaries and expected to share in the program of expanding the Church."[5] Randolph did her part. In 1888 she closed her dressmaking shop one afternoon each week and volunteered at the Hudson County prisons and the White Rose Mission, a refuge for black women in New York City.[6]

As an AME Zion Methodist, Randolph joined a small band of Protestant women allowed to "freely exercise their spiritual gifts."[7] In 1898, the year Violet Johnson organized a Baptist church in Summit, the AME Zion Church licensed Randolph as an evangelist, making her eligible to preach and hold revivals, but ineligible for pastoral assignments.[8] The door to clerical leadership opened unexpectedly when Randolph turned a one-time permission to lead the congregation into a historic church revival during the illness of her pastor. Activist Bishop Alexander Walters ordained Randolph a deacon in 1901 and an elder in 1903, qualifying her for pastoral service.[9] Between 1897 and 1909, Randolph pastored several working-class congregations in New Jersey and New York, generally working without a "stated" or contracted salary. Once the church stabilized, she was "replaced by a 'nice young man' and reassigned to another problem church."[10]

Despite her preaching ability, the support of mentors, and demonstrated leadership, Randolph's denominational advancement was circumscribed. Zion women remained in subordinate roles in the clerical ranks and in the Woman's Home and Foreign Missionary (WH&FM) Society. Finally in 1904, when presented with evidence of the slow growth of missionary societies, the primary funding source for foreign missions, the Board of Bishops allowed Zion women to manage the department. The women restructured the WH&FM, formed their own executive board, and held separate conventions; financial matters remained with the all-male board.[11] Bishops' wives, originators of the WH&FM, "began losing their official positions to other missionary-minded women who felt the need to broaden the leadership."[12]

The shift benefited Randolph. In 1912 she became Secretary of the Bureau of Supplies, the department responsible for collecting all donations of clothing, medicine, literature, and other material for foreign missions, and later president of the national and state WH&FM societies.[13]

While Randolph's gender may have been a liability in the clerical ranks, her "curiosity as a woman" proved an asset in the New Jersey Woman's Christian Temperance Union (WCTU). Sitting at the window of her dress shop in 1892, she witnessed a melee at the saloon across the street, one of many that earned Jersey City the reputation of being a city "under the dominion of the rum traffic." As police placed an "intoxicated and noisy" young man in a patrol wagon, Randolph, "speaking aloud . . . said, if I had my way I would close every saloon before midnight. A white woman standing near, a president of the WCTU[,] told me 'if you feel that way come and join the WCTU and help us bring about prohibition.'" Randolph joined the white Jersey City WCTU. As she later reminisced, "Thus as a WCTU, Christian Endeavor, Kings Daughter and Sunday School Teacher I soon developed into a Bible student discovering that one can do a real telling work for God and humanity."[14]

Randolph's reputation soon spread among temperance women. In June 1899, "Mrs. Randolph, a colored woman, spoke on the 'Afro-

American'" at the regular meeting of the white Hudson County Temperance Union.[15] In February 1900, while on a tour to build up temperance unions in the Northeast, National Superintendent of Work among Colored People Rosetta Lawson "spent two weeks in Hudson County . . . [where] the dear sisters there were untiring in their efforts to push forward our cause."[16] Following Lawson's visit, the WCTU organized a "colored" union with eleven members and representatives from the various churches, including Randolph, as vice presidents.[17] That summer at the WCTU School of Methods in Ocean Grove, Randolph shared the platform with white state and national officers, including a white South Carolinian who "enjoy[ed] New Jersey's gathering of the clans." The "colored sister . . . ably presented" the topic "Total Abstinence among Colored People; Encouragement."[18] Randolph had traveled a great distance from the post-Reconstruction South to interracial Christian activism in the North. America's entry into World War I marked another turning point.

The July 1917 annual meeting of the State Federation signaled the rising visibility of the predominantly working women and their organization. "Women of national character" joined them, including YWCA National Secretary Eva Bowles, New York City Equal Suffrage League President Addie Hunton, and National Association of Colored Women (NACW) President Mary Talbert.[19] The presence of white WCTU presidents and influential men of the Federation of Colored Organizations and the state National Association for the Advancement of Colored People (NAACP) provided further evidence of NJSFCWC's visibility.[20] Many would become perennial visitors seeking the Federation's endorsement.

As Randolph oversaw a morning session devoted to Federation business, Suffrage chairwoman Mary Goodwin announced that the past president of the white New Jersey Woman Suffrage Association (NJWSA) and fellow East Orange suburbanite, Dr. Mary Hussey, was inviting the NJSFCWC to "become identified with the suffrage work in this state." The verbal invitation "precipitated a heated discussion" on the status of the NJWSA and the Federation of Women's Clubs, two exclusive white women's organizations. To avoid disrupting the meeting, Randolph tabled the matter pending further information.[21]

To the black women's surprise, Hussey and suffrage president Lillian Feickert appeared that afternoon to provide "more information on suffrage." Three years earlier NJWSA had moved its headquarters from Newark to suburban Plainfield, nearer to Feickert's home and the suburban locus of suffrage support. With the black club women meeting at the Mount Olive Baptist Church in Plainfield, a white suffrage representative could easily make an appearance. It is striking that both the former and current presidents felt these black women merited their immediate presence. Clearly, they considered black women's support for suffrage a positive good for the cause, and they expected black women to become politically active and vote when they became enfranchised.

Hussey, the initiator of the invitation, "sketched briefly the organization and development of woman suffrage nationally and locally."[22] The black women might have heretofore been invisible to the white suffragists, but they had more than a passing familiarity with suffrage, nationally and locally. Given their participation in the men's Colored Republican Clubs and the WCTU, they understood what was at stake should suffrage legislation remain stalled.

Contrary to the white suffragists' conjecture, the black women's reluctance to become "identified" with the white women's suffrage campaign stemmed not from a lack of knowledge, but from an awareness of the color line in the suffrage movement. In 1911, for example, white women in three suffrage organizations formed the Joint Legislative Committee to press for a suffrage amendment to the state constitution. Black women were not included.[23] Moreover, they had endured white suffragists' scathing criticism following defeat of the suffrage referendum in 1915, when white women blamed the presence of black women poll watchers for causing "responsible" citizens to vote against suffrage.[24] Now that white women were turning to them to further their cause, black women had reason to be wary.

By 1917, the political ground had shifted. When thirty-five-year-old Lillian Feickert became State Woman Suffrage Association president in 1912, the organization had a homogeneous membership of only two thousand white upper- and middle-class women. Barred by the state constitution from submitting the same amendment to the electorate more than once in five years, NJWSA abandoned the state referendum in favor of the federal amendment strategy championed by the National American Woman Suffrage Association (NAWSA). Faced with a state legislature unwilling to support either suffrage or prohibition and anti-suffragists claiming to represent the majority of New Jersey women, Feickert calculated that adding African American women to the pro-suffrage column was a political necessity.

It is unlikely that Feickert intended to speak that Thursday afternoon. However, following Hussey's dismal performance, she "spoke at length and in detail" on the status of states with full and partial suffrage, the relation of woman suffrage to the war, and the relation of the white Federation of women's clubs to the suffrage association, "individually and collectively."[25] Feickert did not reveal details of her plan to have black women identify with the suffrage campaign; the politically savvy black women were equally reticent. Yet, as all understood, numbers mattered. Black men voted in New Jersey, and their wives and daughters might convince them to vote for suffrage. Adding nearly three thousand black club women and the thousands of black women they represented would be a political coup.

New Jersey's black club women and white suffragists joined forces. In a post-session meeting, Randolph, Feickert, and NACW president Mary Talbert hammered out the details. Within two weeks, a committee of ten women equally divided between the Federation and the Suffrage Association submitted an agreement that formalized black women's membership on NJWSA's Executive Board, the formation of black women's local suffrage organizations, and NJWSA's subvention of costs for organizers and activities.[26] Ratification by the respective boards transformed New Jersey's suffrage campaign into a biracial and cross-class movement. Despite the contentious initial meeting, Feickert became a steadfast friend of the African American women. For their part, the black women converted their suffrage participation into a political force.

In a circular headed "Bringing In the Colored Women," Feickert acknowledged being "a speaker at a wonderful meeting of colored women" and assured the white women that the "speakers and officers were all most intelligent, thoughtful and worthwhile women."[27] She failed to mention that she had initiated the contact and met with them at their behest.

Based on Feickert's redacted account, historians of New Jersey's suffrage movement have incorrectly characterized the African American women as supplicants, marginally involved in the critical years of the suffrage campaign.[28] Such a reading not only obscures black women's agency and political acumen, it also ignores the image of black womanhood the State Federation had constructed by 1917. Though the national suffrage organization agreed to put suffrage on hold for the duration of the war in return for Woodrow Wilson's promise not to oppose a federal amendment when the war was over, Feichert recruited the black club women, made them welcome, and understood their value to the cause.

Working Women and War Work

America's entry into World War I on 6 April 1917 catalyzed black working women in New Jersey's cities and suburbs. While middle-class white women viewed war work as an opportunity to advance their suffrage claim—in support or opposition, black women discerned possibilities for racial and economic advancement, possibilities captured in the slogans "No Color Line" and "Come Out of the Kitchen, Mary." The black press reported, "Race women are rapidly deserting the cook stove and the wash tub to take her [*sic*] place at the machine, the looms and the engines of the factory." A Baptist publication "advise[d] ambitious young men and maidens of the high tone type to write their friends north for information [and] at once enter the new fields of industry, domestic service and manual labor."[29] The optimism notwithstanding, the color line tightened in ways that African American women could not have anticipated at the outset of a war waged to make the world safe for democracy.

Within fifteen days of the United States's declaration of war against Germany, the War Department's Council of National Defense created the Woman's Committee, officially the Committee on Women's Defense Work, to supervise women's public work. In early June the Woman's Committee distributed copies of President Wilson's war message and launched a national registration day of patriotic service, registering volunteer and wage-earning women through a network of state, county, city, and town divisions. The Woman's Committee identified twelve departments for war work, including Registration, Women in Industry, Child Welfare, and Liberty Loan. In mid-June National Food Administrator Herbert Hoover handed the committee its first task, to preserve and expand the existing food supply.[30]

By the end of June the New Jersey Division of the Woman's Committee, funded by the state and municipalities with contributions from private citizens, had distributed food registration cards and formed local committees throughout the state to weigh and measure babies, establish milk stations, create health and recreation centers for children, and provide safeguards for women in industry. When the leaders, suburban Ridgewood resident and president of the white Federation of Women's Clubs Lillian Stockton and suffragist Lillian Feickert, brought the leading women's organizations into the Woman's Committee, the State Federation of Colored Women's Clubs was conspicuously absent, though Feickert would give a suffrage speech to the organization only a few weeks later.[31] In a similar act of omission, the national Woman's Committee included more than fifty white women's groups but ignored the National Association of Colored Women, although representatives sat on the general committee.[32]

Contrary to the national and state examples, the mayor of Summit included African American women among the civic, social, and religious organizations on the suburb's Woman's Committee. Violet Johnson represented black women of the newly formed Woman in Industry Club. The suburb's Italian and native-born white working women had their respective Woman in Industry Club representatives.[33]

Throughout the war, black women contended with discriminatory rules of engagement. For example, in only five weeks the state's middle- and upper-class white women raised $12,000 to purchase, equip, and operate the whites-only Soldiers' Club at Camp Dix for a year. Within weeks of its opening, Summit's middle-class white women received permission to staff the club, and young white women entertained enlisted men at dances on Friday nights and officers on Saturday nights.[34] As a poignant coda, after two meetings officials at Camp Dix denied the State Federation of Colored Women's Clubs' request to establish a clubhouse for black soldiers.[35]

With good reason, African Americans questioned America's commitment to democracy. At its national war conference in May 1917, the biracial NAACP demanded fair treatment at home *and* support for the war, even as it cited colonialism and hostility toward darker races as the cause of the belligerence. In contrast, the pastor of a thirty-two hundred member Baptist congregation in Harlem urged withholding support until the Wilson administration had assured the extension of civil rights at home. As many struggled to balance patriotism and protest, racial violence in East St. Louis and Houston increased African American disaffection.[36]

Unable to ignore African American discontent, in October 1917 President Wilson appointed as Special Assistant to the Secretary of War Emmet Jay Scott, an officer at Tuskegee (Alabama) Institute. Based upon Scott's recommendation, by mid-1918 most southern states had organized black men in segregated auxiliary councils.[37] To shore up support among white women, in late September 1917 Wilson established the House Woman Suffrage Committee and positioned suffrage as a war measure.[38] Black women's concerns would have to wait.

However, black women did not wait. By the time the national Woman's Committee convened its initial meeting in Washington, D.C., many had already begun their own home-front battle for social justice. In early May, New Jersey women raised money for the Woman's Auxiliary of the Fifteenth Colored Regiment, a New York City organization supporting the military enlistment of black men. In November they helped establish the Circle for Negro War Relief "to promote the welfare of Negro soldiers and their dependent families," contingents ignored by the Red Cross and discriminated against in neighborhoods where black soldiers were quartered. Considered "the nearest approach to a Red Cross . . . through which colored people cooperated during the war," the Circle for Negro War Relief originated in New York City and its suburbs and within a few months had over sixty units throughout the country. Black women provided services that "ranged from the making of comfort kits to the furnishing of chewing gum . . . [and] the supplying of victrolas and records."[39]

Determined to demonstrate their "Loyalty as Americans," New Jersey's black women worked in segregated organizations as well as biracial coalitions, based on local sentiment and their threshold for racial discrimination. Red Cross participation, for example, rested with the elite white women who controlled local chapters. As members of the Summit Red Cross, black women enrolled in a home nursing course and knitted socks, sweaters, and wristlets. In Freehold they worked in a separate auxiliary that operated in the same location and under the same supervision as white women in the Monmouth County Red Cross.[40] Members of Paterson's black Fortnightly Club cooperated with the Passaic County Red Cross to provide service at Camp Merritt, an embarkation site about ten miles northwest of New York City.[41] In contrast, black women in Hackensack, a suburb about eight miles from Camp Merritt, organized savings bond and War Stamp drives on a completely separate basis after the local Red Cross prohibited their participation.[42] In some locations, such as Cranford, a suburb eight miles southwest of Newark, black women avoided the Red Cross and independently prepared surgical dressings, hospital bed socks, and suits of pajamas. Similarly, the Newark Colored Women's Volunteer League, a branch of the Mayor's Woman's Committee, established a canteen for black soldiers in rented space near Camp Dix and, with the Community Service Clubs of Orange, Montclair, and Burlington, chaperoned dances and sponsored poolrooms, picture shows, canteen and café services, and entertainment.[43] As one contemporary observed, black women navigated a minefield of "local conditions, racial antipathies, and ancient prejudices."[44]

Ultimately, it was sexual politics rather than patriotism or unity across the color line that prompted a reassessment of black women's participation in the war effort. Fearful of the sexual immorality to which recruits and enlisted men might be exposed, the War Department's Commission on Training Camp Activities (CTCA) partnered with the Young Women's Christian Association (YWCA) to organize a program for women and girls, especially black and white working women in communities surrounding army and navy training camps.[45] By January 1918 the YWCA had expanded its staff from one black national secretary and nine paid workers to twelve national workers, three field supervisors, and sixty-three paid workers with an increased budget for work center management.[46] With the color line starkly drawn in the Red Cross, black women gravitated to the YWCA.

Under the YWCA program, black women established Hostess Houses that offered rest, refreshments, and entertainment for black soldiers and visitors. In April 1918, a year after America's entry into the war, the first Hostess House opened at Camp Upton, Long Island, New York. YWCA Special War Work Secretary Lugenia Burns Hope, a social reformer and wife of the president of Morehouse College (Atlanta), managed the New York facility and the nationwide training of Hostess House supervisors.[47] Despite the inadequacy of in-camp programs for African Americans, Hostess Houses provided an alternative space for black soldiers and their families and "brought [them] in contact with high yet simple standards of social intercourse."[48] Black women in the Jersey City

Central Railroad Waiters' Association and the Somerville YWCA Uplift Club regularly volunteered at the Camp Dix Hostess House.[49]

Significantly, YWCA affiliation enabled New Jersey's black women to stabilize programs in which they had been involved for years through their missionary societies and women's clubs. As part of the YWCA's "Colored Work," Violet Johnson formed the Girls' Patriotic League and Y "Uplift" clubs for young girls and expanded the Woman in Industry Club to include domestic workers from neighboring suburbs. In the early 1900s Summit's white middle-class women had created the Woman's Institute as a club for white native- and foreign-born working women and offered classes in dressmaking, millinery, cooking, and embroidery. Black women were excluded. As a war measure, the elite women opened the Woman's Institute to all who signed a loyalty pledge, including Johnson and her clubs for women and girls.[50]

Work patterns of black and white women changed markedly during the war. Because of racism, however, black and white women experienced the war differently. The labor structure remained racially segregated in spite of worker shortages caused by the military draft and the departure of European immigrants.[51] As white women moved into industrial positions vacated by men, few African American women could escape domestic service. Even when able to move into the industrial or manufacturing sector, employers restricted them to the lowest job categories. Further, as women's wages increased, so did opportunities for exploitation in factories, hotels, railroad yards, and private homes. In August 1918 the Division of Labor created the Women's Service Section (WSS) to mediate working conditions for women in select industries, including wages, hours, and assignments.[52] The service sector remained outside the purview of any government agency. And as many black women discovered, any change in work patterns that appeared to shift power to service workers redounded to their detriment.[53] Paradoxically, as surveillance of black women's bodies increased, safeguards for their working conditions decreased.

Not only did black and white women have disparate war experiences, they also valorized war work differently. Historian Felice Gordon argues that New Jersey's white middle-class women used war work to highlight the incongruity between the war for democracy and the powerlessness of women.[54] For black women, the stakes were much higher: war work provided evidence of their womanhood.

Notwithstanding the government's prurient interest in their sexual activities and disregard for their economic well-being, ordinary black women refashioned initiatives intended to inoculate service men from their sexual contagion into housing, employment, and self-improvement programs. For example, though the War Department viewed the Woman in Industry Clubs and Girls' Patriotic Leagues as ramparts protecting soldiers from dangerous black, single, or working women, African American women considered them community fortresses. After the war, they converted many into permanent YWCAs.[55] Johnson transformed the Woman in Industry Club into "The Home Away from Home," a haven for black women and girls.

By mid-1918 black women's "quiet struggle" began to bear fruit.[56] The Secretary of War ordered the Red Cross to register black nurses and assign them albeit on a segregated basis to military hospitals and camps, including Camp Dix.[57] To stem reports of black unrest due to discriminatory treatment, Special Assistant Emmet Scott recommended forming a national black woman's subcommittee or subcommittees in each state. Aware that white southerners feared that organizing black women would disturb race relations, the Woman's Committee appointed NACW member and poet Alice Dunbar-Nelson as field representative to organize segregated committees in southern states. The committee deemed it "superfluous" to organize black women in northern states, Dunbar-Nelson later recalled.[58] More likely, white northern women had convinced the national committee that they were already working with black women.

Certainly, in New Jersey that was not the case. The Woman's Committee ignored black women's organizational strength and maintained a façade of interracial cooperation. State Chairwoman Stockton waited a year before contacting the State Federation about appointing someone to "learn the system of work" in the Council of National Defense office. Despite the public slight, NJSFCWC's Executive Board voted to "cooperate with the Council."[59] The war ended the following month. Further, when the National War Savings Committee appointed women to conduct the Liberty Loan Campaign, the New Jersey Council of National Defense named Florence Randolph to head the "drive to colored people."[60] Nationally, African American women acquitted themselves well during the Third Liberty Loan Campaign, raising more than $5 million dollars, including $300,000 for the Red Cross.[61] In New Jersey, black women's contributions helped fund the Negro Welfare Employment Bureau, an unfunded Labor Department agency belatedly created to assist black migrants and residents in finding employment.[62] Again, Stockton ignored Randolph and her organization. Deeming this one affront too many, the black women penned a terse letter, "regretting that the services of Mrs. Randolph, duly appointed member of the Committee . . . were not needed."[63] From the perspective of New Jersey's black women, Dunbar-Nelson's characterization of relations with the Red Cross as "not altogether a pleasant one" could have been extended to other white women's groups.[64]

The war drew the color line in unpredictable and dizzying ways across New Jersey's cities and suburbs. As an example of the contingency in moral and spatial choices available to northern women during the war, both Johnson and her white employer sat on the suburb's Mercy Hospital Committee.[65] While a domestic servant seemed an unlikely choice for this elite committee organized to provide emergency relief, Johnson parlayed these contacts into patrons for her Girls' Patriotic League and Post-War Reserve Clubs. With public concerts for Thrift Stamps, the NACW's Colored Soldier Memorial, and Johnson's scholarship fund, the young girls served as ambassadors between Summit's increasingly fractious white and black residents.[66]

From Civic Duty to Civic Righteousness

For much of 1917–1918 the social and economic dislocations of war occupied Johnson and Randolph. The harsh winter revealed the limits of municipal charity and industrial capitalism. Beset by discriminatory hiring practices and a scarcity of decent housing, the welfare of black migrants and communities fell largely to black working women, the long-time residents.[67]

When the State Federation convened its second wartime session in July 1918 at Bordentown Industrial Training School, the women focused "not so much on the war . . . but . . . the aftermath."[68] After singing "America" and the Federation song and receiving greetings from the

NACW and the white Federation of Women's Clubs, they listened to prominent women who provided a national perspective. Alice Dunbar-Nelson gave an update on the Woman's Council of National Defense; the director of the YWCA Colored Industrial Section discussed the Girls' Patriotic League; and Sarah Willie Layten, president of the Baptist Woman's Convention, spoke on the "exodus from the South." The CTCA representative shared insights on prohibition and NJWSA president Lillian Feickert examined suffrage as a war measure.[69]

At the evening session, Florence Randolph sought to locate the Federation within the historical moment. "[W]hen we selected as our motto three years ago, 'Work and serve the hour,' we little dreamed . . . of this day of service . . . to the world and the nation as well as . . . to the race," she told the audience of black and white women and men attending the open session. "The close of this dreadful war will usher in a new era for the Negro people of this country. . . . Much of the responsibility of preparedness rests with the womanhood of the race."[70]

With prophetic authority Randolph asserted, "God is calling [the Negro] woman to come to a knowledge of Him and then to go into the cities and towns and help struggling humanity" by fighting for "Right against Wrong." As "the homemakers, the wives, the mothers, the great fountain from which purity must spring, yea, the very salt of the earth," black women enjoyed a special relationship with God. And now God was calling them—"women of great ability" and "women who feel they have no ability," the "educated, trained Negro woman, whether trained in the school house or by personal effort"—in a "united struggle" for "a better womanhood, better homes, a better community life" and for "equality before the law, to down race discrimination, segregation, jim-crowism, mob violence and lynch law."[71]

Referencing the pernicious *Plessy v. Ferguson* "separate but equal" doctrine, Randolph presented the case for action. "For the last twenty years the lines have been tightened around the Negro in America, and each year some new law, some new enactment against us as a race has been made. So far as the Negro is concerned there is no north, south, east or west, it is simply a matter of numbers and circumstances."[72] The war had exacerbated the structural evils spawned by Jim Crow segregation and created new social ills. Southern migrants escaped "labor conditions, lack of opportunity, oppression, mob violence and lynch law," only to encounter "new and untried conditions" in a "new and untried climate." Segregation and migration had created a "growing, alarming problem"—"rundown sections [in] almost every town": the "problem within the problem" that male-led churches and institutions failed to address. Thus, Randolph pronounced, "If our organization means anything at all, it must mean RACE HELPFULNESS AND UPLIFT."[73]

Randolph outlined an ambitious role for ordinary black women. They would advocate for just laws and moral institutions; and, with the "real tangible work" of the Federation's Civic Department, they would redeem a nation torn asunder by Jim Crow. "So long as we are denied the full privileges of citizenship, so long as in our cities and state, we have jim-crow [sic], segregation, and other offensive measures, we must have a wide awake Civic Department," Randolph asserted.[74]

On a warm July evening, operating in the liminal space between middle-class respectability and working-class reality, Randolph conflated the rhetoric of racial uplift and the language of civic righteousness to empower black working women to confront northern economic and social disorder and usher in the Kingdom of God.

In Reformation and Lutheran theology, the purified and reformed state embodied civic righteousness and ensured a godly community. For nineteenth- and twentieth-century American Protestants, civic righteousness was a generative force for social action in the personal and social holiness of redeemed converts, inspiring the abolition and the Social Gospel movements. New Jersey's black church women embraced civic righteousness as the basis of their public activism.[75]

Occupying discursive space at the intersection of personal behavior and civic institutions, the Civic Department would help "protect our rights in our own state as American citizens." As a physical place with an employment bureau and rooms open to women and children, it would function as a mediating structure where physicians, ministers, and businessmen and women could give lectures and provide educational programs. "This," Randolph averred, "is the purpose for which the New Jersey State Federation came into existence[:] To grasp the opportunity now before us . . . to accomplish a great work for God and Humanity."[76]

Randolph placed "social and personal purity" and "religion, education [and] the franchise" in the civic realm and equally necessary for a "solid, healthy nation."[77] Historian Evelyn Brooks Higginbotham argues that "a conservative and moralistic dimension" within the politics of respectability privatized individual behavior and racial discrimination and placed the "social and symbolic representations of white supremacy" outside the authority of government regulation.[78] Buffeted by Jim Crow in northern garb, this group of predominantly working women rejected that formulation in favor of "systemic and united efforts" to protect the "rights and liberty" of "every self-respecting Negro who desires protection of his rights under the law."[79]

* * *

Convinced that the wide-awake "Negro woman" required the ballot for political reform and personal protection, Federation women entered the suffrage battle with religious fervor. A month before the Bordentown meeting, "Rev. Mrs. Florence Randolph" spoke at the "Suffrage War Conference" in Newark along with other "prominent" women, including the presidents of the white Federation of Women's Clubs, the State WCTU, and the State Homemakers Association.[80]

Though suffragists and their opponents declared a truce for the duration of the war, the battle for public opinion continued. In August, Summit resident and president of the State Association Opposed to Woman's Suffrage denounced suffragists as unpatriotic "for continuing their work in wartime" and commended anti-suffragists for "their devotion to the Red Cross and similar activities to the exclusion of all other interests." She warned, "[E]very dollar given to defeat Woman Suffrage is a dollar towards winning the war, because Woman Suffrage in America will 'give aid and comfort to the enemy.'"[81] The heated rhetoric notwithstanding, the decision lay in the hands of the all-male congressional delegation.

The vote on the federal suffrage amendment came in October 1918. The New Jersey congressional delegation was a wild card, as U.S. Senator David Baird demonstrated. With the Senate only two votes shy of the two-thirds majority required for passage, Baird voted against the amendment.[82]

As the public image of suffrage in New Jersey became one of biracial sisterhood, national politics played out much differently. Racist sentiment plagued the suffrage movement.[83] When the Northeastern Federation of Colored Women that included NJSFCWC as an affiliate applied for membership in the National American Woman Suffrage Association (NAWSA) in March 1919, President Carrie Chapman Catt feared that admitting six thousand black women would antagonize southern congressmen and therefore attempted to block the application. At the NAWSA Jubilee Convention in St. Louis that same month, Catt acquiesced to southern white women's plan to disenfranchise black women and supported states' rights over universal woman's suffrage. As NAACP Assistant Secretary Walter White sardonically observed, "[I]f they could get the Suffrage Amendment through without enfranchising colored women, they would do it in a moment."[84]

Finally, on 21 May 1919 the U.S. House of Representatives passed the suffrage amendment, and the Senate followed on 4 June. Neighboring New York and Pennsylvania ratified the amendment within weeks of its passage by Congress. Ratification in New Jersey would have to wait until January 1920, after the November 1919 election.[85]

With their eye on Trenton, New Jersey suffragists intensified their campaign. In July 1919 Feickert organized the Woman Suffrage Committee on Ratification, an umbrella organization comprised of five statewide and eleven local women's organizations. Reflecting the dramatic change in black women's public presence, the Suffrage Committee included NJSFCWC as a constituent member, with Randolph on the Executive Committee.[86]

In August the Suffrage Committee fired the opening salvo in the 1919 campaign before a cheering crowd at the "Big Suffrage Rally" in Asbury Park. Violet Johnson and Florence Randolph were among the "prominent women" who vowed to "Fight Opponents of the Federal Amendment at the Polls."[87] Over the next months the interracial suffrage committee changed the dynamic of the primary election. Whereas both state parties had been anti-suffrage and anti-prohibition the year before, suffragists gained official, though lukewarm, suffrage planks in the Democratic and Republican platforms.[88]

With suffrage neutralized, enforcement of the Eighteenth Amendment for prohibition, not the Nineteenth Amendment for suffrage, became the differentiating factor in New Jersey's bitter 1919 "Applejack Campaign." Intertwined since the 1890s when a vote for one was tantamount to a vote for the other, prohibition and suffrage had become shorthand for political division and control.[89] Enforcement in New Jersey, one of only three states that failed to ratify the Eighteenth

Amendment, remained an open issue nine months after passage of the Eighteenth Amendment and national prohibition. Vowing to make the state "as 'wet' as the Atlantic Ocean," Democratic gubernatorial candidate Edward I. Edwards of Jersey City stood for states' rights and nullification; his Republican opponent Newton A. K. Bugbee of Mercer County vowed to uphold the law.[90] Ultimately, the election hinged on the muscle of the Hudson County Democratic machine.

Despite the Woman Suffrage Committee's lobbying, pro-suffrage candidates suffered a stunning defeat. Republicans gained control of the legislature and Hudson County Democrat Edwards won the governorship. Amid a national postwar shift to the Republican Party, New Jersey Democrats had made anti-prohibition a winning gubernatorial issue. With both Republicans and Democrats opposed to woman suffrage, the "applejack campaign" was a referendum on prohibition alone.[91] Suffrage remained an open question.

On 4 January 1920 the New Jersey legislature took up the suffrage amendment and a cautiously optimistic Woman Suffrage Committee opened its headquarters in the state capital. At the end of the month Florence Randolph and Carrie Chapman Catt addressed more than twelve hundred women at the interracial Woman Suffrage mass meeting in Trenton. The rally concluded with the presentation of a petition with 140,000 signatures arranged by counties and towns to the newly elected Democratic governor, Republican president of the state senate, and Republican speaker of the house.[92]

When legislative hearings began in early February, Florence Randolph and Lillian Feickert addressed the all-male white legislators. The Senate ratified the federal amendment the same day. Stalled by a Democratic filibuster, the Assembly passed the amendment a week later, making New Jersey the twenty-ninth state to ratify the Nineteenth Amendment. The network of African American, foreign-born, and native-white women had succeeded in removing suffrage as a divisive issue.[93] That evening suffragists celebrated with an interracial victory banquet in Newark. The state suffrage organization disbanded and formed the New Jersey League of Women Voters (LWV).[94]

Republicans welcomed the newly enfranchised women into the auxiliary Women's Republican Committee. Lillian Feickert served as vice chairman and Randolph as one of ten at-large executive committee members.[95] Appointed by the all-male regular committee to lead the enrollment of women for Warren G. Harding's presidential bid, Feickert and Randolph evidently exceeded expectations, for on the first day of voter registration in mid-September election boards could not accommodate the number of women who appeared. In Essex County alone, which included the city of Newark and a ring of residential suburbs, the total number of registered voters doubled.[96]

Amid ideal weather and a promising political forecast, black women cast their first presidential vote on 2 November 1920. In Essex County, where women comprised a majority of the voting age population, voters delivered a resounding victory for the Republican ticket and elected to the Assembly two white women, Jennie Van Ness and Margaret Laird, and a black male physician, Dr. Walter Alexander.[97] Although a local victory, African American women viewed it as affirmation of their political acumen. They also claimed a part in the Republican rout in the state and Harding's presidential win. More than a test of black women's ability to mobilize between August and November, the election demonstrated the strength of their cross-class network developed over years in missionary societies, the WCTU, and the Federation.[98] Black women's participation in the suffrage campaign and election earned them a place in the state's politics. They would have to fight to keep it.

Civic Righteousness and "The Home Away from Home"

White and black women expected to exercise public influence commensurate with their new status earned in war and suffrage. For Summit's black women war work and victory at the polls confirmed their call to civic righteousness and portended a new day for the "wide-awake Negro woman." For Summit's elite white women, war and suffrage reaffirmed their privileged status.

Violet Johnson used the exigencies of war to expand her activism. Working with white women on Summit's Woman's Committee, she formed the Woman in Industry Club and the Girls' Patriotic League. When the white women converted the Woman's Institute into the YWCA, Johnson "realized that the best she could do was inadequate without an independent institution to carry on her work." Thus in 1918, "principally on faith she took over a small apartment which was capable of looking out for the creature comforts of four or five girls" and established the Industrial Home for Working Girls, "The Home Away from Home."[99]

Personal experience and a commitment to civic righteousness buttressed Johnson's faith. As her friend Alice Dunbar-Nelson explained, "Miss Johnson came to Summit herself when she was a young girl, and knows the needs of a girl for a home, companionship, protection, and recreation after working hours. She studied the problem for years."[100] Johnson also studied Summit's white women and recognized that though the YWCA National Board had opened professional positions to college-educated black women, activities in local branches remained under the control of white women with a dubious commitment to sisterhood across race and class lines.[101]

Johnson soon outgrew her apartment and with the aid of white women procured a row house on Glenwood Place, a working-class section surrounded by upper- and middle-class homes in the center of town. There she created a "homey and pleasant" atmosphere "where young colored girls, who are employed by the day, may have comfortable rooms, a good bath, a place in which to receive friends, and to have recreational activities." Johnson set "restrictions as to conduct, hours and association" and, as the institution grew, employed a resident matron. Girls with money paid a small fee for room and board; those unable to pay stayed "through the kindness of Miss Johnson, who also finds employment for them, without charging any fee." Over the years, Johnson provided a home for more than eight hundred young women, including teachers and students.[102]

"The Home Away from Home" occupied space at the intersection of conflicting constructions of gender, race, and class. For middle-class white women, it was the site from which Johnson "furnished much of the best help in Summit families."[103] Moreover, with Johnson ensconced in her independent institution, white women could be confident that the newly formed YWCA would remain their exclusive domain, thereby obviating the threat of interracial leadership or the specter of social equality. For that tacit concession, they gladly assisted Johnson and permitted her Girls Reserve Clubs to use YWCA facilities, albeit on a segregated basis. Thus, they could appear to comply with the YWCA National Board's objective on interracial cooperation as they reinforced lines of race and class.

For black women, "The Home Away from Home" represented "more than a YWCA"; it was "a beacon of light" and Johnson the "lighthouse keeper."[104] Johnson subverted the middle-class discourse of home and created a place of safety and security, power and protection, respectability and resistance for black women and girls. Endorsed by both the State Federation and the Baptist Woman's Convention, "The Home Away from Home" served as a sanctuary and a training ground, a veritable fountain of purity and the salt of the earth. Removed from the gaze of white women and black men, working women exercised leadership and organizational autonomy as they reified the wide-awake Civic Department.

Nothing more clearly illustrates Johnson's ability to transform middle-class symbols into the practical work of civic righteousness than the "Health Meeting" held at Fountain Baptist Church in 1923. On a Sunday afternoon in May, Armita Douglas, state chairwoman of the Federation's Civic Department, subverted the politics of home and the "Better Homes" discourse to affirm black women's place in the overwhelmingly white suburb.

In the wake of the 1921 recession, Vice President Calvin Coolidge launched the national "Better Homes in America" campaign that linked "the building and perfecting of national character and the building and adorning of a home" to American family values.[105] Similarly, in language redolent with religious overtones, Secretary of Commerce Herbert Hoover extolled the single-family home as the "ark" of "security, independence and freedom" and the nuclear family as the "unit of modern civilization," and disparaged high-density rental and boarding houses as "unsanitary and dangerous quarters . . . for nomads and vagrants."[106] With the trope of the single-family suburban home at the center of the perfected national community, the exclusion of working-class citizens from the civic ideal could not have been more starkly drawn.[107]

Douglas presented a different vision of home. "A city of homes is a City Beautiful just insofar as all its homes are beautiful and sanitary," she began. "I am here to tell you women to acquaint yourselves with your town and its needs, and when you come to vote you will know how to vote for its best interests. Bring up in your clubs the issues on which you are to vote."[108] Affirming black women's claim to a place in the overwhelmingly white suburb, she added, "You have taken root, and you are going to make your city the best city possible. Summit is known as the most American town in New Jersey. . . . You are Americans. You have been here a long time. Be proud of it."[109]

Douglas rejected the trope of the idealized middle-class mother and instead reinforced black working women's commitment to communal responsibility and service. "The best mother is not the mother who stays at home all the time and gets a flower once a year," she concluded. "There is [sic] home and educational and social work . . . to be done, and there are girls outside our own home who have not the surroundings they should have. Those girls are your problem."[110]

Responding to Douglas in the segregated section white Summit had forcibly created and in the church it had helped erect out of civic duty rather than religious conviction, the "visibly impressed" Republican mayor conceded that the local government did not provide municipal services equally, but then reflexively blamed black residents, asserting, "This section of Summit can be made much more beautiful, if you would work together."[111]

The mayor's disingenuous comments evidently affected the white president of the Town Improvement Association (TIA) who, after citing her group's efforts to stimulate interest in Clean-Up Week, apologetically added that "all were distressed over the housing conditions and hoped for their betterment." Belatedly, she invited Johnson to "openly work" with the TIA.[112] Johnson and her former employer would again be members of the same women's organization.

Though billed as a "Health Meeting," the interracial audience grasped the multilayered message. As the local paper reported, "[C]oming on Mothers'[sic] Day in Better Homes' year and at the close of Clean-Up Week, and having to do with all the conditions that surround the homes of Summit, the first speaker might fittingly group as synonyms the three words—'mother meaning home and home meaning mother, and civics concerning both.'"[113] Though she had failed to convert the mayor, Johnson had gained a key ally. The influential white women's group would prove beneficial as the campaign for better homes gained momentum in the mid-1920s and 1930s.

* * *

War, prohibition, and suffrage gave black women clear public roles, which they seized. Though more often beneficiaries of the ignoble rather than the "splendid," to paraphrase Dunbar-Nelson, they transformed missionary service, temperance reform, and club women's uplift into Christian activism and institutionalized civic structures begun as denominational endeavors.[114]

New Jersey's black working women came to see themselves as agents of democracy and racial progress. As church women in the secular club movement, they were called "to Work and Serve the Hour." As working women in increasingly segregated spaces, they remained committed to a broad vision of community, organizing separately when necessary and forming interracial alliances with the WCTU, the YWCA, and the Republican Party when possible.

Nonetheless, employment discrimination, residential segregation, and racial violence in the North increased during and after the war, especially as the northward migration of African Americans continued. As racial proscription hardened into racial segregation, Johnson and Randolph used their organization and the ballot as instruments of personal and political power. In quotidian yet significant ways, they fashioned beacons of light from ersatz materials. They prevented their communities from foundering under the high tide of racial segregation and the low tide of the Great Depression.

4

"Unholy and Unchristian Attitude"

Interracial Dialogue in Segregated Spaces, 1920–1937

The suffrage campaign had mobilized women, but when it came to race matters white and black New Jersey women faced real trouble. The commonality they had found in temperance and suffrage began to crack at its apogee. White New Jersey simply would not address racial discrimination as it grew in the 1920s. Jim Crow had gained more than a foothold in the North.

Post–World War I America was riven by labor unrest, racial violence, and social dislocations. The national landscape had changed dramatically. The economy shifted from agricultural production to industrial consumption and the migration of black and white citizens changed the geography from rural to urban. Race and labor riots in the North rivaled the mob violence and lynchings that had long characterized the South. Violent attacks against soldiers still in uniform and women and children in their homes and churches increased. As mainline denominations stood silent, the limits of American Protestantism were all too clear. W. E. B. Du Bois, a National Association for the Advancement of Colored People (NAACP) founder and editor of the *Crisis* magazine, sounded the battle cry of a New Negro post-war militancy: "We return. We return from fighting. We return fighting."[1] Democracy abroad demanded democracy at home.

Violet Johnson and Florence Randolph prepared for a "glorious" fight against the unchristian acts that ranged from discrimination in housing, employment, and education to mob violence, lynching, and abuse of women. "[I]n the great task of reconstruction before the nation, Negro women have their greatest opportunity, the chance not only to serve but to save America in this crucial hour," Randolph averred.[2] African Americans had earned the right to full citizenship and protection from "Humiliation, Discrimination, Brutality and Crime against our race."[3]

Randolph and Johnson amassed their own arsenal of democracy. No longer fighting a "southern problem," northern black women's language became more demanding and their remedies more varied as they sought to defend social and political gains against a rising tide of white supremacy. They combined direct political action with moral appeals to the American conscience. They demanded government intervention to end mob violence and declare lynching a federal crime. They tried to engage white club women in the Anti-Lynching Crusade and to ally with white church women in the interracial movement. Both the secular and religious attempts at a united womanhood withered under the white heat of American racism. White club women wrapped themselves in class privilege, and white church women lacked power.

Amid shifting constructions of race, gender, and citizenship, the discourse on civilization clashed head-on with black women's vision of civic righteousness. Black women's fight for just laws and moral institutions exposed cleavages in the woman's movement. They lost white women as allies just as southern black women began to build interracial ties with white women's organizations.

Despite their best efforts, these Christian activists could not stem the rise of the Ku Klux Klan or the segregation sweeping into civic and religious spaces in the 1920s and 1930s. Class and color politics, a color-coded economic structure, rising property values, and the devastation of the Great Depression eroded the slim gains they had made. Even as economic and social discrimination solidified and race relations deteriorated, black working women remained committed to a vision of community based upon Christian principles and the indivisibility of race and gender—and class. They turned segregated spaces into sites of resistance and socialized a new generation of women as Christian activists.

United Womanhood: Suffrage and the Anti-Lynching Crusade

The "Red Summer" of 1919 removed any doubt as to the state of race relations. The end of war in Europe had not resulted in peace at home. From April to October approximately twenty-six race riots erupted in the country, including one in the nation's capital. Many northerners considered riots a southern problem, until the weeklong Chicago riot in late July resulted in thirty-eight deaths.[4]

Violet Johnson responded with righteous anger. As chairwoman of the State Federation's Anti-Lynching Department, she "respectfully ask[ed]" Woodrow Wilson, "president of a country in which colored men, as well as white men, have laid down their lives for the principles of freedom," to convene and "personally preside" over a conference to address the "race differences which have now become appalling" and "universally destructive . . . ultimately to both races." Quoting from Wilson's Fourth of July speech aboard the *U.S.S. George Washington*, Johnson wrote, "If the 'kind of freedom America has always represented is a freedom expressing itself in fact,' we pray you to lead America to prove it now before a world that has brought Democracy for all peoples." Reminding the president of his "many months in France in an earnest effort for interracial harmony," she "beg[ged]" for "a like skilful [*sic*] attention to interracial harmony here" to "preserve the honor of the country."[5]

Johnson urged federal intervention to end state violence—the "sending of white troops only to crush colored men into submission"—and mob violence. She rejected the specious connection between rape and lynching that white southerners and northerners reflexively made. "Excuse for lynching colored men and for rioting against them is everywhere made on the ground that colored men assault white women's honor," Johnson averred. "As a student of American history you know that the story of the assaults white men have made on colored women's honor is written on the faces of our race."[6]

As African Americans had done since Reconstruction, Johnson based her claim for justice on the Fourteenth and Fifteenth Amendments, and added the social capital African American women had accrued as national and international defenders of democracy during the war. She closed the letter by asking the president "to permit colored women and white women to come before you with representative men from the two races and confer as to wise methods before the nations of the world."[7] African American women had struggled for their country during the war and expected to stand as partners with white women and black and white men in creating a civilization based on democratic principles.

When the State Federation met in July 1920 in the "aftermath of war," the women addressed the disjuncture between assertions of American democracy and the discrimination and violence directed at African Americans. National Association of Colored Women (NACW) President Mary Talbert declared, "Democracy means to us a land of just laws, where color does not count. According to this standard America is not a democracy." Stressing that African Americans had fought "for that democracy they did not possess," Talbert assured the women that she would "speak out clearly and forcibly on conditions in America as regards the Negro" as one of ten delegates to the International Council of Women in Norway in September.[8] Lillian Feickert, white vice chair-woman of the Republican Women's Auxiliary Committee, added that a united womanhood stood ready to lead in "getting rights as citizens. . . . Then it is up to us to see that every woman does her part to help make clean, *just laws*, and see that they are enforced."[9]

Feickert had come a long way in her understanding of black women's formulation of civic righteousness and just laws; not all white women had mastered the learning curve. The white State Federation of Women's Clubs representative confessed that "it [was] brought to her attention for the first time that . . . a line of demarcation [existed] between the races on club work." Following Violet Johnson's "report on Lynching [*sic*] and abuse" that "led to much discussion," the white club woman experienced a conversion and "spoke eloquently . . . of the necessity for closer unity" in club work. She "promised to take the message to her people."[10]

Despite such promises, black women questioned white women's commitment to a united womanhood or just laws. At a Federation meeting early in 1921, Randolph, a Republican Women's Auxiliary Committee officer, discussed the "controversy concerning the Conference of the leading women" in the nation's capital that dismissed evidence of voter suppression, "especially Negro women of the South."[11] Though Feickert spoke earnestly at the same meeting on suffrage cooperation in the state, Federation women considered the absence of southern black women at the polls a key measure of the Republican Party's commitment to black equality.

When the Federation met in Summit in 1921 for its sixth annual conference, the women pressed their fight for just laws in a resolution to President Warren G. Harding, a Republican for whom black women had vigorously campaigned the previous year. "[We] feel that the condition of the law-abiding Negro population . . . is sadly in need of amelioration [that] can be accomplished only by a determined effort on the part of the Federal Government to enforce the Fourteenth and Fifteenth

Amendments." Federation women sought reparations for victims of the recent Tulsa riot, enforcement of the federal law against peonage, and passage of a federal anti-lynching law.[12] Black women's fight had to be the government's fight.

The following year, the newly enfranchised women carried the fight to the national NAACP meeting at Bethany Baptist Church in Newark. Federation women maintained a high profile at the convention focused on the Republican failure to pass the Dyer Anti-Lynching Bill. Like Johnson, many were members of the Newark branch of the NAACP and the convention planning committee.[13]

On the Sunday preceding the official opening, NAACP members spoke at local churches on the importance of the Dyer Bill, first introduced by Missouri Congressman Leonidas C. Dyer in 1918 and now languishing in a senate committee since January.[14] In the afternoon Federation women joined the impressive line of women dressed in white and the thousands of marchers carrying American flags to the sound of muffled drums in a "silent parade" through downtown Newark. Young boys carried a banner inscribed with the poignant message "We Are Fifteen Years Old. A Boy of Our Age Was Roasted Alive Recently." Other banners read, "Lynch Law Must Go" and "Pass the Dyer Anti-Lynching Bill." Johnson, her friend and NAACP Trustee and Anti-Lynching chairwoman Nannie Helen Burroughs, Florence Randolph's daughter, and other Federation women rode in three cars prominently bearing the inscription "NEW JERSEY FEDERATION OF COLORED WOMEN'S CLUBS."[15] The procession ended with a "monster" meeting at the Newark Armory.[16]

Over five days convention delegates and visitors discussed antilynching, peonage, and the perfidy of the Republican Party. For Federation women the high point was Tuesday, Women's Day. NAACP field worker and YWCA national officer Addie Hunton presided over the "Women as Citizens" session at which former NACW president Mary Talbert received the NAACP's Spingarn Medal, the first African American woman so honored. Representatives of white women's organizations shared the podium and "urged a united womanhood without race discrimination and prejudice." The National Council of Jewish Women representative spoke movingly of black and Jewish women's shared commitment "in their work for better humanity." Recalling women's work for abolition and temperance, the president of the white Federation of Women's Clubs stated, "Christianity does not include race prejudice and a double standard of morality." The League of Women Voters president added, "I realize that you are suffering at the hands of my own race"; and the Woman's Peace Party representative assured the audience that "all women stand for peace and brotherhood and are opposed to peonage, mob rule and lynching." The white NAACP board member encouraged support "for the work that is to be done by the colored women" and "cautioned against the loss of woman power, which also means loss of man power."[17]

The evening's main speaker, "silver-tongued orator" and NACW president Hallie Q. Brown, "demanded that colored women of America be accorded the rights which are their due," based upon their loyalty from the American Revolution through fifty years of suffrage activism to the sacrifice of "400,000 sons" in the war.[18] In the fight against "that terrible crime, the lynch law," she stated, "[o]ur women must do the work. They must set an example even to the white women." Black women would lead America to a moral and political reformation. Brown urged "an intelligent use of the ballot . . . a powerful weapon for the righteous man and the righteous woman."[19]

The attention to black women's rights at the interracial and intergender NAACP convention contrasted sharply with the lack of discussion a year earlier at the ceremony unveiling sculptures of suffrage pioneers Elizabeth Cady Stanton, Susan B. Anthony, and Lucretia Mott in the nation's capital. Prior to the National Woman's Party convention, a delegation of black women visited founder and leader Alice Paul to discuss Mary Talbert sharing the report on the suppression of black women's votes in southern states in the 1920 election.[20] Despite entreaties from influential white women, Paul refused. Contending that black women suffered at the polls because of their race, not their gender, she steered the convention toward a "feminist" program, a move designed to maintain the support of white southern women at the expense of black women.[21] In Newark, black women announced their leadership of a "unified" campaign for social justice.

Within a week of the NAACP convention, Mary Talbert outlined plans for an Anti-Lynching Crusade in which black women would "unite a million women to stop lynching" and "by sacrifice and self-denial" pledge at least one dollar to support the year-long campaign.[22] In the quasi-religious Anti-Lynching Crusade, black women combined fasting, national days of prayer, and church rallies with direct political action. They lobbied congressmen and threatened voter retaliation against political candidates who failed to support the federal anti-lynching bill.[23]

Anti-Lynching Crusaders resolved to unite women, regardless of class, color, or religion. Historian Rosalyn Terborg-Penn concludes that the anti-lynching crusade was "perhaps the most influential link in the drive for interracial cooperation among women's groups."[24] Unfortunately, cooperation proved elusive in the polarizing decade of the 1920s. For example, claiming they did not wish to cooperate in the creation of another women's organization, the YWCA National Board declined Mary Talbert's request to endorse the Anti-Lynching Crusade.[25]

White and black women would not unite. In her analysis of women's activism after suffrage, scholar Estelle Freedman identifies three political options available to women: separate feminist action in the National Woman's Party, moderate action in the League of Women Voters, or mainstream partisan politics.[26] The Anti-Lynching Crusade offered a fourth option, a united women's campaign formulated within the discourses of civilization and civic righteousness. For Freedman the "devolution" of women's culture in general, and the proliferation of separate female institutions in particular, resulted in the decline of feminism. Clearly, as the Anti-Lynching Crusade illustrates, black and white women could not overcome disparate constructions of gender and race. When it came to race relations northern white women elected to remain uninformed and uncommitted, while southern white women, as historian Jacqueline Dowd Hall concludes, remained impervious.[27]

Black working women continued their campaign for social justice. Violet Johnson, a "real live wire" in the movement, helped to organize a local Summit NAACP branch to foster "the betterment of civic and economic conditions among colored people locally" and "better understanding and better inter-racial conditions nationally."[28] Federation women disseminated resolutions that linked obstacles to "our progress as individuals, as a group and as a people" to the "racial, economic and social disturbances which have threatened the very foundation of the nation." "There can be no peace until all nations have peace with their hearts, and love and charity towards their neighbors," they cautioned.[29]

The Anti-Lynching Crusade provided a national context for local issues and promoted the growth of the NAACP; however, the women failed to reach their goal. Nationally, the Crusaders raised less than $13,000; New Jersey Crusaders contributed only about $1,500, a result no doubt of the lingering impact of the 1921 recession.[30] Nevertheless, New Jersey's black women remained committed to federal anti-lynching legislation and the eradication of the personification of mob rule and lynching, the "hyrdo-headed [sic] monster known as the [Ku] Klux Klan."[31]

Throughout the 1920s the Ku Klux Klan established an almost un-broken chain of klaverns along the Atlantic seaboard from Long Island, New York, to Cape May, New Jersey.[32] Headquartered in Newark, the New Jersey Klan operated about fifty klaverns in the northern part of the state alone and boasted of the one at Princeton University, the Anglo-Saxon preserve.[33] Though primarily targeting Jews and Catholics, the well-organized Jersey Klan extended its program of terror and intimidation to African Americans, immigrants, and labor unions with nocturnal cross burnings, daytime automobile processions, and parades of masked marchers.[34]

The masked order did not spare the "ideal suburb." On a Saturday night in early October 1922, Violet Johnson and other Summit residents could observe a thirty-foot cross burning against the western sky as part of an initiation ceremony in an abandoned quarry in a neighboring sub-urb. Two years later the quarry again served as the initiation site for about two hundred men and one hundred women.[35] In November 1923 the Klan burned thirteen crosses in Newark and surrounding suburbs; visible from New York City, the flaming crosses lit up the night sky from Saturday night into Sunday morning.[36] Despite reports of its demise in the 1920s, the Klan continued its reign of terror into the 1930s, advertising open air lectures and mass meetings, including a full-page ad inviting Knights to a "Protestant Christian" Easter Union Service officiated by two ministers.[37]

Undaunted, black women continued their campaign for federal anti-lynching legislation and an end to the economic and political conditions that promoted mob violence. They appealed directly to "the church, and civic organizations of our community [to] arouse the conscience of the American public to the disgrace of this terrible blot upon our boasted twentieth century civilization."[38]

When the Federation's Executive Committee met in Summit in January 1924 at the home of a domestic servant and president of the local Colored Women's Club, they invited presidents of three leading white women's clubs to join them for the business meeting and social hour that followed. The white women shared in the hospitality of women who worked as maids, cooks, and laundresses in white homes. The Fortnightly Club president and wife of a Standard Oil executive expressed interest in the black women's club work and offered assistance; the Town Improvement Association president requested their endorsement of the marriage bill that required a health exam prior to issuance of a license. The white Federation Club officer sought their support on women's and children's welfare matters, including a child labor amendment, appropriations to purchase forest lands, and additional funding for the state college for women.[39]

After acknowledging their comments, Florence Randolph asked the white women to endorse the Dyer Anti-Lynching bill. "With lynching abolished," she stated, "this country will be better qualified to lead the world in peace."[40] The white women demurred. As historian Molly-Ladd Taylor concludes, white women refused to consider racial violence as a women's or children's problem.[41] Despite repeated attempts by African American women to position anti-lynching as an issue on which all women could unite, federal intervention remained a bridge too far.

However, white Summit could not ignore the black women. When queried by the local editor about the Daughters of the Confederacy's proposal to erect a statue honoring the mythical "Old Black Mammy of the South" in the nation's capital, one woman, probably Johnson, replied, "Yes, we have been talking about it here. We feel it was very nice of the southern white people to think of it, of course; but we feel it would be more honoring if they'd pass the anti-lynching bill or put up a memorial to the colored soldiers who died in the World War." The "rather impressed" editor complimented the women and reprinted a verse from the previous Sunday's local NAACP meeting: "They are slaves who fear to speak/For the friendless and the weak;/They are slaves who fear to be/In the right with two or three."[42] When the Republican Party adopted an anti-lynching plank at the 1924 convention in Cleveland, the editor gave a public nod to "[t]he negro [*sic*] women of Summit who have worked so heartily to have the Dyer Anti-Lynching Bill passed."[43] Unfortunately, the women could derive only fleeting comfort. Fearful of the Ku Klux Klan's political clout, the national parties failed to denounce the terrorist group or take a firm stand against lynching during the presidential campaign.[44]

United Womanhood: Church Women and Interracial Dialogue

Failing to win over white club women, black working women tried to arouse the conscience of white church women. However, persuading church women to take action to end racial violence and protect the rights of African Americans proved equally challenging.

In 1923 following the launch of the Anti-Lynching Crusade, the Council of Women for Home Missions declared, "[T]he time [is] ripe for every churchwoman in every community to ask herself searching questions as to whether she is treating her Negro neighbor in the Spirit of Christ." "Stimulated" by the white women of the Southern Commission on Interracial Cooperation (CIC), the northern-based interdenominational board of white mainline Protestants formed the Committee on Negro Americans "to consider . . . organizing the women of the North for the purpose of creating a spirit of cooperation between the races." The white missionaries proposed a year-long study of the 1919 Chicago race riot and a "program of activities to remove misunderstanding . . . and to encourage mutual good will."[45] While far short of an endorsement of the Anti-Lynching Crusade, white Protestant women had moved beyond their 1920 "Christian service" program to eradicate "the dangerously insidious modern tendency toward indecent clothes, indecent dancing and 'tunes of African jungle syncopation.'"[46]

White northern church women were not alone in searching for a Christian response to the racial violence sweeping the country. The Federal Council of Churches of Christ (FCC), the quintessential institution of the Social Gospel and liberal Christianity, did not consider race relations a legitimate religious concern until the horror of the 1921 Tulsa pogrom. Belatedly, it created the Commission on Negro Churches and Race Relations and, following the launch of the Anti-Lynching Crusade

in 1922, designated the second Sunday in February 1923 as "Race Relations Sunday" to coincide with President Lincoln's birthday.[47] In New
Jersey white Baptists attempted to form "closer relationships with the
colored churches" by appointing a black minister to an underfunded
liaison position.[48]

The limits of American Protestantism were all too clear. Shifting
cultural understandings of race and gender generated a Protestant crisis. Mainline Protestants seemed more concerned with controlling the
postwar militancy of the "New Negro" and retaining patriarchal hege-
mony than practicing an inclusive Christianity.[49] White church women
lost much of their independence as the Protestant hierarchy merged
their organizations with male boards or eliminated them altogether in
a movement against the feminization of religion. Historian Gail Bederman concludes that by the 1920s "American Protestants had effectively
masculinized their churches." As feminine morality and manly domi-
nance became increasingly antagonistic, white missionary boards com-
missioned a study on women's status in the church.[50]

Black church women found themselves equally marginalized as re-
vised constitutions reduced their organizations to auxiliaries and undermined their leadership in the very churches they had sacrificed to
maintain.[51] Though an ordained pastor, Florence Randolph spoke wist-
fully of organizing an interdenominational missionary department
within the State Federation, secure from the control of male boards.
Similarly, in a comment on the increasing dissonance between the
priorities of church women and men, Violet Johnson confided, "The
churches keep one's time so filled that one can hardly get in for any other
interest."[52] Yet the churches still needed women, even if they scarcely
deigned to recognize them, as Randolph discovered in 1925 when the
New Jersey Conference appointed her pastor of another fledgling congregation in Summit.

In an effort to circumvent constraints, church women developed interracial conferences as sites for creating a distinctly gendered religious
activism. The first interracial meetings occurred in the South, where
between July and October 1920 black and white southern women met to
discuss ways to improve race relations. The July meeting followed the biennial session of the National Association of Colored Women (NACW)
held at Tuskegee (Alabama) Institute. At the subsequent meeting spon-

sored by the Southern CIC and the Women's Council of the Methodist Episcopal Church (South) ninety-one white and four black women continued the dialogue in Memphis, Tennessee, and initiated a model for church women's interracial meetings.[53]

In September 1926 a select group of eighteen black and thirty-two white church women from fifteen states gathered in Eagles Mere, Pennsylvania, about four hours from Philadelphia, to explore ways to "promote work for interracial goodwill and cooperation." For the Church Women's Committee (CWC), a committee within the FCC's Department of Race Relations, the coming together of fifty women, northern and southern, black and white, with guests from national Jewish and Catholic groups, represented "a new stage of progress in grappling with the interracial problems by religious forces."[54] Over two days the women discussed topics ranging from methods in local interracial work to white and black women's employment and housing segregation.

One white attendee rated the conference "the deepest spiritual experience" of her life and a glimpse of "the Kingdom of God."[55] While not all feedback rose to such sublime heights, the organizers believed they had erected a platform for a unified Christian womanhood. Through "close informal contacts . . . in personal conversations, and by a spirit of fellowship" with a purely educational objective, the planners had precluded "the emotional tension between northern and southern white women which frequently develops when they meet to discuss the race problem" and "the fear and suspicion which Negro women have of reactionary sentiment generally expected from the South." "The prevailing attitude . . . seemed to be liberal, democratic and Christian."[56]

The First General Interracial Conference, officially sponsored by the FCC's Department of Race Relations, the Council of Women for Home Missions, and the YWCA, reflected white southern thinking on race and race relations. With assumptions of white superiority and innate racial antagonism, progressive white southerners sought to ameliorate, not eliminate, Jim Crow practices by softening the most violent aspects without dismantling the structural apparatus. The southern model provided the language for public discussions of race relations.[57]

The CWC viewed education as the solution to America's race problem, a position promoted by the burgeoning field of sociology and FCC Secretary of Race Relations, George Haynes. An ordained African

American minister and Columbia University Ph.D. in sociology, Haynes believed that education based upon Christian principles could engender "happy experiences and memory . . . within and between groups," and thus create an "interracial mind" to counter racial and class separation in social, civic, and public life.[58] Further, he contended, interracial conferences could stoke a "consciousness of racial worth" and "a belief among Negroes that they must fight and contend to secure citizenship rights."[59] The CWC fashioned social science analysis into a religious tenet: "[I]nterracial action must be preceded by interracial thinking." To distinguish their modern scientific approach from missionary paternalism, the CWC added, "[W]omen of our churches, white and Negro, need to learn to work *together*, rather than one *for* the other."[60] Unfortunately, thinking often became a substitute for action.

The church women's program centered on promoting interracial education and sociological studies, expanding Race Relations Sunday to Race Relations Week, and encouraging legislation and industries to mitigate the "limited opportunities for Negro women in employment." They also recommended "specific lines for study and experimentation," such as employing African American women stenographers and clerks in denominational offices and social agencies, and improving the "understanding between housewives and domestic workers."[61] Though the CWC had the potential to expand the role of religion—and of religious women—in society, the middle-class church women lacked the authority to implement their program.

Nonetheless, the church women celebrated their "liberal, democratic and Christian" attitude, even as they sidestepped the pressing issues of segregation and mob violence. Instead, they "encouraged . . . preventive measures" and discussions in the press "to create proper sentiment and right public opinion" against lynching. Moreover, they concluded, only "*forced* segregation" qualified as "an invasion of what we stand for in a democracy."[62]

It would be easy to attribute the modest proposals to the predominance of white southern women at the conference. Their role on the planning committee and as session leaders indicates the deference paid to southern views on race. Most northern Protestants preferred to clasp hands in racial unity with their white sisters and brothers rather than step across the color line in support of social justice.[63]

Whether at the urging of black conferees or northern white women's interaction with them, the CWC invited four black women, including Florence Randolph, and four white women to join the permanent committee.[64] The black women's presence resulted in a noticeable shift. Eight months after Eagles Mere, in May 1927 an equal number of black and white church women met at the Quaker Woolman School, about fifteen miles from Philadelphia, for a regional conference. Informed by reports from African American sociologists and social workers, the women explored northern manifestations of Jim Crow: white resistance to share work space with black employees, the exclusion of black doctors from hospitals and clinics, biased textbooks in public schools, impediments to black home ownership, and violence against those who moved into white neighborhoods. They deemed all these to be legitimate religious issues.[65]

In September 1928 the CWC returned to "delightfully inaccessible" Eagles Mere for the Second General Interracial Conference.[66] "[B]efore a big open fire, and [with] prayers," sixty women declared themselves "representative[s] . . . of the two great races which together hold the future of American civilization in their hands" and "spokesmen [sic] for thirty-one denominations and organizations whose membership number millions of American women."[67]

Identifying themselves as more than mere auditors in the discourses on race, religion, and civilization, the church women excoriated American Protestantism for not "taking the lead in promoting a liberal and firm policy on interracial comity and justice." Hobbled by "inertia, indifference and ignorance" and a "misplaced emphasis on form and ceremony," the Christian church, they concluded, suffered from a "failure to realize that the great function of the church is to practice vital religious living and to understand that the great social problems of peace, industry and race relations are the churches [sic] responsibility."[68]

Florence Randolph's influence could be detected throughout the two-day conference in which African American women comprised more than half the session leaders. To prevent irritations and disagreements from derailing the conference, Randolph ensured that "a strong spiritual note was struck" by interspersing devotional prayers and songs amid spirited discussions. Following one particularly intense session in which black women "asked some pointed questions" and "gave the hypocrites an uncomfortable fifteen minutes," Randolph "brought it all back to sugary sweetness and love with closing prayers."[69]

An impressed Alice Dunbar-Nelson observed, "That was an interesting group of women who met . . . to discuss the church and its relation to the interracial question. . . . [A] more representative body of both races would be hard to find. And for two days . . . they carried out a most crowded program of breathtaking scope. . . . [A]nd you rather felt breathless from rushing so fast and so far into the realm of applied religion and social science and the race question and reports of what has been done and what can be done, and what yet remains to be done."[70]

Yet like many black women, Dunbar-Nelson remained skeptical. "It is easy for inter-racial gatherings to deliquesce into sentimental experience meetings or love feasts," she lamented. "It takes real courage on the part of both groups to stick to cold, hard, unsentimental facts, and to pay homage to the God-of-Things-As-They-Are. . . . It was the colored women, by the way, who kept the discussion on a frank and open plane . . . who insisted that all is not right and perfect in this country of ours, and that there is a great deal to be done by the right thinking church women of both races."[71]

The following year in a "new departure," the church women convened the first statewide interracial conference in Trenton, New Jersey. Florence Randolph and Violet Johnson were among the seventy-six black and white delegates representing twenty-one communities. Over two days at the Stacy-Trent Hotel, speaker after speaker told of bleak conditions in education, housing, and labor. They delineated "what it means to be a Negro in New Jersey" and presented a "clear picture of life of the Negro citizens and race relations."[72]

Although the conference preceded the onset of the Great Depression by several months, the much vaunted prosperity of the twenties had clearly bypassed many of the state's black residents. Some had never fully recovered from the severe recession of 1921; others suffered from discrepancies between civil rights statutes on the books and discriminatory hiring practices. For black men systematically excluded from skilled trades and black women restricted to domestic service or the laundry and tobacco industries, economic prospects remained low.[73] Segregation, absentee landlordism, and structural barriers to home ownership created an endemic housing shortage made worse by inflated rents for dilapidated, unsanitary, and overcrowded space. Particularly poignant were reports of children forced to attend inferior segregated elementary schools, of high school students barred from vocational classes, and of graduates denied admission to state colleges.[74] Though they exhorted delegates to abandon the idea of "Negroes as especially inferior" and to take "a personal stand for justice and fair play in all relations of life," the church women could only recommend forming more local interracial committees and stimulating the right community attitude.[75]

When the Second New Jersey Interracial Church Women's Conference met in Trenton in 1930, the more than one hundred delegates and visitors had ample evidence of the economic depression gripping the nation, though few apprehended its depth or duration. On the first day conferees listened to presentations on African and African American ethnology and the influence of African American visual and literary art on American culture. The day ended with an exhibit from the Newark Museum's renowned African art collection and an anti-lynching lecture by the NAACP's Walter White.[76]

The second day's discussion of "Open and Closed Doors in Economic Life" painted a sobering picture that substantiated what many of the delegates had experienced or at least witnessed. In the six months since the October 1929 market crash, New Jersey's black residents had suffered more than at any time since the recession of 1920–1921. Employment discrimination created severe hardship, especially white employers' practice of dismissing unskilled labor, a label applied to most black workers regardless of actual skill level. The conference ended somberly with a review of local activities.[77]

Northern church women continued to hold interracial conferences and to share sociological studies on racial discrimination in employment, education, housing, and health.[78] In Summit white women invited George Haynes to speak on interracial harmony at the YWCA in 1929, and in 1938 the Women's Federated Missionary Societies held the World's Day of Prayer service in Randolph's AME Zion church, the first in an African American church.[79] Conferences created a discursive space for church women's leadership. However, when it came to action, the Interracial Conference Movement suffered from a limited vision, a lack of funds, and a need to appease a myriad of stakeholders.

The Great Depression: Less Interracial Dialogue, More Segregated Space

The Great Depression exposed the limits of the church women's interracial conference movement and the unwillingness of white northerners to address racial discrimination. Contraction of the hierarchically racialized and gendered job market further undermined the economic position of black working women, those already on the lowest economic rung. Unemployed white men displaced white women in the labor force and black domestic servants lost jobs to unemployed white teachers, stenographers, and typists. White employers and laborers resorted to violence and intimidation to expand the economic color line and force African Americans from the workplace. Black families suffered in a downward spiral of unemployment.

For Florence Randolph the "unholy and unchristian attitude . . . against the colored people of Summit" and the "big effort . . . to keep all negroes [*sic*] unemployed" amounted to the criminalization of color. "[W]hat are you trying to do," the Methodist pastor asked, "make criminals out of negroes? Force them to steal to keep soul and body together, so that an entire race . . . [is] discriminated against for no other reason than that God Almighty created them black?"[80]

In an open letter to her fellow suburbanites, an outraged Randolph declared, "[T]he odds are against the negro [*sic*]. He is last hired and the first fired." Affluent white housewives in Summit and neighboring Short Hills colluded "to dismiss all colored help and to spread propaganda to discourage those who were employing them."[81] "Honest, Christian, praying people" who made every effort to obtain work repeatedly heard "'no colored wanted,' or 'my husband is opposed to colored people,' or 'we do not employ colored, we are going to rid the town of colored people.'" Town officials expended scarce resources on a program of "preparedness against crime [and an] enlarged police force . . . minimizing the wrong acts committed by white people and magnifying the same wrong acts committed by colored people." Having named the sin, Randolph offered redemptively, "It is the duty of every Christian minister and worker . . . to speak out for the right and against the wrong. Summit cannot pose as a Christian town and be unjust to any portion of her citizens. . . . Jesus Christ stood firm against race hatred."[82]

Jim Crow segregation outpaced interracial committees and conferences. In 1923, for example, a public hospital in a Monmouth County shore town unabashedly announced that following a renovation "[i]t was found possible to give the colored patients a roomy ward with a sunny piazza" distant from white patients.[83] More often white New Jerseyans resorted to violence to demarcate white space. For two days in April 1926 white mobs in Carteret, an industrial suburb twenty-five miles from Summit, physically attacked a black Baptist congregation during worship and burned the church. Roving bands of white men and boys clubbed and prodded men and women who resisted, set homes afire, and in a weeklong reign of terror kept more than six hundred black residents from their homes and hundreds more from their jobs with threats of lynching.[84]

The public response was muted. "This was not in South Carolina or Georgia, but in Middlesex County, New Jersey[,] where the people are supposed to be civilized and educated[,] above resort to lynch law," stressed a Newark editor who condemned the violence without questioning the underlying structural causes. "In a different environment, Jews, Italians or Poles might have been the objects of attack. In the Carteret affair we see the fruits of the seeds of intolerance and hatred so widely sowed by the Ku Klux Klan."[85]

From his pulpit in suburban Orange the state chairman of the Baptist convention's interracial commission decried, "We have been horrified by Armenian massacres and Russian pogroms . . . . The atrocities done by these people have made us use the terms 'unspeakable Turk' and 'savage Russians,' but other nations have the right to reproach us for the treatment accorded native-born Americans with a different colored skin." Though he called the riot "indefensible from every angle," the minister ended with the specter of interracial sex, "I hold no brief for the whole colored race. I am aware of their serious defects. . . . I do not want my children to marry theirs. Neither do they."[86] When the NAACP requested contacting the governor to send the National Guard, the minister proposed to investigate Sunday school and public school literature on race relations and to arrange a meeting with the Ku Klux Klan to "tell the negro's side of the question." His appeal for a "square deal" and Christian "brotherhood" probably sounded like a tinkling cymbal to the Carteret victims who, according to the State Colored Women's Republican Club vice president and pastor's wife, had previously appealed to the town council for protection following defeat of the Democratic machine by an active black plurality.[87]

In 1928 the color line erupted in Summit in the first weeks of the school year as real estate valuation and public education collided. White middle-class parents refused to send their children to "the colored district," a school with all-white teachers and a white principal, because of the "predominance of colored pupils over white pupils in the lower classes."[88] The school board reacted immediately and gerrymandered district lines to reassign nineteen black and ten white students to different schools. Not satisfied, eighty parents and a number of property owners demanded the removal of more black students. When the school board hesitated, white parents enrolled their children in "white" schools.[89] Thus, without signage or statute the suburb nullified state civil rights laws, violated school policy, and created a segregated school system. It assigned lower grade students based on color and segregated upper grade classes and extracurricular activities.[90]

As segregation in Summit schools intensified, black women devised creative strategies of resistance. One long-term AME Zion resident and state Republican and Federation Club member opted to tutor her child at home and incur a fine, rather than comply with his assignment to a remedial class.[91] Violet Johnson formed the Junior Republican and Junior State Federation clubs for girls and the mixed-gender Senior Student Council and Literary Debating Club "to promote wholesome amusement and intellectual uplift" for high school boys and girls. "Miss Violet" recruited black and white professionals and educators as interlocutors and mentors. Meeting at Johnson's "Home Away from Home," the students elected their own officers, researched African American history and literature, and explored a range of religious and political topics as they gained the leadership experience their public schools denied them.[92]

Perhaps nothing more clearly demonstrates the invidious progression of Jim Crow in the northern suburb than events at the Summit YMCA. Organized in 1886 as a marker of middle-class Protestantism, the "Y" provided commodious dormitories, a pool, gymnasium, game rooms, and separate lobbies for men and boys. The iconic three-story red Devonshire brick building with its terra cotta trim and copper roof

symbolized early twentieth-century muscular Christianity and suburban affluence.[93] In 1929 following a four-month "study" and only eight
months after George Haynes had spoken at the Summit YWCA on
"Inter-Racial Harmony," the YMCA Board of Directors peremptorily
implemented a "year's experiment" with a segregated "colored" branch.
Housed in a two-room apartment some distance from the "white"
YMCA, the new "colored" branch received a mere $2,000 of the YMCA's
$26,000 budget.[94]

At the formal opening of the Lincoln YMCA, Violet Johnson extended greetings to a hundred guests, including the president of the
white YMCA and the white chairwoman of the "study" committee. The
main speaker, National Secretary of the YMCA Colored Works Department Channing Tobias, pronounced the Lincoln YMCA, if not the modest facility, of "vast importance to the colored people of Summit" and
"an opportunity to make a positive contribution to the welfare of the
community, just as any other group of any race." Rather than view the
Lincoln Y as another brick in the wall of segregation, Tobias challenged
the black suburbanites to construe it as a weapon in the fight for full citizenship. "[E]very opportunity given, every game played, every camping
facility opened—are to the end that we may perfectly reflect that perfect
image of manhood, Jesus Christ." The newly appointed branch secretary
presented the segregated space more prosaically as a much-needed community center for adults and youth of both sexes and a "dependable employment service."[95] Whatever Summit's black residents felt about this
latest drawing of the color line remained part of the hidden transcript.[96]

The editor of the local paper unhesitatingly shared his viewpoint. A
week earlier he had fulminated over the racist action of a white Brooklyn rector who announced during Sunday service that the five black
parishioners were no longer welcome in the Episcopalian parish. The
indignant editor wondered "if the reverend expects to find a 'Jim Crow'
department in Heaven when he gets there."[97] Now that Summit's YMCA
had expelled African Americans and demarcated yet another public area
as white space, the editor struggled with "parallels and contrasts" between "the color line" drawn by elite white northern civic and religious
leaders and the southern-born rector. Pursuing a torturous line of rea-
soning, he concluded that the rector had acted with *benevolent* motives
"in a most unfortunate way." Segregation *per se* was not unchristian;

rather it was *forced* segregation that created "ill-feeling." "What would have been thought of the Summit Y.M.C.A.," the editor queried, "if instead of cordially co-operating with the colored people in organizing a branch of their own, it had issued a *pronunciamento* to the effect that 'No Negroes were wanted in the Y.M.C.A.?'" Presumably responding for "our colored friends and neighbors," the editor found nothing objectionable about segregation, provided it followed a "decent procedure" and not "some arrogant exclusion policy on the part of the white people."[98]

Satisfied that it had behaved with good form, albeit without African American input, white Summit swiftly consolidated the latest instantiation of white superiority and consigned recreation for black youth to the high school gym.[99] Later when the white "Y" announced that because of the importance of swimming to civic safety, the gym and pool would be open to "all boys" from Summit and neighboring towns, all boys needed no other marker.[100] Having forcibly demarcated space to conform to an imagined community, white Summit understood it to mean *white* only and required black Summit to view it similarly.

After six years of a separate but unequal arrangement, in 1935 the YMCA board announced that due to "financial difficulty" and "the increased use of physical equipment by our own boys," the Central "Y" had severed all ties with the "colored" branch.[101] Jettisoning any pretense of a study, the white board moved with all deliberate speed.

Black Summit also acted swiftly. Forced either to relinquish all claim to civic space or to maintain an independent, though severely straitened, beachhead, Summit's black citizens chose the latter and incorporated the Lincoln YMCA as an independent institution. The organizational objective reflected their faith and resistance in the midst of the prolonged economic depression: "The Lincoln Young Men's Christian Association accepts the principle of Jesus that persons are more important than things."[102] Confronting white civic and religious leaders who exercised coercive control over the town's economic resources, private as well as New Deal public funds, black residents demonstrated their understanding of community.

The Lincoln YMCA Women's Auxiliary became the lifeblood of the segregated institution. Working women organized fund-raising projects and initiated cultural and civic programs open to African Americans in Summit and neighboring suburbs. Florence Randolph chaired the Reli-

gious Committee and instituted Sunday Vespers as an interdenominational space for religious and social programs. Under Violet Johnson's
leadership the Annual Lincoln-Douglas [sic] Tea became a forum for
discussing major civic, political, and religious topics that attracted black
and white participants from throughout New Jersey and the New York
metropolitan area. Johnson organized the Women's Progressive Sewing
Club for adult women to earn money during the Great Depression. She
formed the eponymous Violet Johnson Progressive Club for the small
group of young professional women and wives of local doctors and dentists who were "trying to live up to the name and standard of Miss Violet
Johnson."[103]

When Channing Tobias returned to Summit in June 1936 to install
the officers of the independent Lincoln YMCA and Women's Auxiliary,
he found an organization that had risen to the challenge of making a
positive contribution to the community.[104] Set adrift amid the economic
dislocation of the Great Depression with limited space and limited resources, working women transformed the Lincoln Y into a thriving cultural and civic space.

* * *

In May 1937 Pastor Randolph hosted the State Interracial Conference
of Church Women at her Summit church. The interracial conference
and luncheon could only hint at the discursive distance black women
had traversed. They had sustained their communities against nearly
insuperable odds and had expanded the discourses on justice, race,
and Christian womanhood during a period of social and economic
retrenchment.

However, Randolph and Johnson had little to celebrate. The conference theme, "Race Relations in New Jersey—Church Women, What
Next?" expressed the dilemma of the white and black women of the state
and region. After years of meetings, intense discussions, and trenchant
sociological studies, the church women conceded that there remained a
"great lack of knowledge on the part of the public about the problems of
housing, education and living conditions of the Negroes and a great lack
of sympathy with the sufferers."[105]

Johnson and Randolph did not need a conference to know that decades of interracial women's alliances had not eliminated lynching, mob

violence, segregation, and economic discrimination or resulted in federal intervention to protect the rights of African Americans. Paradoxically, the conferences had placed race relations in a mediated framework and provided cover for a church that silenced its prophetic and egalitarian message. Further, interracial conferences had not created a united womanhood. In many ways, African Americans in Summit, in New Jersey, and in the nation as a whole were worse off in 1937 than they had been in 1917. Nonetheless, New Jersey's black church women continued their program of civic righteousness, this time based on civil rights. They carried their fight for social justice to electoral politics.

5

"Putting Real American Ideals in American Life"

Church Women and Electoral Politics

By the time Tennessee ratified the Nineteenth Amendment in August 1920, African American women in New Jersey were already "an important factor in politics."[1] They carried their religious convictions into the political arena, convinced that "Negro women have the opportunity now as never before to stand out prominently in putting real American ideals in American life."[2] Those real ideals rested on Christian principles.

Unlike black women in the South who suffered disenfranchisement, northern black church women carved a role as political actors. Defining politics as "nothing more than [the] Science of Government" and political parties as "the instruments by which thinking men and women first promulgate and then practice principles [for control] of the influence which surrounds the place they call their home," they believed that good government could transform society.[3] Their duty was to ensure that "every woman does her part to help make clean, just laws, and see that they are enforced."[4] Having learned organizational effectiveness in their missionary societies and temperance unions, they formed county, ward, and district clubs and led campaign rallies with the sonic and visual markings of religious revivals. Their registration drives and successful get-out-the-vote campaigns turned formerly Democratic wards into Republican victories.

In 1922 they formalized their political activism in the New Jersey Colored Women's Republican Club (NJCWRC). Initially stimulated by the Republican Party's desire to organize black women for Warren G. Harding's 1920 presidential bid, the statewide organization represented a shift in ordinary women's sense of themselves as enfranchised citizens with a singular purpose. The ballot was a sacred instrument and they were agents of moral redemption.

By the time they gained the right to vote in 1920, New Jersey's black women had tried for decades to effect progressive social change without participating in electoral politics. Initially they claimed space based upon their Christian service. Later they contended that their sacrifices as women and mothers during World War I had earned them the right to be heard. Finally, in the 1920s and 1930s they demanded a place as independent actors in the electoral process. As they discovered, the intersection of race, gender, and class was fraught with complications within the Republican Party and in politics at large.

The Colored Women's Republican Club formed alliances with newly enfranchised white women. However, rather than converging, the priorities of New Jersey's middle-class white women and black working women diverged after suffrage. White women adopted a purely feminist agenda, while black women held to the objectives of civic righteousness. Further, as women recognized that the party apparatus remained in the hands of white men, although women constituted the majority of the voting age residents in many areas, the relationship between white suffragists and the state Republican Party became strained. White men marginalized white women, who in turn tried to eliminate black women from party positions.

Yet black women had practical reasons to remain loyal to the party of Lincoln. Besides, Democrats offered few inducements to leave. As one pundit remarked, African American women were the least likely to "hop out of the Republican frying pan . . . into the Democratic fire."[5] With few illusions about the relative merits of the political parties, Johnson and Randolph tried to hold in creative tension a critique of the American political system and their commitment to civic righteousness. It would take years for their disaffection to grow into a Democratic realignment.

From Social Reform to Legislative Politics

After 1920 black women added politics to their service. With the ballot in hand, they could "strengthen and uplift institutions and bring them to a higher degree of moral worth." For example, in 1917, after listening to a "very touching report" on black women released from prison, Federation women noted plaintively, "[T]here is little hope for the girl or woman just out of prison unless there is a stronger and purer hand to help her."[6] Moved by the report, Prison Reform Committee Chairwoman Mary Burrell solicited data on the number of African American parolees and parole officers, "if any." The responses painted a bleak picture. Only one of New Jersey's five penal institutions housing women employed African American officers, though many judges agreed that black officers would have a "most salutary effect" on black prisoners and probationers.[7]

Believing that the ballot could amplify voices and open doors, in 1921 as chairwoman of the Legislative Department, Burrell contacted county judges directly with a resolution that read in part, "fully realizing [our] duty as citizens in this commonwealth, and appreciating the helpless and unfortunate condition of many of our women and girls who find their way to our courts of justice, we believe that they can be helped and sooner placed on the right road to reestablishment in society by being cared for by persons of their own race."[8] The direct action by the newly enfranchised women prompted one judge to send two girls, "strangers to the county," home to their parents following arrest on a serious charge.[9]

Wishing to effect structural changes, the women lobbied the officials they had helped to elect. Since power resided in the county where freeholders or commissioners managed major expenditures, Burrell contacted a white woman freeholder to arrange a visit to the State Home for Girls in Trenton where twenty-eight girls from the Newark/Essex County area were housed and an equal number paroled. As a test of their "sincerity," the freeholder asked the women to provide a volunteer to work in the probation office.[10]

Over the course of a year, Federation member Lottie Cooper regularly attended court and made one hundred and fifty calls on probationers. "Few can appreciate the number of Colored girls and women who are arrested daily and until now there has never been a Colored woman in the Court to intreceed [sic] for them," Cooper told her Federation sisters. Every Friday fifteen probationers reported to Cooper, who provided them with food, shoes, and medicine. In addition to taking them to the New York Hippodrome and entertaining them with a Christmas party, Cooper had "prisoners paroled in [her] custody[,] made investigations, . . . visited the jails" and counseled others to avert recidivism. In one case she "secured the confidence of a young woman who was in trouble, assisted and encouraged her to change her way of living." Though the work was varied and exhausting, Cooper noted enthusiastically, "Other cities have Colored police women. Let us hope and pray the day is not so far distant when we can be as fortunate."[11]

Mary Burrell was well equipped to shift from social reform to legislative politics. Born in Virginia in 1886, the home care nurse had gained extensive experience in women's organized work prior to moving to New Jersey with her husband and sons in 1913. In addition to chairing the Executive Board of the Virginia Baptist Missionary Society, Burrell was also a founder of the Richmond Hospital and the Virginia State Federation of Colored Women.[12] During the 1920 election, as chairwoman of the Essex County Colored Women's Republican Club, Burrell "turn[ed] a Democratic ward into an overwhelming Republican majority" and sent Dr. Walter Alexander to the state assembly, making him New Jersey's first black legislator.[13] Before black women could vote, New Jersey black men held no significant elective positions.

After suffrage, Burrell collaborated with Assemblyman Alexander to draft a bill giving judges the power to appoint probation officers. The bill successfully passed both houses over the governor's veto. Burrell's most notable lobbying effort was in support of the Civil Rights Bill of 1921. Drafted by Alexander, the bill banned discrimination in all public accommodations, including restaurants, hotels, theaters, and beaches as well as in public education from primary grades though college.[14]

In the move from reform to legislative action, Burrell contacted the legislative chairwomen in the National Association of Colored Women's Clubs (NACW) and the white State Federation of Women's Clubs "in order to get their help and guidance as the work was new."[15] Burrell cooperated with her white counterpart to support maternalist legislation on marriage and divorce, women's industrial employment, the Mother's Pension Bill, and infant welfare.[16] She also partnered with newly elected white Assemblywoman Jennie Van Ness on a prohibition enforcement bill enacted over the Democratic governor's veto.[17] In recognition of her extensive legislative work, the New Jersey legislature granted Burrell floor privileges for an entire session.[18]

Yet as black women discovered, their ability to influence public policy had limits. Burrell could not count on white women's support for anti-lynching and civil rights legislation. And even their legislative victories were not unalloyed successes. The probation reform legislation, for example, permitted the judicial appointment of volunteer as well as paid probation officers. Although Lottie Cooper passed the required examination and was on the eligible list, she remained a volunteer officer throughout 1921 and 1922.[19] Further, black women funded their lobbying activities from their meager earnings and during their leisure hours, placing an extra constraint on their political activism. Nonetheless, the women believed that with the ballot they could reform civic institutions and promote just laws.

"Good Government of Men and Measures"

By the time Florence Randolph convened the first statewide political conference of black women in August 1920, they were already organized for action. Determined to "promulgate and then practice principles" grounded in the Golden Rule and "professedly American," they formed County Republican Clubs with ward and district units that blanketed urban and suburban communities with get-out-the-vote drives and rallies.[20] They held educational "suffrage meetings" in local churches and halls to encourage women to become "active factors in the political life of the community." They explained the electoral process and evaluated party platforms to save the newest voting citizens from "fumblings and mistakes in the future."[21]

In Essex County, an area that included Newark and the surrounding suburbs, "county chairman for colored women" Mary Burrell held more than forty-six "suffrage meetings" and gave more than thirty speeches in support of Warren Harding and the Republican ticket. In September she hosted a "great meeting" at which Florence Randolph and other black and white, state and national party leaders spoke.[22] Black women contributed to the Republican tidal wave.

Despite their electoral performance, white and black Republican women remained in subordinate positions on auxiliary women's committees and in the State Women's Republican Club where Lillian Feickert served as president and Florence Randolph one of several vice presidents. In 1921, after the state legislature granted women the right to serve equally on regular party committees, white women filled the majority of the committee positions designated for women, leaving few seats for black women.[23]

Nonetheless, New Jersey's black women gained power that eluded southern African Americans. Randolph, for example, served as a member-at-large of the Republican State Committee and on the board of the New Jersey League of Women Voters. In the South, Republicans maintained a "lily white" structure and only white women could join the League.[24]

The state's black women formalized their political activism in early May 1922 when two hundred delegates from seventeen counties gathered in suburban Plainfield for the "record breaking" Colored Women's Political Conference. The women organized the Colored Women's Republican Club, elected Florence Randolph president, and organized county and local units throughout the state.[25]

At the close of the Plainfield conference, Mary Burrell motored to Atlantic City to attend Lillian Feickert's Women's Republican Club forum. Feickert outlined two aims for the predominantly middle-class white women's political group: raise the registration of women of voting age above 55 percent and demand more attention for "women's legislation."[26] Absent from the list was the federal anti-lynching bill or federal enforcement of southern black women's voting rights. One month later black women would march through downtown Newark to protest congressional inaction on the Dyer Anti-Lynching Bill and join the nationwide Anti-Lynching Crusade.

By the summer of 1922 New Jersey's black women were seasoned political actors. In August, Violet Johnson and other Federation women joined their sisters from the Empire Federation of New York in a special train car to attend the National Association of Colored Women's (NACW) biennial session in Richmond, Virginia, and Washington, D.C.[27] Following the dedication of the Frederick Douglass Home in Anacostia, a contingent visited Capitol Hill to lobby key senators on the Dyer Bill.[28] Upon her return to Summit, Johnson organized a local unit of the Colored Women's Republican Club with forty-five women at The Home Away from Home.[29]

The church women valued their interlocking relationships with the State Colored Women's Republican Club, the State Federation, and their local missionary societies and boasted, "We have gained experience by availing ourselves of every opportunity to cooperate with all agencies that make for good citizens, a better understanding and closer sympathy with our neighbors."[30] Violet Johnson, for example, was a National Training School trustee, Baptist Woman's Convention vice president and field worker, State Federation and Summit NAACP vice president, State Federation Anti-Lynching Department chairwoman, and president of the local missionary society and Colored Women's Republican Club. Industrial clerk Ida Brown was first vice president and chair of the State Federation Executive Board, a state Colored Women's Republican Club organizer, president of the Jersey City Helping Hand WCTU and the Jersey City Sixth Ward Colored Women's Republican Club, and vice president of the trustee board at her local Methodist church.[31] Colored Women's Republican Club members carefully differentiated their political aims from those of white women and black men. Unlike white middle-class women in the Women's Republican Club and League of Women Voters, they organized out of a desire for common action and a willingness to serve. As "intelligent [women who came] together for strength, for inspiration, for information," they would ignore differences based on education, dress, or physical appearance. "[O]ur salvation," Randolph proclaimed, "lies in . . . A CAREFUL STUDY OF POLITICS, OF GOOD GOVERNMENT OF MEN AND MEASURES AND THEN, SUPPORTING THE BEST MAN."[32]

The hotly contested 1922 senatorial campaign tested black women's unity and determination to vote their convictions and not their emotions. U.S. Senator Joseph Frelinghuysen stood at the center of an NAACP attack because of his absence on a crucial vote on the Dyer Bill. Yet Frelinghuysen, a Republican, realized the importance of the African American vote. In a telegram to delegates at the NAACP Convention in Newark, he declared his "continued effort" to enact the legislation, adding, "Civilization and humanity demand it. It is justice long delayed."[33] NAACP delegates were not in a forgiving mood.

Denied a place on the legislative ticket for the upcoming fall election by the County Republican Committee, former Assemblyman Walter Alexander urged black voters to withhold support if the Republicans did not "accede to the just demands of the colored race and give . . . equal rights with whites as guaranteed by the constitution." Alexander saved his most "caustic remarks" for Congressman R. Wayne Parker, an opponent of the Dyer Bill, and Senator Walter Edge. Edge had not stated his position. "Maybe he thinks that by the time he will look for office again we will have forgotten, but he is mistaken," Alexander grimly warned.

As for Parker, he quipped, "I want to say that Congressman Parker is retired right now."[34]

In November, black women broke with black men and the NAACP and joined white women to vote for Frelinghuysen, the prohibition candidate.[35] Despite the united woman's vote, Frelinghuysen lost to the "wet" Democrat Edward I. Edwards. However, true to Alexander's prediction, the New Jersey electorate "retired" Congressman Parker.

As the 1924 presidential election neared, the second in which women would vote, black women were determined to be a significant factor in the race between Republican Calvin Coolidge and his running mate Charles Dawes and their Democratic opponents John W. Davis and Charles W. Bryan. When the NACW convened for its biennial meeting in Chicago that August, New Jersey women were there, including NACW Chaplain Florence Randolph who opened the Sunday session with a prayer. Before leaving the city, representatives from forty states formed the National League of Republican Colored Women (NLRCW) and elected Violet Johnson's dear friend Nannie Helen Burroughs president and Hallie Q. Brown national director. The NLRCW's slogan captured black women's political resolve: "We are in politics to stay and we shall be a stay in politics."[36]

New Jersey's black women intended to be the "stay" that stiffened the resolve of the black electorate and the Republican Party. They formed NLRCW county units and Coolidge-Dawes clubs in cities and suburbs and extended their organization to precinct and street captains.[37] In April 1924, the Jersey City Sixth Ward Republican Club hosted a Coolidge Club Dinner with more than one hundred guests, including the president of the Eighth Ward Coolidge Club and white and black county and state committee men and women. Later that month, the Essex County Colored Women's Republican Club held a mass meeting at a local church; the white woman county delegate and party leaders from around the state attended.[38] Demonstrating what historian Evelyn Higginbotham calls a new political consciousness among black women nationally, the working women's grassroots mobilization and careful study of the issues led white and black party leaders and candidates to seek their endorsement.[39]

The bitter 1924 Republican senatorial primary between Hamilton Kean, the "dry" candidate, and the incumbent Senator Walter E. Edge, a "modificationist" on prohibition, once again pitted black women against their gender and race allies.[40] Calling Edge's nomination "offensive" to African Americans, former Assemblyman Alexander charged that during his term as governor in 1917–1918, Edge, an Atlantic City businessman, had failed to make any important black appointments or support black candidates in his home county and had created a Jim Crow annex in the Labor Department. Moreover, Alexander contended, out of fear of offending white patrons and harming the shore economy Edge colluded with two state senators to weaken the civil rights bill Alexander introduced in 1921, resulting in a meaningless law that denied damages to victims.[41] White women opposed Edge because of his efforts to weaken the Eighteenth Amendment.[42]

Black women stood by Edge despite his avoidance of the Senate's Dyer vote, because he subsequently entered a supportive anti-lynching statement into the congressional record. Though white Republican women called for a "no vote" and black men wanted to reduce him to "a copper," Edge defeated Kean in the primary and went on to win the general election.[43] Whereas black women defied black men and voted with their gender for prohibition in 1922, they voted for their race and anti-lynching in 1924.

While their political behavior most often branded them as party loyalists, New Jersey's black women guarded their independence. Unlike white women who "did not realize the value of the vote" and black men "ready to sell . . . their own race . . . for a mess of pottage," they intelligently assessed the political landscape.[44] As State President Florence Randolph explained, "The right-thinking, honest Negro, would hardly recommend joining the Democratic Party for . . . with some exceptions it is the party of corruption in the North and [l]ynch law in the South. On the other hand, the Republican Party in its struggle to keep 'lily-white,' will use the Negro with many fair promises before the election and abuse him after."[45] Black women would cast their vote for good government and good measures.

The 1928 presidential election that pitted prohibitionist Herbert Hoover and Charles Curtis against "wet" Alfred Smith and Senate Majority Leader Joseph Robinson was a pivotal one for New Jersey's black women. Al Smith, the Catholic governor of neighboring New York, had a strong Democratic organization in New Jersey, and based on overturning prohibition and extending state services, made a strong bid for the black vote.[46] He won many adherents but most African Americans remained loyal to the party of Lincoln, seemingly none more than the women of the State Colored Women's Republican Club. The senior women's division and the newly created junior division coordinated a successful get-out-the-vote campaign. Meeting in churches and homes throughout the state, they established Hoover-Curtis Clubs, distributed pledge cards, and adopted the National League of Republican Colored Women's step-by-step plan for calling and managing meetings and rallies.[47]

In the intense campaign, black women injected their understanding of justice and civic righteousness. Hoover was "a man of broad sympathies" who understood the problems African Americans confronted and who would "apply his scientific mind to those problems for a just and fair solution."[48] Their activities paid off. The heavy turnout on Election Day resulted in a Republican landslide. Hoover carried twenty of New Jersey's twenty-one counties; Republican gubernatorial, legislative, and Summit municipal candidates swept to victory. According to NLRCW President Nannie Burroughs, the party of "prosperity, projects, protection, and peace" defeated the party of "rum, race, and religion."[49]

Their partisan enthusiasm notwithstanding, black women remained clear-eyed when it came to the Republican Party. Even a rock-ribbed Republican like Burroughs conceded that Republicans were "justly charged with some 'sins of omission' and dereliction of patriotic duty." Nonetheless, the well-organized Colored Women's Republican Club claimed Hoover's 1928 win as their own—a moral victory for social justice and "general relief from demoralizing evils, rather than personal rewards for party fealty."[50]

And there were demoralizing evils aplenty. Nationally and locally, black women demanded enforcement of the Reconstruction Amendments as well as the Eighteenth *and* Nineteenth Amendments, a position that contrasted with white Republican women who stressed enforcement of only the Eighteenth Amendment.[51] Second, they looked to Hoover and the Republican Congress to combat segregation. Echoing Violet Johnson's 1919 proposal to Woodrow Wilson, black women called on Hoover to appoint a national, nonpartisan, biracial Welfare Commission to investigate and relieve the civil disabilities of disenfranchisement and discrimination, especially in travel, civil service appointments, relief work, and the military. Finally, the women requested the appointment of two African American women specialists to work in the Children's and the Women's Bureaus to "parallel the work that is being done . . . primarily for white children and women and incidentally for colored children and women."[52] Black women voiced their demands; unfortunately the Republican Party listened with a tin ear.

Undaunted, they claimed rhetorical and moral space in the public sphere. Violet Johnson's Summit Colored Women's Republican Club invited all state chapters to a New Year's Day Emancipation Proclamation Celebration in 1929, the first such commemoration to be held in the suburb in thirteen years.[53] The local editor urged support for "the biggest affair ever held in Summit by colored people." Selectively ignoring the dramatic increase in discrimination and segregation in the suburb and the state, he contrasted the position of Summit's black residents with that of black southerners and reminded white residents that the "people of African descent have formed a considerable and useful factor in the civic life of this city, and their interest in this anniversary must command the general sympathy of all citizens."[54]

The celebration was a civic and political success. The women energized their political and religious networks and attracted white and black Republicans from across the state. They demonstrated their political strength with a program that combined civic discourse and partisan rhetoric. They delineated their political priorities and raised salient social issues before a broad audience of politicians and voters. Initially black women based their claim to respect and a public presence on their Christian service; later they demanded a place in the public discourse because of their sacrifice as women and mothers during World War I. After nearly a decade of suffrage, New Jersey's black working women had earned the right to speak for themselves and their community. In the aftermath of the 1928 campaign, they claimed a place in the civic community and the electoral process.

Florence Randolph presided over the Emancipation Celebration and Violet Johnson delivered the major address. Mary Burrell joined them on the podium along with national, state, and county Republican committeemen, Urban League officers, and Summit's Republican mayor. A fifty-voice jubilee chorus and two mixed-voice quartets lent the air of a religious revival to the event. Unlike in 1916, no one criticized the women for politicizing the Emancipation Proclamation.[55] Indeed, they used the event as a political rally for three more years. How black women would convert their public visibility and Christian convictions into political power to remedy social ills remained an open question.

Church Women and the Politics of the Great Depression

The winter of 1929–1930 was an especially hard one. By year-end 1929, shantytowns appeared in formerly bustling cities and suburbs, making "relief the real industrial problem of the state."[56] Newark alone experienced a 25 percent drop in employment.[57] Employment, wages, and take home pay steadily declined. The Lincoln YMCA's employment bureau soon became its most widely utilized program. Dismissing optimism as "extravagant" and pessimism as "foolish," the YMCA secretary urged black residents "to better matters by courageous effort and by a spirit that matters are no worse than facts compel us to admit."[58] Never having fully participated in the era of prosperity, New Jersey's working-class residents, black and white, were early casualties of the economic depression.

By February 1930, Summit's municipal leaders abandoned hope of an imminent recovery. Not until fall, however, would the Republican mayor and city council attempt to address the high rate of unemployment.[59] In the interim, managing relief cases that had nearly doubled in the first months of the year fell to the Overseer of the Poor, the Co-Operative Services Association, and a voluntary Committee of Ten comprised of representatives from the "central" and Lincoln YMCA branches, the YWCA, and the police department. Organized by the mayor to "cope" with the unemployment situation, the Committee of Ten identified only temporary jobs such as cutting firewood in East Summit and building a retaining wall at Memorial Field, the public park dedicated to war veterans.[60] These feeble measures did little to relieve the despair gripping the suburb.

When Violet Johnson's "dear friend" Nannie Burroughs sought contributions from Summit's white middle-class women for the National Training School in Washington, Johnson responded on the difficulty "to interest friends . . . during this period of unemployment." As one who relied on these affluent donors for her own work, Johnson commiserated, "You have my sympathy because I know what you're up against." A trustee of Burroughs's school, Johnson promised to fulfill her personal commitment of $25, a princely sum in desperate times.[61]

Though the Great Depression crossed color and class lines, the effect was disparate. For example, when the Co-Operative Services Association attempted to distribute raw skimmed milk at a site visible from the train station, elite residents protested that the milk station would attract unemployed families who wished to take advantage of the suburb's largesse. When the milk station finally opened in a less visible location, only persons certified as "entitled" based upon residency and prior employment, not need, received milk.[62] Summit officials, like those in other suburbs, tried to close its borders to those in need.

The city's worst fears seemed to have been realized when in mid-July 1931 a "floating population" of twenty-seven "colored men" appeared at the Co-Operative Services Association seeking work. Upon being told the suburb had no work or food for them, one man replied, "I'm good and tired of starving to death." The press reported, "The unemployed colored folks feel that race discrimination may have something to do with their position."[63]

Ever ready to defend the suburb against such charges, the local editor countered that the "majority" of the men were not "bona fide residents," but merely "persons who . . . drifted here from other sections of the country, doubtless drawn here by reports . . . that colored workers have been doing well here and that those out of work have been pretty well cared for." Conceding the "inherent right" of the unemployed to move about freely, the editor justified the refusal to feed or employ them on the basis of fairness, the need to take care of "our own unfortunate," and the "limit to our capabilities in this direction." He vehemently denied the charge of drawing the color line, asserting, "[T]he inference that in Summit there is discrimination because of color is distinctly unfair and unworthy. Colored people who have lived here any length of time know that their race gets a fair break here at all times." Voicing the tacit contract that prevailed in the suburb, he added, "If a man lives on the square, is industrious and sober he will not have cause to complain because of discrimination here on account of the color of his skin."[64] No matter its veracity, the statement served notice to black residents to behave, or else.

Having taken steps to reify the color line during the prosperous 1920s, Summit's white elite used the dislocation of the Great Depression to expand its compass and specify the conditions under which the suburb would tolerate African Americans. The poor, unemployed, and homeless were suspect; aid was for the "entitled." Ironically, at the same time the suburb expelled the unemployed black men, the "central" YMCA opened its dormitory rooms to other "transients," unemployed middle-class white men.[65] As would be the case throughout the Great Depression and the New Deal, the politics of class and color converged with economics to sanction official discrimination and harden the lines of color and class.

By the fall of 1931, the state and municipal governments could no longer ignore the widespread unemployment. In early September, Republican Governor Morgan Larson appointed a state director of unemployment and in October formed the New Jersey Emergency Relief Administration modeled on New York State's temporary relief program initiated by Democratic Governor Franklin Roosevelt.[66] Forced into action by more than two hundred "citizens of the United States and residents of Summit" who signed a petition demanding work or property tax relief, the mayor and city council with promised state assistance established a $1,000 public works fund to provide two weeks of work for "jobless but willing hands," an insufficient measure amid ever-widening distress.[67]

Conditions worsened. By early November the Emergency Unemployment and Relief Committee reported that one out of every seven Summit families was in "urgent" need and hundreds of residents unemployed. The needy included those who "have seen investments, the home, position and income swept away" as well as those who "probably, have never known much luxury in their own lives, but have been happy and good citizens, giving their children shelter, food and a share in our community life."[68] Identifying the deserving based on color and class had become a futile exercise, though Summit officials attempted to do just that, requiring meticulous registration and classification by race, sex, and degree of need.[69]

Ideologically opposed to government relief, Summit's Republican leaders implored residents to provide "Summit Relief for Summit Folk" and "make the Golden Rule a reality in Summit."[70] Need far outstripped the resources of the voluntary community chest and residents' ability to provide jobs at homes or businesses. As the Relief Committee's attempt at a citywide clean-up and vegetable garden failed, the suburb shed its relief roles and jobless white men went door-to-door offering to paint mailboxes for ten to twenty-five cents "or anything you care to give."[71]

Still, the Great Depression was not an equalizer. In fact, it had the opposite effect. White Summit no longer disguised its racist practices. An outraged Florence Randolph lifted the scrim. "[W]ithout fear of successful contradiction," she stated, "the odds are against the [N]egro."[72]

Against this backdrop of economic displacement, the State Colored Women's Republican Club convened in Summit for its Eleventh Annual Conference in August 1931. Delegates and visitors, many of whom had traveled more than three hours by bus from as far as Atlantic City, filled Fountain Baptist Church.[73] The women's attendance reflected their assessment of the political landscape. With an anti-prohibition plank in the Democratic platform and a call for repeal in the Republicans', the upcoming gubernatorial election would center on the economy—a referendum on "Hoover Prosperity" and the opening volley in the 1932 presidential race.[74] A Democratic victory in 1931 would increase the prospects for a Democratic presidential win in 1932; an outcome that black women feared would portend greater economic and racial discrimination.

The women devoted the Summit conference to the gubernatorial candidacy of U.S. Senator David Baird, Jr. State vice presidents and committee heads led roundtable discussions. Prayers, songs, and scripture suffused the political rally that included speeches by white state, county, and city officials.[75] Black men prominent in state and national Republican circles promoted Baird's candidacy with topics such as "Baird, the Business Man," while also casting him as a "friend to the farmers." Speakers praised his performance as governor and one spoke on "Congress and the Negro."[76]

Throughout the summer and fall of 1931, the Colored Women's Republican Club and its junior division campaigned enthusiastically for Baird. They hosted luncheons and dinners in homes and sponsored concerts and forums throughout the state. At one event Chicago Congressman Oscar DePriest, the first African American elected to the U.S. Congress since Reconstruction, headlined the program.[77] During the campaign black women astutely combined campaigning with social out-reach, on one occasion donating the proceeds of a concert held at the Lincoln YMCA to Summit's unemployed.[78]

While the Colored Women's Republican Club campaigned vigorously for Baird, the NAACP campaigned as vigorously against him. Thus, the National League of Republican Colored Women president and NAACP trustee Nannie Burroughs refused to speak for Baird, even when invited by her friend Violet Johnson.[79] The NAACP launched a retaliatory campaign against Republican candidates who had supported Hoover's Supreme Court nominee Judge John J. Parker, who as a North Carolina gubernatorial candidate in 1920 opposed black women's voting registration and declared that African Americans as a class did not desire to enter politics.[80] The NAACP made Parker's nomination a litmus test for Republicans. New Jersey Republican senators David Baird and Hamilton Kean had voted to confirm Parker's nomination to the bench. When Baird resigned from the Senate to run for governor, he remained in the NAACP's line of sight. National and state NAACP officers conducted an intense campaign in New Jersey and outlined their opposition in the pamphlet "Why the NAACP Should Defeat Baird."[81] Black women stood by their candidate.

Baird's Democratic opponent, A. Harry Moore, derided the Republican government that caused the economic depression. "Where is the job for every man . . . where the chicken at every table and the automobile for every workingman that we were to have under Hoover prosperity?" Moore demanded.[82] In an election in which both parties made a bid for the African American vote, the candidates leveled charges and countercharges of "bossism," fraud, and voter intimidation. Moore claimed, for example, that black citizens in the southern part of the state needed "protection" from Republicans intent upon controlling their vote.[83] Black women took umbrage and construed the statement as evidence of the Democratic Party's penchant for impugning black voters. The women would remind voters of the offensive comment during the 1932 presidential election.[84]

Nonetheless, some black voters formed the A. Harry Moore Colored League; many because they supported the Democratic candidate, others because they supported the NAACP's national boycott of pro-Parker senators.[85] Violet Johnson's endorsement would have been a coup for the Moore backers and some alleged she had come into their camp. Her disclaimer appeared under the headline "IS NOT SUPPORTING MOORE." Johnson tersely stated, "I have been annoyed by the use of my name in a Newark newspaper in connection with the alleged opposition by colored voters to the candidacy of David Baird. . . . I have not attended any conference of colored voters opposed to Baird, nor have I committed myself in any manner." She ended with an avowal of loyalty as a "Republican and naturally favorable to the candidates of the party."[86] Just as they voted their own mind in 1924 and 1928, black church women would determine their political course based upon their priorities, not those of the NAACP.

The Colored Women's Republican Club closed the 1931 campaign with a "large and enthusiastic" rally at the Lincoln YMCA. Speakers included local white party leaders, mayoral and council candidates, and the lone African American on the National Republican Committee, Assistant U.S. Attorney General Perry Howard. The noisy procession of Democrats and A. Harry Moore supporters marching through the streets was no competition for the enthusiastic Baird backers.[87]

To the black women's astonishment, Baird's Democratic rival won by a landslide. Though some African Americans who did not want to vote for either Baird or Moore stayed away from the polls, Moore garnered 80 percent of the statewide black vote in what amounted to a "rebuke" of Hoover. Baird carried only four counties, his home county of Camden and three other southern counties. The *Summit Herald* defiantly reported, "Summit did not participate in the Democratic landslide," though the remainder of the county went for Moore.[88] Democrats also swept the state legislature. In spite of the Democratic rout, Summit's black women could derive satisfaction from the heavier than usual voter turnout; 72 percent of registered voters went to the polls.

If African American women had expected to be rewarded for their fealty with changes in unemployment and relief operations, they were sorely mistaken. The referendum to remove relief administration from municipal control to a centralized county board went down to a stunning defeat along with Baird. Home rule and local control remained intact, despite worsening conditions.[89]

When the 1932 presidential campaign began, Violet Johnson's endorsement still mattered. Calling her "a respected and honored leader of the Negro race," the *Summit Herald* reported on one of Johnson's stump speeches under the heading "MISS JOHNSON ASKS SUPPORT FOR HOOVER." "Vote for a principle," Johnson urged. "[V]ote for Hoover and don't swap horses in the middle of the stream for conditions will be worse." She emphasized loyalty to the Republican Party rather than a commitment to Hoover's policies. "You will hear much about Hoover being to blame for the present economic conditions, but if you read your papers and study your history, you will find that after every war there has been a depression. We must decide as to which of these two great parties is to be given the privilege and power of directing the affairs of our government for the next four years."[90]

In a succinct history lesson Johnson cautioned, "Don't be influenced by promises from either political party, for they are as pie crusts—easily broken. . . . Ask yourself the question, 'Who is it that makes the laws of segregation, discrimination, Jim Crowism and humiliation suffered throughout the South where Democrats control and deny the Negro any voice in affairs of State?'" Speaking directly to African American women, Johnson challenged her auditors "to vote your own honest conviction and not to be influenced by what others say, but to read and study the issues, and find out what party has done more for the betterment of the Negro race as a whole." She was confident that as informed citizens they would make the right decision. "Let us show our appreciation by voting to re-elect Mr. Hoover as our next President."[91]

Throughout the 1932 presidential campaign, black women used multiple channels, from grassroots organizing to mass media broadcasting. Johnson gleefully reported to Nannie Helen Burroughs, "I had the thrill of my life when I heard your name announced over the radio to have been one of the speakers." Though Burroughs became ill on the campaign trail and the "lady announcer" read her speech, Johnson found much to celebrate. "All of the speakers were very good and of course I enjoyed your message. I'm right tipsy listening to the speakers. And between listening to them and putting up my winter curtains, I feel batty." Still, she expressed concern for her friend's health on the arduous campaign trail. "I'm so glad the campaign is nearly over, because if it doesn't end soon you'll kill yourself."[92]

Renowned as excellent vote-getters who could draw a crowd and deliver a compelling message, white and black pols welcomed black women on the hustings. When the white Summit Republican Club presented leading white male candidates at a rally at the Lincoln YMCA, Colored Women's Republican Club veteran Mary Burrell "almost 'stole the show' . . . with her keen, intelligently phrased exposition of why Summit Negroes should vote the Republican ticket."[93]

Whatever their dissatisfaction with the Republican Party locally and nationally, black women used every means to "arouse colored voters for the G.O.P."[94] They believed that the race's well-being hung in the balance. As Johnson confided to Burroughs, "I'm afraid if Hoover doesn't get in we'll all die. I'm doing my bit trying in a small way to help the cause."[95] In addition to speaking and placing articles in newspapers, Johnson reproduced Burroughs's speeches and articles for use at club meetings and distribution to the black and white press. Johnson also sent copies of her speeches and articles to Burroughs. Johnson hoped the multiple channels would be a "stay" for "some of these weak-kneed republicans [sic] going over to the other side."[96]

Though the Great Depression had taken its toll and dampened Johnson's partisan fervor, an untested Roosevelt and an unwelcoming party were not sufficient to lure her to the Democratic fold. Wary of the party of "segregation, discrimination, Jim Crowism and humiliation" in the South and urban bosses who maligned black voters in the North, black women could not discern a place for their voice or convictions in the Democratic Party.[97]

Three days before the election and with a subdued and perhaps realistic assessment of the Republican Party and its candidate, Johnson confided to Burroughs, "All we've got to do is pray and have faith."[98] On Election Day, Roosevelt's promise of change triumphed over Hoover's commitment to the status quo. Roosevelt won forty-two of forty-eight states and carried New Jersey by a narrow margin; Summit gave Hoover a two-to-one edge and the county remained in the Republican column.[99] Black women in New Jersey would stay with the Republicans. They had no reason to expect just treatment from the Democrats.

At the close of the campaign, an exhausted Burroughs penned a note to Johnson that expressed hope over experience. "Well the republicans [sic] will have four years to plan and stage a comeback," she wrote. "The party will doubtless be made over from top to bottom and if they do not consider the National League of Republican Colored Women in the making we are going to battle with them. I think they are coming to their senses after this sound beating."[100] Black women had remained faithful to their party even when others had abandoned it. They expected a reward.

As the nation waited to see what a Roosevelt administration would deliver, Pastor Florence Randolph appealed to a higher power: "We pray Thee that in the coming year men may think less of race, of color, of creed, and more of human souls; that a man may not suffer because he is white, brown, red, or black. We believe . . . Thou didst understand thine own plan when Thou created of one blood all nations to dwell upon the face of the earth."[101] In the midst of economic devastation and racial injustice, Randolph's prayer was intended for human ears as well as the divine.

Randolph blended her appeal for justice with an avowal of patriotism. "We love the town in which we live [;] we love the hills, the parks, the green grass and the blue sky. . . . [W]e are not anarchists, not reds, not bomb-throwers. . . . [W]e don't belong to the underworld who are trying to wreck the American system, who refuse to become American citizens. . . . We love our country and expect to remain here until Thou shalt come."[102] In other words, African Americans' claim to the protection and privileges of the Constitution was inviolable.

Burroughs's prediction of a party makeover was far too optimistic. Their public defense of the Republican Party notwithstanding, New Jersey's black women did not ignore the discrepancy between their experience and the party narrative of linear progress. As signatories with black men to the National Colored Republican Conference statement in 1923, they had threatened to bolt the party unless it ended its lily white policy and ensured equality of party membership to black Republicans, North and South.[103] In 1931 they petitioned the state Republican Committee to grant them "more recognition" and a "square deal" in party and government administration and protested white women's efforts to eliminate them from the Women's Republican Club by reducing the number of positions.[104] Having formulated an oppositional discourse of civic righteousness, black women did not bracket their religious convictions or their experience of race, gender, and class upon entering the political arena. Nor did they confuse political attitude with political behavior.

Neither should we. As historian Glenda Gilmore cautions, to do so would misrepresent the agency and the "political aspirations" of black women.[105] The political experience of New Jersey's black women suggests that the seed of the Democratic realignment of 1936 was sown prior to the Great Depression, though it took years to germinate. Remaining in the Republican fold was less a measure of satisfaction with the party of Lincoln than a pragmatic assessment of options. Despite their partisan rhetoric, black women's relationship with the party that consistently failed to respond to their demands for just laws and moral institutions was an uneasy one. The breakup was long in the making.

By 1936 black women conceded that Republicans had not come to their senses. After seven years of economic and civic depression, four years of discriminatory relief, and even more years of Republican perfidy, Burroughs encouraged African American women to vote for "Justice and Jobs," for "the man" rather than the party.[106] With little to lose—and perhaps something to gain, New Jersey's black women went to the polls and helped reelect Franklin Roosevelt.[107]

* * *

Historians continue to debate the movement of African Americans to the Democratic Party and the realignment of 1936. They emphasize either economics or the so-called civil rights appeal of Democrats and the New Deal. Both Evelyn Brooks Higginbotham and Nancy Weiss, for example, argue that in the four-year period between 1932 and 1936 African Americans moved from a position of unfailing Republican loyalty to vote Democrats into office based upon New Deal economics. Harvard Sitkoff, on the other hand, contends that the New Deal embrace of civil rights induced black Americans to abandon the party of Lincoln. Combining the economic argument with racial appeal, Patricia Sullivan argues that Democrats successfully wooed African American voters with New Deal relief jobs and blandishments like the 1936 multicity celebration of the seventy-third anniversary of the Emancipation Proclamation.[108]

Yet as Gilmore reminds us, focusing on a single election rather than the longer history of political behavior can be misleading.[109] Indeed it is important to explore the beliefs and experiences of black women as well as the marginalization of women and black men in the Republican Party to understand the realignment of 1936. Black women mobilized a Republican political machine in the 1920s and early 1930s. The Republican Party and its candidates did not reward them for their work or support their agenda, and it lost their votes.

Because of their political acumen and the public respect accorded them in political campaigns, it is easy to forget that most New Jersey Colored Women's Republican Club members wore uniforms and aprons; they scrubbed other people's floors and tended to other people's children; they had to work quietly behind male denominational and NAACP leaders. However, when these same women entered the political arena, they received the respect often denied them in other spaces. They operated on the principle of one woman, one vote. They made it impossible to deny that black women were more than their work or that they had identities as women and citizens in their own right. When they cast their ballots, more than an election was at stake. They were "working for the 'upbuilding of the country'" and black womanhood.[110] The Republican Party had given these women alternative roles as politicians. Abandoning those political roles for Democrats, a party that might take no notice of them, was risky. But desperate times called for desperate measures.[111]

6

"Carthage Must Be Destroyed"

Health, Housing, and the New Deal

"If because of injustice and poverty we should leave the rooms where we slept all night without fresh air because of no windows and should pass through dingy, dirty halls to get a little sunshine and fresh air in the street, may our fortunate fellowmen not stand ready to deport us into further misery," Reverend Florence Randolph prayed in December 1932.[1] More than piety led Randolph to link justice and housing in her public prayer, for only the election of Franklin Roosevelt competed with housing as a discussion topic as the year drew to a close.

The Great Depression and the New Deal profoundly affected black church women's activism. Questions of fitness for citizenship and black women's respectability regained currency as the economic depression exacerbated structural and social fissures and recovery policies divided citizens along gender, race, and class lines. Federal housing programs reinforced the trope of the suburb as the preserve of the white middle class, and new zoning and health ordinances turned black homes and black bodies into contested sites.

Demographic changes altered the suburban landscape and further racialized space. While the regional press printed reports of a "Negro invasion," Summit's black population remained relatively stable, though the rate of increase outpaced that of whites, nearly doubling between 1920 and 1930 from 4.8 percent to 8.7 percent of the total population of over fourteen thousand. By the mid-1930s, Summit's population climbed to over fifteen thousand and the black population peaked at about fifteen hundred, or nearly 10 percent.[2] As the population increased, so did competition for space.

The Great Depression aggravated old fault lines and New Deal polices created new ones in the six-square-mile suburb. National housing standards valorized racial space, while the federal financing of building loans and home mortgages transformed the single-family detached house in a homogeneous neighborhood into one of the most potent symbols of suburbia. The Federal Housing Administration (FHA) established by the National Housing Act of 1934, was the "spark plug" in a middle-class housing boom that ignited a suburban land grab and solidified New Jersey's reputation as the quintessential suburban state.[3] Anxious to secure their investment, real estate interests and white home owners racialized the single family home and public space as middle class and white. Housing became the flashpoint between an expanding white middle class and a besieged black community. With passage of the National Housing Act of 1937, known as the Wagner-Steagall Act, that provided federally backed mortgage insurance for low income rental housing, the national housing debate intensified. The state's role expanded as taxpayer dollars placed federally subsidized single-family homes within the reach of white middle-class families and consigned black and white working families to public housing.[4]

Federal subsidies for owner-occupied and rental housing changed the contours of the discourse in Summit. Economic returns superseded moral concern for the rights of black citizens to private and civic space. For the black working class, the New Deal became a "raw deal" and the National Recovery Act the "Negro Riddance Act" as the New Deal language of "slum clearance and removal" framed discussions of race, class, and citizenship.[5]

Violet Johnson and Florence Randolph fought back. They used religious, political, and civic programs such as Church Women's Interracial Conferences, Health Week celebrations, and garden clubs to disrupt the discourse. They enlisted white allies to battle ordinances that branded black women's bodies as diseased and black residents as a contagion. With limited resources and few friends they staved off the most pernicious attempts at racial cleansing and educated a new generation in the struggle for just laws and moral institutions.

Church Women and the Politics of Housing and Health

In early October 1932, African American sociologist and Director of Research for the National Urban League Ira De Augustus Reid appeared before the Summit Civic Association, an organization of elite white men, and declared that housing in the ideal suburb was less than ideal. Further, Reid called "unfounded" the "popular rumor [that] colored people are rapidly filtering" into Summit because of its relief work. Although 20 percent of the suburb's relief went to African Americans who comprised only 8.7 percent of the population, they were not transients. The average African American family had resided in the suburb six years, and 90 percent were nuclear families with a husband, wife, and a small number of children. Moreover, black residents owned homes at a rate higher than the state average, despite the "remarkably high" female working population.[6]

Nonetheless, Reid informed the white civic leaders, housing conditions "were worse than anticipated." The average monthly rent was the sixth highest of the sixty municipalities studied and, on a per room basis, the third highest. "In other words," Reid emphasized, "local colored people are getting less for their money than in other parts of the state." He attributed Summit's "bad" housing to "a triangular laxity of city, landlord and tenant."[7]

Reid painted an equally disturbing picture of education in the suburb. While the percentage of foreign-born residents masked the racialized structure of the educational system, Summit had "more illiteracy than was anticipated."[8] Only 40 percent of black children entered high school and a smaller number graduated. Reid correlated the high arrest rate of black youth, the lack of recreational facilities, overcrowded housing, and the high school dropout rate.[9]

"In summary," Reid stated, "Summit is largely a city of commuters who, seeing little of the needs of social service as they go to and from work, little understand the needs of the community." Noting a "paradoxical fact," he added, "The white population seems indifferent toward the welfare of the Negroes yet is developing increasing resentment over their presence."[10]

Reid proposed several remedies: renovate tenements that had not already deteriorated into "slums"; enforce health codes to correct windowless rooms, high rents, and overcrowding; provide occupational and vocational guidance and recreational activities for youth; employ black teachers; and increase social interest in housing. He also recommended forming an interracial committee of "influential individuals" interested in ameliorating the social and economic situations that inevitably lead to "dissatisfaction and unsocial actions."[11]

From April to September 1931 Reid and a fifteen-person team had "quietly and unobtrusively" conducted interviews on education, employment, business, health, recreation, citizenship, and race to assess the "advantages and disadvantages" accruing to African Americans. A Columbia University-trained sociologist, Reid conducted his work under the aegis of the New Jersey Conference of Social Work's Interracial Committee and the Department of Institutions and Agencies, which published the findings in *The Negro in New Jersey.*[12] The Federal Council of Churches (FCC) Church Women's Committee on Race Relations had made improving housing, health, and education a major thrust of the interracial conference movement. Although unable to stem Jim Crow segregation in northern communities, the interracial movement promoted the formation of interracial committees, including that of the State Conference of Social Work.[13]

According to Reid, the interracial committee selected Summit "for the review of Negro life because of its non-industrial character." And with a black population smaller than the 10 percent considered the point at which racial and social friction surfaced, "conditions here were thought to be better than average."[14] As the survey revealed, however, racial conditions were less a matter of numbers than of daily practices, structures, and the attendant material reality.

Reid's explanation for the Summit study notwithstanding, it is more likely that Florence Randolph and Violet Johnson influenced the selection. As members of the Conference of Social Work and leaders in state and regional religious and civic organizations, they believed they could form an interracial team of "influential lay persons" to "discuss and work out practical and satisfying solutions" that would serve as a model for the state.[15]

For years prior to Reid's study, Johnson had attempted to focus public attention on the discrepancies in housing and health in this affluent New York City suburb. In 1915 she inveighed against the quality and quantity of housing available to workers, especially black workers. Following the 1923 "Health Week" celebration at Fountain Baptist Church that highlighted discrimination in housing and municipal services, Johnson cooperated with the elite women's Town Improvement Association (TIA) to strengthen housing and health ordinances. Over the decade, the TIA had effected some minor improvements;

however, public interest in housing and municipal services for low income workers all but disappeared during the suburban housing boom of the 1920s as developers razed manor homes and created middle-class subdivisions with restrictive racial covenants, and realty interests tried to reify the vision of the suburb as a middle-class Anglo-Saxon preserve.[16]

Throughout the 1920s and 1930s black women used "Negro Health Week" celebrations to mobilize support in the politics of housing and health. Begun in 1915 by Booker T. Washington and revived in 1917 by the National Negro Business League with suggestions from Nannie Helen Burroughs, in 1932 the United States Public Health Service (USPHS) promoted national recognition through the Office of Negro Health Week.[17] Skillfully exploiting the maxim "germs know no color line," black women connected germ theory and racial anxieties to convert reluctant allies. In her analysis of public health activism, health historian Susan Smith concludes that through the "gospel of health," African American women in the North and South mobilized at the community level and, working with black professionals and white officials, "altered ever so slightly the focus of public health policy." They turned National Negro Health Week into a "grassroots movement with possibilities for social transformation."[18]

In Summit, Violet Johnson and Florence Randolph blended sermons and lectures with health education and examinations. For example, during Health Week in 1935, African American physicians, dentists, and nurses conducted free clinics for babies, children, and adults at the black Baptist and Methodist churches and the Lincoln YMCA. The culminating celebration held on the last Sunday in April conflated civic, political, and religious themes and featured a gospel chorus, sermons, and lectures by ministers, physicians, and dentists from Summit, Newark, and surrounding suburbs.[19]

To Summit's white middle class, National Negro Health Week looked like another racial uplift program. In actuality, it was much more. Through a program of health education, Johnson and Randolph linked individual hygiene and environmental sanitation to housing and gained the attention of the county and state health and housing departments.

But the business leaders Ira de Augustine Reid faced that October day were not ready to acknowledge the problems in their midst. The elite men of the Civic Association accused Reid of "distort[ing] the facts."[20] The presentation ignited a public debate on housing for low income workers and the place of African Americans in the affluent suburb's civic life.

Private Space, Public Debate

Negro Health Week celebrations in the 1930s were timely, if not prescient. Two months after Ira Reid exposed Summit's substandard housing and its correlation to tuberculosis, the local board of health initiated an assault on black working women's bodies. Armed with a new health ordinance that mandated semiannual health examinations for all domestic servants, Health Officer Dr. Henry Dengler began an aggressive anti-venereal disease campaign. Refusal to submit resulted in a $50 fine.[21] By the second week in January 1933, Dengler had examined more than two hundred women and classified sixty-eight as "diseased." Six months later, after examining an additional nine hundred and eleven domestic servants, he announced that of the eighty-six "affected," sixty-five were "colored" women.[22]

Although the USPHS authorized compulsory examinations as part of its national anti-syphilis program, in the absence of standardized protocols the sensitivity and specificity of testing could be substantially inaccurate depending on the quality of the laboratory and the serologic test. Therapeutics for treatment and follow-up also varied based upon local resources. Moreover, as medical historian Allen M. Brandt argues, "The suggestion, knowledge, or inference of immoral behavior by a patient may also have led to a tendency to identify non-specific infections as venereal."[23] Health officials generally restricted mandatory testing to high-risk populations, such as women arrested on charges of prostitution, men accused of vagrancy or sex offenses, and pregnant women. In contravention of the logic of sexual transmission of venereal infection, Dengler required all domestic servants to submit to semiannual examinations. Newark and suburban Englewood and Tenafly enacted similar ordinances.[24]

Local health officials usually worked closely with African American physicians, social workers, and health professionals to conduct educational programs, especially during Negro Health Week, and the health examiner issued a certificate of health based upon results provided by a health clinic or private physician. In Summit, Dengler conducted the testing himself. Historian Natalia Molina locates public health "as a key site of racialization," one in which "[h]ealth officials not only incorporated their racially charged visions into policies and ordinances that targeted ethnic communities but also helped shape the ways mainstream populations perceived ethnic peoples."[25]

Summit's black working women comprehended fully what was at stake. Yet, consistent with the *culture of dissemblance*, they maintained a studied silence, shielding threats to their respectability, and enlisted allies to repel the attack on their womanhood. Prominent white middle-class women immediately voiced opposition to the ordinance. Referencing the prevalence of white men's sexual abuse of black women, one wondered where was the protection for the domestic servant? Another questioned the legality of the examinations for American citizens and charged the health board with "petty terrorism," offering as evidence the eight notices she had received within forty-eight hours. In one instance, before the employer could have her private physician examine a couple, they protested with their feet and left Summit. Some employers simply refused to comply.[26] Despite white women's protestations, Dengler refused to rescind the ordinance, though he reduced the fine from $50 to $25 and pledged to hire a woman doctor; that eventually became a white public health nurse.[27]

Not all white women opposed the invasion of private space. The Summit WCTU and the TIA endorsed compulsory examinations, and the State League of Women Voters (LWV) advocated syphilis testing as part of a social hygiene program that included premarital testing and sterilization of the mentally "unfit."[28] In suburban Montclair, twenty-five "socially prominent" LWV and American Red Cross board members demonstrated their support by taking the serological test themselves; two brought along their maids.[29] Nationally, white women's groups ardently supported the "syphilis war."[30]

In 1937 and 1938, under the New Deal Works Progress Administration (WPA), the USPHS increased local funding to fight the "social evil." New York City and Chicago led the way; several New Jersey suburbs received awards for their programs. Dengler earned recognition for his "excellent work" in the "examination of public food handlers and domestic employees" and received out-of-state requests for information on Summit's "model" ordinance.[31]

Nationally, the NAACP denounced compulsory examinations as a pretext by white employers and housewives "to exercise their prejudice against Negroes."[32] African Americans understood, as historian Martha Ritzdorf argues, that health and zoning ordinances are never neutral; rather, they are part of a "culturally bound discourse . . . that both persuades and informs . . . about values and attitudes."[33] In her study of black working women in pre–World War I Atlanta, historian Tera Hunter contends that white officials used public health to invade the privacy of poor black and white women's bodies and create "public moments of relief" by "repeatedly depicting black women as bearers of filth and contagion." These performances reaffirmed the authority of the white elite and "impress[ed] subordinates with claims of its right to rule." Medical historian Allan Brandt suggests that "syphilophobia" reflected anxiety over the status of the white middle-class family and women's changing roles in the 1920s.[34] These forces seemingly converged in Depression-era Summit.

To mollify opponents, Dengler recommended hiring a full-time "Colored Public Health Nurse," thirty-one-year-old Lulu Hawthorne Ader, RN. The Mississippi native completed her nurse's training at Tuskegee (AL) Institute, earned a graduate nursing degree at an Alabama hospital, and previously served as superintendent at Newark's private Booker T. Washington Community Hospital. Her excellent credentials notwithstanding, hiring an African American woman in such a visible position was so unprecedented that the city council delayed her appointment to "meditate further upon this step." Initially able to hire Ader only on a probationary basis, Dengler overcame the city council's resistance by pointing to a growing black population and intimating an increase in venereal disease.[35] Moreover, with WPA funds to cover Ader's salary, he could align the suburb with the national campaign to combat "the Social Evil."[36]

Ader received a mixed reception from Summit's black residents. Church ladies and the Lincoln YMCA's Women's Auxiliary welcomed her with a community-wide reception. Others refused to admit the visiting nurse into their homes. Although Dengler did not state it publicly, Ader was expected to conduct a surveillance of the black bodies and homes that he and the white nurse had been unable to access.

Within three months the "Negress Health Nurse" proved her value. She visited two-thirds of Summit's black families, recorded and indexed the sanitary conditions in each home, advised fifteen mothers on the care of their babies, gave health advice to more than four hundred individuals, and spearheaded the opening of a clinic for tuberculosis testing. She also uncovered a number of delinquent venereal disease cases that were returned to health clinics.[37] In the end, Dengler may have gotten more than he bargained for: Ader converted him into becoming an advocate of sanitary housing. The availability of New Deal funds undoubtedly helped.

Ader joined the small cadre of black doctors and dentists drawn to Summit by the African American and Italian residents who constituted their clientele.[38] Despite their middle-class status, black medical professionals were not exempt from white surveillance and censure. Their private transactions quickly became public.

In 1933, twenty-nine-year-old dentist Dr. Norman Hill and his twenty-six-year-old wife, daughter of the local Baptist pastor, purchased a home on DeForest Avenue, a street of well-maintained single family homes one block north of Springfield Avenue, the suburb's main thoroughfare. To ensure a successful transaction, the young dentist retained a white agent to consummate the purchase. Shortly after settling into his new home, Hill's white neighbors, "who admitted that they did not wish to have him in their neighborhood," "induced" him to sell.[39]

The humiliation visited upon the Hills was mild compared to that suffered three years earlier by Hill's colleagues, dentist Errold Collymore and physician A. M. Williams, who purchased homes in an exclusive section of Westchester County, a New York City suburban area. Dr. Collymore frequently visited the Lincoln Y and Summit residents would have followed the events in White Plains. Alleging that the "Negroes' Invasion" would lower property values, someone burned a seven-foot cross on Collymore's lawn and a mob of five hundred white middle-class homeowners and the White Plains Realty Board picketed both doctors' homes. When the doctors refused to sell, the white YMCA executive board threatened to close the "colored" Y. The board relented and merely removed the black doctors from their positions as committee chairman and secretary and discharged the newly hired YMCA secretary. Belatedly, the White Plains Ministers Association of eleven white and two black men denounced the timing—during Holy Week—of the mob violence and the firing of the Y secretary.[40] They remained silent on the morality of segregated housing and the sanctity of the home.

In complete disregard for the suburban apotheosis of private domestic space, white middle-class northerners readily invaded black homes and black women's bodies. By casting the black family as an alien invader and the black female domestic as a contagion, white suburbanites justified mob violence, economic retaliation, and the use of government power to redefine public and private space and create imagined neighborhoods as white space.[41] Such attempts to demarcate space and reify whiteness resulted in vertiginous contradictions, as in 1937 when Health Officer Dengler, without a hint of irony, stated, "Due to racial prejudices that should not exist, because they are never intelligently explained, the Negro residents . . . often have conditions made undeservingly hard for them."[42]

A year later Dengler fomented a controversy that demonstrated how broadly he construed his powers. In October 1938 twenty-seven-year-old African American entrepreneur Spencer Logan, a suburban Plainfield resident and former Rutgers University student, prepared to open a soda fountain and luncheonette in the central business district. After expending between $500 and $1,000 to renovate and equip the building that had stood vacant for three years, Logan filed the requisite application and paid the $10 fee for a business permit, which the city clerk signed upon receiving the building inspection notice and a letter certifying Logan's clean legal record.[43]

Subsequently, Dengler altered the procedures to require city council approval and a letter attesting to Logan's "worthiness." Since Logan had not complied with the retroactively inserted requirements, Dengler ordered the clerk to return Logan's fee and application with the official signature crossed out. Though advised by his attorney to withdraw the application and cut his losses, Logan demanded a hearing before the city council. In a surprise move, the city council announced plans to widen Springfield Avenue at the exact location of the building Logan intended to lease.[44]

In one of the ironies of history, the building owned by the Irene M. Consa estate stood opposite the Summit Opera House on Springfield Avenue, a site that had generated a firestorm when Violet Johnson's church attempted to purchase the property in 1915.[45] In a reprise of old roles, business and residential interests along "the avenue" formed a coalition to defend white space, citing potential parking complications and competition for white-owned restaurants.[46] As a striking indication of changed race relations, twenty years earlier white residents had opposed black *ownership* of space demarcated white. By 1937 *renting* space was prohibited. Along with ice cream, jukeboxes, and black teenagers, Dengler saw the soda fountain as a black space that would attract African American residents seeking leisure in the center of town and within proximity of the elite white teenage ballroom and game hall, making them all too visible.

The Consa daughters had paid taxes on the non–income producing property for the past three years and were not willing to lose rental income to preserve a white boundary. A coalition of the Consa sisters, African American church women, and more than two hundred black residents packed city hall for the council meeting. Speaking on Logan's behalf, Violet Johnson's protégé, a Fountain Baptist Church member and Colored Women's Republican Club organizer, informed the city council that black residents had invited Logan to Summit, because "the colored people really have no place where they can go and be served ice cream."[47]

The city council ignored the wishes of the church women and the Consa sisters. And ostensibly to spare him pecuniary loss due to the street widening, the Republican city council "thought it unwise to grant Spencer Logan, a Negro, his application."[48]

In language made familiar by the New Deal, Logan "appeal[ed] for fair play and the right to determine [his] own economic destiny." As a businessman seeking a square deal, not welfare, he accused the city council of denying his "civil rights as guaranteed by the Fourteenth Amendment" and requested a second hearing "on the basis of exemplification of American ideals of Democracy, the rules of sportsmanship and . . . [the] opportunity . . . for the employment of young Negroes."[49] Charging the council with "discrimination, the color of the man," Logan's lawyer added, "If he doesn't get his rights here, he is going to get them elsewhere."[50] Faced with threats of civil rights violations by Logan and the Consa daughters, the city council capitulated and allowed Logan to open his business after a three-month delay.[51] Logan received no compensation for legal fees or lost revenue.

For Logan and the church women who had invited him to Summit, this was a civil rights victory not for one black man but for the race. Logan had successfully championed individual masculine rights with the aid of church women who regarded civil rights as granted by God, protected by the Constitution, and transcending race and gender.[52] Summit's African Americans could now get an ice cream soda and listen to New Jersey native Count Basie's "One O'Clock Jump" in the center of the suburb.

The Politics of Public Housing

For New Jersey's working class, the availability of suitable housing was a perennial problem. In the nineteenth century white upper- and middle-class women established settlement houses and encouraged the passage of state and municipal tenement laws to aid European immigrants.[53] In 1901, members of Summit's Presbyterian Church organized the Neighborhood House in North Summit as "a center for worship, work, fellowship and fun" for the more than one hundred Assyrian and Armenian families of silk workers who lived in the tenements mockingly dubbed "Weavers' Arms."[54]

Housing for African American workers did not receive public attention until the harsh winter of 1916–1917 revealed the limits of industrial capitalism and municipal charity. Migrating laborers and their families taxed New Jersey's nineteenth-century housing stock and perforce lived in outdoor tents, railroad boxcars, stables, or any other structure offering shelter. Emmet Scott, Special Assistant to the Secretary of War, complained, "Industries in New Jersey have utterly failed to provide housing which would enable their negro [sic] help to live decently and in enough comfort so that . . . they would be stimulated to become useful and efficient."[55]

In the absence of business or government action, black church women intervened. "The mature negro [sic] residents of the city and suburban towns have been kind and generous in helping the southern stranger," Scott noted. "They have collected money to send numbers back home, and when the bitter cold weather began they collected and distributed thousands of garments."[56] Black women opened their homes and worked with the Newark Negro Welfare League, an interracial social services group focused on housing. In early 1917 many attended a national conference on "Negro Migration" sponsored by the National Urban League and the Russell Sage Foundation to address the causes and consequences of migration and adjustment in a new environment.[57]

Relying only on their resources and a few white women's clubs, the State Federation of Colored Women's Clubs established community houses, supported industrial clubs, and formed social and political organizations to ameliorate the economic and social plight of black workers.[58] Though noble, these efforts did not alter the politics of housing or the racial practices of developers, realtors, and landlords. The housing boom of the 1920s bypassed black workers, and the Great Depression and New Deal added economic injury to racial insult.

In 1932, armed with Ira Reid's list of housing offenders, a Summit committee of white local and state officials conducted their own legally required but rarely performed inspection. After two weeks, the committee reported a "[f]ailure to find any instance of laxity on the part of the local Board of Health." The state health inspector suggested that "conditions may have changed" since Reid's initial survey. Less generously, the state tenement inspector charged Reid with deliberate distortion, adding, "If those are considered bad, the critics should see some in other cities." The local relief administrator claimed to have proof of an influx of "colored persons" who, having "learned one must live here at least two years before eligibility for relief," lied about their status.[59]

Dismayed by the committee's report, Summit's black women began a sanitary housing campaign. In what would become a multiyear undertaking, they built on their relationship with the TIA and formed relations with white religious groups. When the white Presbyterian Young People's League conducted a month-long forum on "The Negro in America" in 1936, Florence Randolph used the occasion to contrast the "closed opportunities" in suburban Summit with more progressive racial practices in Jersey City, an urban Democratic stronghold. The Lincoln YMCA secretary drew attention to the "economic deadline" that limited aspirations and restricted employment opportunities for Summit's black citizens. African American physicians presented graphic evidence of "railroad flats" that violated city health ordinances and contributed to high morbidity and mortality rates.[60]

The church women's long campaign generated a shift among some residents. When the black doctors returned to the Presbyterian Church the following year, the white State Board of Tenement Houses supervisor and a chastened state inspector accompanied them and spoke movingly of the need for improved housing.[61] In his annual health report, Commissioner Dengler exhorted, "Let the good people of Summit take their eyes off China, India, Africa and other distant lands for a little while, if necessary, and concentrate them on Negro housing and slum clearance matters in Summit. Let us not forget to give our own neighbors a good chance to live."[62]

White religious leaders broke their silence. The Episcopalian rector and chairman of the interdenominational Community Service Commission deplored the "virtually slum conditions [that] prevail in Summit."[63] In language intended to touch middle-class taxpayers in their pockets and move them to action, the president of the Presbyterian men's Bible class opined, "The slums don't pay much in taxes, but taxpayers have to pay a lot for the slums."[64] Following the appearance of FCC Commissioner George Haynes, who called for "constructive, creative thinking to prevent clashes" between nations, classes, and races, the YMCA board chairman acknowledged that "problems in Summit in the field of housing and race relations . . . urgently cry out for a Christian solution."[65]

White realty interests remained impervious to the call to Christian conscience. With rare enforcement of housing or health codes and virtually no penalties for violations, landlords had little incentive to improve housing for low-income workers. Moreover, the women's campaign overlapped with a real estate boom in middle-class suburban housing. Spurred by the availability of federally subsidized loans for single family homes, housing became a flashpoint between an expanding white middle class and a besieged African American community.

The 1937 Wagner-Steagall Act turned housing for low-income workers into a national issue and brought the power of the state into the debate.[66] The availability of federal subsidies for rental housing changed the contours of the public discourse in Summit, not only on housing but on African American claims to civic space. Historian Suzanne Mettler argues that New Deal policies transformed American governance by institutionalizing a two-tiered system of federalism versus localism.

Though Mettler focuses on gendered citizenship in social and labor policies, her conclusion applies as well to New Deal policies that subsidized owner-occupied and rental housing, thereby altering the real estate industry and accelerating the racialization of housing patterns.[67]

New Dealers may have conceived of their programs as racially neutral, but local governments often administered them in discriminatory ways. In the hands of local administrators who had little reason to change the status quo, federal funds intended to build low income housing and improve neighborhoods fueled efforts to banish African Americans. Colored by New Deal language of "slum clearance and removal," housing became a marker of race and class and a valorization of citizenship.

Glenwood Place and the Politics of Race and Space

Early in 1938 Glenwood Place emerged as ground zero in the eruption of the color line when the newly organized Franklin Place Neighborhood Association proposed widening the street to create a buffer between the commercial and residential districts. Located in the center of the suburb and abutting the central business district on the north and an expanding middle-class residential section on the south, the valorization of this strip of real estate changed with the growth of the suburb. Dotted with tenement houses erected in the 1890s, at the turn of the century Glenwood Place was home to European immigrants. By the 1920s and 1930s, fifty black and white working-class families lived in the twelve tenements. Violet Johnson located "The Home Away from Home," an alternative YWCA for single working and professional women, near the curvilinear section where Glenwood Place intersected upper-class Hobart Avenue and middle-class Franklin Place.[68]

Citing numerous health code violations on Glenwood Place and calling the situation unstable, white homeowners declared, "[U]nless the congested area is restricted and reduced, it will inevitably spread to include property which is now preserved and well cared for." Demanding "prompt action," they insisted the city council appoint a housing authority, apply for federal funds, and eliminate the "conditions." With federal subsidies available under the Wagner-Steagall Act, city officials could acquire and demolish the Glenwood Place tenements "with a minimum of hardship to the present tenants" and construct low income housing, presumably some distance from Franklin Place.[69]

As the contest over space intensified, the Republican mayor appointed the Civic Progress Committee, "an informed non-political, non-partisan organization of citizens dedicated to the service of public interest," to formulate a solution for "keeping Summit a very desirable place in which to live."[70] In one of its first public acts, the ostensibly disinterested committee of white men pronounced Glenwood Place a "'Black eye' for Summit."[71] Public officials aligned themselves ideologically with the Franklin Place Neighborhood Association. One reduced the controversy to a simple economic calculation. It cost the city $200 a year to educate a child from Glenwood Place and more than $900 a year for medical care and hospitalization for one man on Glenwood Place; therefore, the suburb should "raise taxes and rid the city of slums."[72] His calculus left no doubt that raising taxes and ridding the city of slums would force black residents out of town.

Soon two newly organized white homeowners' groups, the Second Ward Citizens' Association and the South Summit Civic Association, entered the skirmish. In his study of the politics of home and race, Thomas Sugrue identifies homeowners' associations as the locus of white resistance as well as race and class construction in post–World War II urban America. The Summit experience reveals their roots in 1930s New Deal policies. Association titles denoted their ideologies, with *civic associations* "upholding values of self-government and participatory democracy" and *protective associations* standing as paternalistic defenders of the investment in "neighborhood, home, family, women, and children." These conservative coalitions, Sugrue argues, employed the language of "rights," though they operated out of fear of racial intermingling.[73] In Summit and other New York City suburbs, civic associations represented themselves as protective associations. For example, the White Plains Highland Civic Association, the group that repelled the penetration by two black physicians in White Plains, New York, claimed, "[T]he agitation over the right of the two Negroes to settle wherever they wished should not obscure the right of some 500 white householders who had settled there first and invested the savings of a lifetime."[74]

Although Glenwood Place was home to nearly an equal number of black and white working families, African Americans clearly apprehended the racial animus underlying calls for slum clearance and removal, despite allegations of overcrowding and unsanitary housing. On the eve of World War I, white Summit had been willing to rent space in the center of town to black residents, though denying them the right to purchase. Now, in the late thirties, white middle-class homeowners viewed black residents as inimical to their neighborhood and economic security. Having imagined a *voluntary* segregation in civic institutions, white suburbanites prepared to reify a *spatial* segregation with the aid of the federal government.

If the business and residential interests coalescing to remove working-class residents from Glenwood Place expected their proposal to proceed without resistance, they misjudged their black neighbors. Experienced in the art of resistance and political mobilization, black women organized the Glenwood Place Neighborhood Association, which in contrast to white homeowners, they used to make their claim for American rights as "independent and rooted rather than dependent and transient" citizens.[75]

With a flair for the classics, the local editor captured the moral dimension of the Glenwood Place controversy with the subhead "Carthage Must Be Destroyed."[76] The allusion to the Punic Wars and the destruction of the African city of Carthage by imperious Romans vividly depicted the battle being waged by a white middle class desperate to hold on to its economic and psychic status and willing to use federal funds to realize a version of "racial cleansing."[77] The association's land sterilization involved razing homes and constructing a parking lot.

If Glenwood Place symbolized Carthage, Violet Johnson personified Hannibal. Johnson had led the fight for space for her gender and race for more than forty years. Now in her late sixties and virtually immobilized by chronic ailments, she served as advisor to the Glenwood Place Neighborhood Association and its companion Coordinating Council comprised of "Negro citizens" throughout the city "organized with the objective for home improvement in all its phases. . . . [and] to thrash out the much talked of 'Glenwood place situation' and other problems affecting Negro life in Summit."[78] The women and men leading the organizations reflected the interwar cross-class makeup of the black suburban community. A Baptist deacon chaired the Coordinating Council; Florence Randolph chaired the housing committee; Violet Johnson,

Nurse Ader, a black physician, and the Lincoln YMCA secretary completed the leadership team.[79]

In an open letter that bore Johnson's hallmark political acumen gained from years of Christian activism, the Glenwood Place Neighborhood Association promised "to present [the] matter clearly and impersonally and to make such explanations as [are] necessary for a complete understanding of the subject." Johnson decried the "grievous hardship to the self-respecting residents of Glenwood [P]lace to read almost weekly the exaggerated reports of unfavorable conditions said to exist in that block" and refuted the "pure propaganda" spread by rent-gouging landlords and self-serving neighbors. The "hard working people in the low income brackets" presented their own truth: tenants forced to "pay high rents for houses with bad plumbing and otherwise greatly in need of repairs to insure sanitation." Johnson juxtaposed greedy landlords with the "reasonable and feasible" request to work with the board of health and transform an adjacent rubbish-filled open space into a demonstration garden "to show what can be done in blighted areas."[80]

Johnson also addressed the racial hysteria that conflated class and color, health and housing by questioning the board of health's claim to have identified four "new colored residents . . . afflicted with venereal diseases." "Is the migration to Summit solely colored? If not, are they all free from venereal diseases?"[81] On the eve of World War II, black citizens were under surveillance and under siege.

The Glenwood Place Neighborhood Association succeeded in quelling demands for the immediate destruction of "Carthage." When the Civic Progress Committee reported six months later on "better housing for families in low income groups," it declared that Summit had no "slums" and no residents would be removed. Rather, the committee explained, substandard housing existed throughout the affluent suburb and affected white and black low income residents. Thus it recommended immediate passage of enabling legislation to form the Summit Housing Authority pursuant to constructing public housing.[82]

Having achieved a minor victory, the Glenwood Neighborhood Association and Coordinating Council turned quotidian activities into grassroots political action and representations of "civic pride." For example, the Glenwood Betterment Club would "teach the children community pride and . . . civic conscious[ness]." The "I'll Help" Garden Club would do "its part in beautifying the City of Summit and uplifting humanity."[83] When the statewide garden club held its annual show at the Lincoln YMCA, representatives from neighboring suburbs joined and offered evidence of their ability to turn blighted areas into "beautiful premises" with vegetable and flower seeds. Local club president Nurse Ader and a health commissioner presented cash awards donated by the board of health.[84] Under assault, black residents responded with cross-class and intergenerational unity.

Throughout the summer and fall of 1938, the city council and the five-member Summit Housing Authority (SHA) held open hearings to present the public housing proposal to middle-class white suburbanites. Using a seventeen-point question and answer format adapted from the Montclair Housing Authority, the council chairman explained the SHA's recommendation and the Wagner-Steagall Act of 1937 that enabled the United States Housing Authority (USHA) to lend local governments up to 90 percent of the cost of slum clearance and new low income rental construction. The SHA would have sole discretion in selecting occupants based on Summit residency and means testing. Because USHA guidelines required the elimination of one substandard unit for each new unit, no dwelling would be torn down until new units could be constructed. Thus, the housing project would not increase the number of low income families in the suburb.[85]

Questions eight and nine generated the greatest interest among Summit residents. Question eight asked, "Will any Housing Project be exclusively for colored or white families?" "No," the SHA chairman responded. "The local Housing Authority will not give consideration to any Housing Project to the exclusion of either colored or white occupants." Question nine addressed the economic impact on the private housing market. The chairman assured white middle-class homeowners that the value of their property would remain inviolate. Because the FHA rated newer homogeneous, owner-occupied neighborhoods higher, removal of substandard housing would yield "an appreciable rise in real estate values."[86]

Consistent with other New Deal programs, Wagner-Steagall centralized policy development and federalized implementation. Local housing authorities had sole authority for key housing decisions, including site location, architectural standards, per unit cost, and tenant selection. As such, local communities could use taxpayer dollars to initiate or rein-force racially segregated housing.[87] Summit's public housing would be open to both black and white residents. However, in an inversion of the practice that the national real estate industry would oppose in urban areas after World War II, officials would "decentralize the present low income population from the center of the city," locate public housing on the "outskirts" of the suburb, and maintain the suburban center as white space, thereby ensuring segregated neighborhoods for white middle-class homeowners.[88]

Over the next twelve months, the all-white, all-male SHA finalized the public housing proposal. Summit would construct two federally funded projects in North and East Summit, for fifty families each, at a cost of $478,000 dollars. The SHA based the number and location of units on its survey that identified 462 unfit housing units—214 in the center of town, 138 in East Summit, and 110 in North Summit, 200 fewer units than the Civic Progress Committee had identified two years earlier. According to the SHA, locating public housing on the suburb's periphery offered two benefits: reducing the density of low income housing and minimizing the impact on the public schools. What the SHA did not state was that the new housing would decimate Glenwood Place, remove low income residents from the center of town, and, absent a one-for-one replacement, decrease the number of low income families in the suburb. By September 1939 the SHA had secured federal funding.[89] Only city council approval remained.

The task of selling the public housing proposal fell to SHA Chairman William Darling, president of the First National Bank and Trust Company, the State Title & Mortgage Guaranty Company, and the Summit Real Estate Board. Despite glaring conflicts of interest, Darling had the requisite standing to make the case to key stakeholders. Still, he faced an uphill battle. White homeowners' associations immediately voiced their opposition. Vowing to prevent the suburb "from hanging such an economic and sociological millstone about its neck," the Second Ward Citizens' Association positioned itself on the side of fiscal responsibility and raised the specter of the long-term financial burden to taxpayers from hidden costs and litigation by builders.[90] In a terse statement, the Summit Civic Research Group, formerly the South Summit Civic Association, demanded that the city council "secure the voluntary demolition or abandonment of enough units in order that, together with the uncrowding [*sic*] no additional low cost housing shall be available to people from outside this city."[91] Though most white homeowners understood that public housing was not a poorhouse, many welcomed the use of federal funds to erase African Americans from the suburb's civic and political space. "Elimination" was the only solution.

SHA chairman Darling also failed to convince his fellow realtors who rejected any program that would jeopardize federal financing of private homes and subdivisions. Anxious about an industry still in recovery, realtors voiced pocketbook interests that, they believed, coincided with the social and economic interests of prospective homebuyers who expected their neighbors to be middle class *and* white. The real estate board predicted substantially higher property taxes caused by a decrease in private housing production and an increase in public housing maintenance. The realtors passed a resolution "definitely opposing this project in Summit." With partisan politics ever present, both realtors and homeowners envisaged public housing residents under the sway of a Democratic machine led by a mythical public housing commissioner.[92]

A few white residents questioned the proposal's underlying assumptions. As one SHA member noted, "If the wage scale of domestics and laborers was raised above the mere pittance category, these people themselves would quickly improve their own circumstances. It is impossible . . . to live decently on six or seven dollars a week."[93]

Henry Twombly, a New York lawyer and Presbyterian organizer of the North Summit Neighborhood House, believed that low-cost detached houses built with private capital and supported with enforceable health ordinances would eliminate the slum problem and transform low income workers into responsible homeowners and citizens. A private market solution would retain "the desirable citizens," convert "some of the undesirables" into "good citizens through better surroundings and better housing conditions," and eliminate the irredeemable.[94] Yet, even for Twombly, a long-time friend of Summit's black Republicans, the real "problem [was] what to do with the people now living in Glenwood [P]lace." Furthermore, he insisted, "Many of the residents of Glenwood [P]lace come from employment in Chatham and Short Hills, and these could be eliminated."[95] In other words, the adjoining suburbs should find their own solution to the race problem.

Only the Council of Social Agencies, an umbrella organization formed in the early years of the Great Depression, denounced the racialization of the housing issue. "It is unwise and undesirable to confuse the problem of low cost housing and adequate sanitary regulations with the race issue," the agency cautioned. "Further, it is a mistake to assume that the housing authority project is intended to correct only conditions affecting Negro tenants."[96]

Though the mayor did not appoint any African Americans to the housing authority or any of the committees studying the housing problem, the Coordinating Council designated its own five-person housing committee.[97] There is no evidence that the Republican mayor or SHA acknowledged the black men and women or sought their input.

Contrary to the public outcry, Glenwood Place was neither the most egregious example of substandard housing in Summit nor the "slum" portrayed by the Franklin Place Neighborhood Association. That honor belonged to Weaver Court, the overcrowded and dilapidated tenement in North Summit built next to the silk mill in the 1880s to house immigrant laborers and their families. By 1939 twenty-eight black and white families lived in "the cheapest possible housing in Summit." Coal or kerosene stoves in dingy kitchens provided the only heat in the two- and three-room tenements that lacked bathtubs or indoor plumbing. Toilets were on the stoops and most often in poor working condition. A structurally weak outside stairway provided the only means of ingress and egress. Weaver Court, unsurprisingly, was the best real estate investment in town, annually generating the highest returns for the white absentee landlord.[98] Long the target of the Town Improvement Association, Weaver Court, unlike Glenwood Place, was not in the center of the suburb, abutting the homes of an expanding white middle class.

When it came to housing, black residents had few allies. White Protestant churches had not recovered their moral voice following the fundamentalist debate of the 1920s. The Great Depression drove them further from their Social Gospel heritage. Churches curtailed programs and drastically reduced budgets, by some estimates by as much as 50 percent.[99] The Church Women's Committee and Interracial Conference Movement had the potential to be a moral force but suffered from limited funds and an equally limited vision. Northern white Protestants seemed unable or unwilling to transcend the boundaries of race and class.

When Summit residents gathered in City Hall at eight o'clock on the evening of 25 October 1939 for the final hearing on the housing proposal, uncertainty hung in the air. After seven years of discussion sparked by Ira Reid's presentation, three years of exhaustive state and local studies, and a year of heated public debate, the city council announced its "unwillingness to hurry a decision." It tabled the proposal and committed to "making an exhaustive study of the whole situation, realizing that any policy adopted . . . will have far reaching results on the character of the community."[100]

Five days later in a specially convened evening session that lasted less than ten minutes, the city council, acting as a committee of the whole, a parliamentary procedure that limited discussion and motions and required a unanimous decision for approval, rejected the public housing proposal. The Second Ward councilman cast the negative vote, to the great applause of his constituents.[101] Three days later all members of the Summit Housing Authority resigned.[102]

It is difficult to know precisely what single argument or constellation of arguments in the politics of housing, race, and class scuttled the proposal. What is clear, however, is that Summit's white middle-class homeowners weighed resentment of their black neighbors against their desire for white space and jettisoned any civic or moral responsibility for decent housing for black citizens.[103] It was elimination or nothing.

Stripped of its morality, suburban housing became an instrument of erasure of both the black middle class and white and black working class who were discursively, if not physically, removed from the suburban landscape. White homeowners and realty boards mounted similar campaigns after World War II when municipalities used federal urban renewal funds to achieve racial cleansing.[104]

For Summit's black residents, the city council's decision must have been bittersweet. The possibility of modern, affordable housing had raised expectations. As historian Linda Gordon notes, "The very existence of these federal programs awakened civil rights consciousness and prompted demands for equal treatment."[105] With the collapse of the housing authority, low income workers and renters had little reason to believe that landlords would voluntarily improve the dilapidated housing that yielded high returns for minimal investment. Or that the city or state government would intervene to desegregate the private housing market or enforce building and health codes.[106]

Though black residents had averted the imminent threat of removal, they recognized that their white neighbors desired their elimination. By 1939, on the eve of World War II, black claims for a square deal and equal rights seemed more imperiled than ever in the suburb that was co-eval with their presence and which they had helped to build. The battle of the color line had changed. The question no longer centered on ownership of property; rather it centered on their very presence in spaces constructed as *white*. Without physical violence or visible signage, Jim Crow had moved North to humiliate and intimidate. Nonetheless, as Violet Johnson's resistance from her sick bed demonstrated, the fight for civic righteousness would continue.

* * *

But Violet Johnson would not lead it. Arriving as a twenty-seven-year-old domestic in a village re-creating itself as the ideal suburb, Johnson had spent her adult life leading the fight for civic and social justice for her gender and race. On Tuesday night, 21 November 1939 Johnson died at "The Home Away from Home." Four days later, on Saturday afternoon, Reverend Florence Randolph officiated at the funeral service held at the church that Johnson had founded and at the interment in an unmarked gravesite in her former employer's family plot.

Marian Anderson, the renowned African American contralto, appeared in Summit on the first day of December before the largest audience ever gathered there. Although most of the audience would not have realized it, the concert provided a benediction to Violet Johnson and her allies who promoted civic righteousness, just laws, and moral institutions. Seven months earlier on Easter Sunday, Anderson had performed on the steps of the Lincoln Memorial after the Daughters of the American Revolution denied her the right to sing in Constitution Hall. Now five days after Johnson's burial, the overwhelmingly white Summit audience listened to Anderson's call "to let freedom ring."[107] Despite decades of disappointments, Violet Johnson had died keeping the faith that someday Summit, New Jersey, would become an ideal suburb for all its residents.

Conclusion

"You Just as Well Die with the Ague as with the Fever"

In November 1941 Reverend Florence Randolph, along with Bishop P. A. Wallace and his wife, boarded a train in Newark en route to the African Methodist Episcopal (AME) Zion conference in Virginia. The trio purchased first class interstate tickets so that, as the ticket agent assured them, they would not have to change seats upon crossing the Mason-Dixon Line. However, when the train reached Virginia the conductor ordered them to a segregated Jim Crow car. Asserting her rights as an interstate traveler, Randolph refused; whereupon the conductor summoned "four police for two elderly women and one man." Randolph again refused "and hence was subject to arrest."[1]

Since Bishop Wallace was to open the conference the following morning and Randolph was to preach in the afternoon for the Women's Home and Foreign Missionary Society, she reluctantly "yielded; but was never more anxious to spend a night, and perhaps longer, in a jail." Reflecting on the moment, Randolph lamented, "I felt and still feel I have lost a great opportunity to speak for my grand-children and thousands of Negro youth now in our colleges and trade schools preparing for good citizenship."[2]

As she made her way to the segregated car, "heart beating faster than ever, and Mrs. Wallace suffering from shock," Randolph "began to think of God and the Bible and this thing called 'religion.'" Traveling to New York City no one would summon four police officers to remove her from the train. Yet other anti-democratic and immoral practices limited her exercise of the rights and privileges of "American democracy." "[I]f I retired from my church and desired to spend the rest of my days in Summit, I would not be able to purchase or rent a home to live beyond Glenwood [P]lace or Railroad [A]venue. Then I thought of the white minister and his wife who often worship at my church. . . . [who] discovered to his surprise that there was no restaurant or tea room in Summit where I could eat with them or without them." In an open letter Randolph recounted, "The more I thought of existing conditions in my own northern Christian town—housing, employment, education—the calmer I got about Virginia State laws. And I found all bitterness leaving my heart."[3]

The elderly minister opened her "new red letter testament" and "read what Jesus said" about loving those who hate you and the one who claims to love God but hates his brother. Assaying the systemic and structural evils in the suburb and the nation she mused, "[W]hen I think of some of the merchants with whom I have, and am still spending money, and the things they have said about the housing situation, I agree with the old southerner who says, 'You just as well die with the ague as with the fever.'" Jim Crow in the North was a distinction without a difference, a national symbol of American hypocrisy and the growing chasm between the promise and the reality of American democracy. Randolph signed her letter penned a week before the bombing of Pearl Harbor "Yours for American Democracy."[4]

As the winds of war blew over the ideal suburb, the color line wavered ever so slightly. The increased demand for industrial workers for New Jersey's chemical, weapons, and manufacturing industries transformed issues of race, class, and gender into matters of national defense. For white middle-class women who considered domestic service a "necessary part of the Total Defense of the United States," war mobilization shrank the pool of domestic workers and raised wages, which they blamed on inconsiderate domestic workers who had moved from the kitchen to the industrial "apron shift."[5]

For Florence Randolph and Summit's working women the approaching conflict portended change. Throughout the fall of 1940 and the spring of 1941, four black and fourteen white women on the Summit YWCA Interracial Committee that Randolph helped organize led public discussions, often over tea, on activities affecting "Negro groups in Summit, New Jersey, and the country" and the "Negro's part in the national defense."[6] The Lincoln YMCA's Young People's Forum explored ways that "the youth of today can help to establish liberty, justice and equality for all."[7] When NAACP Executive Secretary Walter White spoke before Summit's reorganized interracial NAACP his subject was "Democracy and the American Negro."[8]

The fight against fascism abroad had finally brought Summit's white people face to face with their own discrimination. Some took the moment to affirm their intentions to achieve equality of opportunity in Summit; others simply were not ready to face the immediate implications of removing the race and class barriers they had so carefully erected. But none could continue to pretend that Jim Crow was confined to the South.

One white civic leader denounced the "Jim Crow" elementary school. The city council introduced an ordinance requiring repairs or demolition of buildings "unfit for human habitation."[9] The chairman of the Summit Interracial Committee appealed for the admission of African American women to the local hospital's Nurses Training School. The United Youth Council protested the Red Cross's practice of segregating blood.[10] The local library hosted an exhibition entitled "'Color,' Unfinished Business of Democracy."[11] The rhetorical shift raised the hopes of black women who had protested against these conditions for decades.

Still, American democracy remained color-coded. The housing ordinance lacked enforcement power or specificity as to what constituted "unfit for human habitation." The Summit Interracial Committee admitted "great difficulty in enforcing the law . . . when it involves a Negro tenant against a white landlord."[12] The YWCA's Interracial Committee acknowledged the impotency of state civil rights laws after its members, one of whom was black, were refused service in an Atlantic City restaurant while attending a conference.[13] The Red Cross refused to accept blood from black women.[14] Segregation in schools continued, and local congregations listened to the annual brotherhood sermon on Race Relations Sunday.

Randolph condemned the "Race Prejudice, Hate, Oppression and Injustice" in international, national, and local affairs in a 1943 essay written for Race Relations Sunday at the request of the Summit Interracial Ministerial Association. "In these strenuous war-torn days, when the entire Christian world is struggling to get its bearings as to the Church and its definite place in world adjustment," she began, "if I were white I would speak in no uncertain language to my own people what I believe to be right, or in other words the truth as I see it respecting the American Negro." Adopting the stance of whites who advised 'the Negro' on 'fitness' for citizenship, she continued, "I would prove my race superiority by my attitude towards minority races; towards oppressed people [and] remember that of one blood God made all nations of men to dwell upon the face of the earth." The minister enumerated Summit's transgressions. "I would speak of the unjust housing problem affecting Negroes, the school problem, the movies, the hospital and certainly the Negro physician, the lack of Negro books in the library, the ignorance of Negro history . . . in our schools." With the voice of a prophet she added, "Whether my argument availed or not I would be conscience free before Him."[15]

Randolph's essay unleashed a firestorm in the suburb and the state. No one disputed her bill of indictment; rather, the controversy centered on whether "race" was a "religious" or "social" question. Though the local editor confessed his reluctance to print the essay in the religion column, white and black readers unequivocally deemed race a religious issue; one that informed the public discourse and affected the country's standing as a world leader.[16]

Yet the promise of an expanded democracy had seemingly crashed on the shoal of white supremacy and a conservative ideology. A few days before African American poet Langston Hughes was to appear at a Summit High School assembly in November 1944, school officials summarily cancelled the program. Stating that "neither race nor color had anything to do with the cancellation," city officials cited Hughes's "tie . . . with a group of people to whom . . . un-American utterances" had been attributed, though the Common Council for American Unity, a liberal organization that promoted national unity and opposed racial, religious, and ideological division, had sponsored Hughes's "goodwill" tour to promote racial understanding.[17] Seven months later Fountain Baptist Church, the church Violet Johnson had founded, hosted Hughes before an audience of five hundred black and white citizens.[18]

In March 1945, four months after the Hughes cancellation, the YMCA invited high school senior girls to join a swimming class. When five African American seniors appeared "in good faith," the YMCA denied them access. "And there in the presence of our white classmates," the girls reported, "we were both humiliated and embarrassed by being told that Negroes were not permitted to use the pool." "Taking advantage of [their] right to freedom of speech" and countering YMCA intransigence and YWCA silence, the girls penned a letter "concerning an example of unfair treatment of a minority group" to the press, "an instrument of democracy and fair play."[19] The protest by the five black girls embarrassed the affluent suburb, especially after a New York tabloid picked up the story.[20]

Violet Johnson would have been proud of her spiritual progeny, the young women she had mentored and the church she had founded. Though the language had changed, black working women's Christian activism still mattered. So did the "vision of the potential strength and influence of a union of Christian women and faith in their willingness to assume responsibility."[21] As Florence Randolph retired from active ministry in 1945, the seventy-nine-year-old minister could take heart that a younger generation of women would speak for American democracy.

* * *

As this book has shown, religion made a difference in black working women's organizational order. In responding to the call to "Work and Serve the Hour," cooks, laundresses, housekeepers, and seamstresses demonstrated profound moral agency from the margins. Over a half century their goals evolved, though their basic strategy, community organizing, remained constant. Whether in missionary societies, the WCTU, the secular Federation of Colored Women's Clubs, or the Republican Party, they transgressed boundaries and crossed lines to advocate for their gender and their race. A commitment to civic righteousness, just laws, and moral institutions, shaped their negotiations for space.

Black women's organizing in the North differed from that of black women in the South. Northern black working women had to organize in liminal space on the edges of white middle-class society, particularly at the end of the nineteenth century. They were few in number, with limited resources. They had to form religious and social networks with African Americans over great distances, and their issues of singularity were different from those of black women in southern communities with established institutions. Moreover, in the emerging suburbs any civic endeavor meant that domestic servants would be directly under the gaze of prominent whites and would require their concurrence to move forward. For example, finding space for a sacred meeting place in Summit proved difficult and depended upon the goodwill of local whites. Even those organizations that seemed autonomous in the North, such as "The Home Away from Home" and the National Training School for

Girls, depended on white society in ways that southern women's organizations did not.

While it was important for northern black women to maintain contacts with influential white people and to use public space in ways that met with the white community's approval, these contacts attenuated over time. As the visibility of African Americans in the North increased, white tolerance for their presence decreased and white suburbanites pursued exclusionary goals rather than cooperation.

In contrast, with larger communities, access to land owned by African Americans, and college-educated enclaves southern black women's organizing followed different trajectories and a different chronology. In the 1880s and 1890s, southern black women were active in church and community work, yet as Anne Firor Scott famously remarked, they were "most invisible of all." Glenda Gilmore argues that because of virulent racism and white fear of African Americans getting out of their "place," black women deliberately wove a cloak of invisibility to organize institutions outside the white community. The exception to that invisibility in the South was the brief collaboration in the WCTU in the 1890s, which succumbed to the politics of disenfranchisement.[22] Thus, northern black women allied with whites more often than did southern women from the 1880s through the 1900s. They created semi-autonomous organizations and achieved civic recognition from 1900 to 1920 at a time when southern black women were invisible to whites. Paradoxically, northern black women lost white women allies after 1920, just as southern black women began to build some interracial ties with white women's organizations.

Moreover, the politics of respectability had different meanings in the North and South. For the most part, especially before 1915, the women discussed in this book were domestic workers in upper middle-class white households. While Victorian culture pervaded their lives, as working women their respectability was never a given and depended on the vetting of their churches and male pastors. Thus, respectability as both a religious practice and a sociological issue required continual vigilance. In the South, where black women were also domestic workers but lived at a distance from white households, respectability was a political issue exacerbated by the rape scares of 1890s politics. From 1900 to 1920, black southern women rebuilt a politics of respectability through racial uplift that gave them little room politically, but afforded their only opening for civic organization.

Further, woman suffrage in 1920 represented a fundamentally different situation in the North than in the South. In the North, black women registered, voted, and became active in party politics, albeit in secondary roles. In the South, attempts by black women to register and vote represented a crisis in the "solution" of disenfranchisement and threatened to bring their husbands, brothers, and sons back to the polls as well. Southern black women, even the few who successfully registered, could not form local, statewide, or regional political organizations or win influence in party politics, although a few did become active in national party politics.

Mary Burrell, a native Virginian, exemplifies the regional differences in black women's organizing. Burrell migrated to New Jersey in 1913 with a wealth of experience in "woman's work" and religious and civic organizing that would have been difficult to acquire in pre–World War I New Jersey. With passage of the Nineteenth Amendment, the breadth of her political activities was arguably greater than would have been possible in her native Richmond. A home care nurse by vocation, she chaired the Federation of Colored Women's Clubs Legislative Department and served as a county and state Republican Party leader and a state representative of the National League of Republican Colored Women. Because of her effectiveness as a lobbyist, the state legislature granted Burrell floor privileges for a year. Though welcomed by white and black male candidates on the hustings and courted by white women to endorse their maternalist agenda, Burrell, Johnson, and Randolph could not depend on white women's support for anti-lynching and civil rights legislation. When white men pushed white women to the fringes of party politics, the distance between New Jersey's white and black Republican women increased. Black women relied on their autonomous organizations to defend their communities.

Further, this book has argued that the course of segregation differed in the North compared to the South. The trajectory of this narrative moves from racial proscription to the *northernization* of Jim Crow segregation. The 1896 *Plessy v. Ferguson* U. S. Supreme Court ruling stands as a signal event in the declension in race relations in the South with a devastating echo in the North. Race relations in the North were in continual flux and often contradictory, particularly in the northern suburbs. Following the end of Reconstruction and the evisceration of the Reconstruction Amendments in the 1880s, African American Protestants were dismayed by the prevalence of racial proscription in American society and churches. Northern black ministers and church women partnered with their white allies to denounce strongly racial violence in the South. Yet because most of the segregation in the North was customary and flexible to a greater degree than in the South, northern African Americans had even more reason to assume these racial proscriptions would wither away.

Thus, northern black Baptists initially denounced *Plessy v. Ferguson* as a "mischievous law." However, as *Plessy* became established law, African American men and women were alarmed by the attempts of "enemies" of the race to "Southernize the North" and by the acquiescence of the federal government in the "nationalism of Jim Crow." The drift of northern capital South, the sanction of Jim Crow cars in interstate travel, the success of the disenfranchisement campaign in the South, and the "strange and studied silence" of northern white Protestant ministers marked a change in the moral landscape. By the 1900s African Americans inveighed against mob violence, American imperialism, and the ideology of white supremacy that fueled both. They appealed to the common sense and moral conscience of white northerners. Yet the effects of southern propaganda, the obsession with black women's sexuality, and the specter of miscegenation in a hierarchical society preoccupied with the discourse of civilization added a sense of urgency to black church expansion and working women's respectability. Thus, Violet Johnson's decision to organize a Baptist church in suburban Summit was as much a religious as a political one.

Twentieth-century suburban segregation was no accident. In the North, from the 1910s to the 1930s black women had to negotiate a place between a growing black population and an anxious and growing white suburban population. By the onset of World War I, northern African Americans no longer saw themselves as fighting a "southern problem." The Great War and the Great Depression compounded the problems of race and class. Anxieties over the future of the white races in the aftermath of World War I, the suburban land grab, and the marketing of the single-family home accelerated the deterioration in race relations.

Demographic shifts and economic dislocations of the 1920s and 1930s ignited a florescence of white racism and metastasized the color-coded economic structure, while New Deal policies further inscribed racial segregation onto the suburban landscape. Once again fitness for citizenship and black women's bodies became part of the public discourse. Black church women combated "Humiliation, Discrimination, Brutality and Crime" as they transformed segregated spaces into sites of resistance. They continued their fight into World War II.

* * *

By reclaiming the voice and public presence of African American working women, this book has shown that black women's Christian activism mattered. Grounded in civic righteousness, they influenced change over the first half of the twentieth century. They built churches, sustained communities, and advocated for just laws and moral institutions. The story of their activism adds another dimension to our understanding of black women's crucial role in the northern civil rights movement, as it illuminates the complicated intertwining of religion and politics, race and gender, and the importance of listening to voices on the margins. By taking the long view of the intersection of race, class, and gender in a localized northern venue, this volume reminds us that women and men experience national and global events in intimate local settings. The volume also affirms that the diversity written into our sacred and secular spaces is no less real or significant because we choose to erase or ignore it. As the twenty-first century weaves more diverse strands into the American religious and civic fabric, may the religious narrative of these ordinary women who worked for wages remind us that in the fight for just laws and moral institutions we can transform immoral places into sites of resistance.

NOTES

INTRODUCTION

1 New Jersey State Federation of Colored Women's Clubs, *Proceedings of the New Jersey State Federation of Colored Women's Clubs Conference and First, Second and Third Annual Meetings, July 1915–1918,1920*, 14, Florence Randolph Collection, MG 1321, Folder 2. New Jersey Historical Society, Newark, New Jersey (hereafter cited as NJSFCWC and FRC).

2 "The colored woman of to-day occupies . . . a unique position in this country. . . . She is confronted by both a woman question and a race problem, and is yet an unknown or an unacknowledged factor in both." Charles Lemert and Esme Bhan, ed., *The Voice of Anna Julia Cooper, Including a Voice from the South and Other Important Essays, Papers, and Letters* (Lanham, Md.: Rowman & Littlefield, 1998), 112.

3 Thirtieth Anniversary Dinner of the New Jersey Federation of Colored Women's Clubs with Florence Randolph, D.D., Founder, Honored Guest, 18 October 1945, FRC, MG1321, Folder 2.

4 Dorothy Thompson, ed., *The Essential E. P. Thompson* (New York: New Press, 2001), 5.

5 *Summit, New Jersey: An Ideal Suburban Home Town* (Newark, N.J.: Civic Publicity Co., 1909).

6 *Ibid.*

7 *Summit Herald*, 24 March 1883.

8 *Summit Herald*, 25 June 1898.

9 *Summit Herald*, 15 May 1923.

10 BTW to Leslie Pinckney Hill, 7 June 1904, *Booker T. Washington Papers* (Urbana: University of Illinois Press, 1977), Vol. 7, 524.

11 U.S. 15th Federal Census, 1930. On New Jersey's "soaring Negro population," see *New York Times*, 18 June 1931, 17; and 27 June 1931, 10.

12 Andrew Wiese, *Places of Their Own: African American Suburbanization in the Twentieth Century* (Chicago: University of Chicago Press, 2005), 25. Wiese identifies "premier" domestic suburbs that "represented both home and workplace" for black workers and their families as Westchester County, New York; Pasadena, California; Evanston, Illinois; and suburbs along the Orange Mountains of New Jersey. Wiese, *Places of Their Own*, 26. Scholars of the "new urban history" have added race and class to the discussion of the suburbanization process prior to 1950. See Kevin M. Kruse

and Thomas J. Sugrue, ed., *The New Suburban History* (Chicago: University of Chicago Press, 2006); Henry Louis Taylor, Jr., and Walter Hill, ed., *Historical Roots of the Urban Crisis: African Americans in the Industrial City, 1900–1950* (New York: Garland, 2000); Shirley Ann Wilson Moore, *To Place Our Deeds: The African American Community in Richmond, California, 1910–1963* (Berkeley: University of California Press, 2000); Myra B. Young Armstead, *"Lord, Please Don't Take Me in August": African Americans in Newport and Saratoga Springs, 1870–1930* (Chicago: University of Illinois Press, 1999); Leslie Wilson, "Dark Spaces: An Account of Afro-American Suburbanization, 1890–1950" (Ph.D. diss., City University of New York, 1991). Often missing from these analyses and one contribution of this book is the more complicated constellation of race, class, gender, and the demarcation of white space within the borders of residential suburbs.

13 New England Baptist Missionary Convention, *Minutes of the Third Annual Session, Held in Newport, Rhode Island, May 18 to May 23, 1877*, 3–4, American Baptist Manuscript Collection, American Baptist Historical Society, Atlanta, Georgia (hereafter cited as NEBMC). NEBMC ministers maintained dual affiliation with white state associations and the Northern American Baptist denomination. James M. Washington, *Frustrated Fellowship: The Black Baptist Quest for Social Power* (Macon, Ga.: Mercer University Press, 1990), 126–127; Leroy Fitts, *A History of Black Baptists* (Nashville: Broadman Press, 1985), 72–98.

14 As Matthew Frye Jacobson argues, a destabilized notion of "race was the prevailing idiom for discussing citizenship and the relative merits of a given people" in post-Reconstruction America. Matthew Frye Jacobson, *Whiteness of a Different Color: European Immigrants and the Alchemy of Race* (Cambridge, Mass.: Harvard University Press, 2001), 9.

15 Joanne J. Meyerowitz, *Women Adrift: Independent Wage-Earners in Chicago, 1880–1930* (Chicago: University of Chicago Press, 1988), 42; also Kathy Lee Peiss, *Cheap Amusements: Working Women and Leisure in New York* (Philadelphia: Temple University Press, 1986), 51, 72–75, 163–184. Peiss's discussion of working-class immigrant women's leisure activities and anxieties about their sexuality and morality characterizes the plight of black working women in the suburbs.

16 Frances A. Kellor, "Sex in Crime," *International Journal of Ethics* 9 (October 1898): 74–85.

17 Frances A. Kellor, "Southern Colored Girls in the North: The Problem of Their Protection," *Charities* 13 (18 March 1905): 584–585. Hazel Carby cites this article as "important evidence that as early as 1905 the major discursive elements were already in place that would define black female urban behavior throughout the teens and twenties as pathological." Hazel V. Carby, "Policing the Black Woman's Body," *Critical Inquiry* 18 (Summer 1992): 740.

18 Mary White Ovington, *Half a Man: The Status of the Negro in New York [1911]*, reprint (New York: American Century Series, 1969), 104.

19 Twenty-one years old when elected Corresponding Secretary of the National Baptist Woman's Convention, Burroughs (1879–1961) founded the National Training

School for Women and Girls in 1909. Evelyn Brooks Higginbotham, "Religion, Politics, and Gender: The Leadership of Nannie Helen Burroughs," in *This Far by Faith: Readings in African-American Women's Religious Biography*, ed. Judith Weisenfeld and Richard Newman (New York: Routledge, 1996), 147–157; Opal V. Easter, *Nannie Helen Burroughs* (New York: Garland, 1995); Sharon Harley, "Nannie Helen Burroughs: 'The Black Goddess of Liberty,'" *Journal of Negro History* 81 (Spring, Summer, Winter 1996): 62–71.

20 Nannie Helen Burroughs, "The Colored Woman and Her Relation to the Domestic Problem," in *The United Negro: His Problems and His Progress; Containing the Addresses and Proceedings of the Negro Young People's Christian and Educational Congress, Held August 6–11, 1902*, ed. I. Garland Penn and J. W. E. Bowen (Atlanta: D. E. Luther Publishing Co., 1902), 324–329.

21 Sarah Deutsch, *Women and the City: Gender, Space, and Power in Boston, 1870–1940* (New York: Oxford University Press, 2000), 71, 74, 114; Wanda A. Hendricks, *Gender, Race, and Politics in the Midwest: Black Club Women in Illinois* (Bloomington: Indiana University Press, 1998), 61. Deutsch ignores the complex structure of African American society in Boston. It is unlikely that women of the National Federation of Afro-American Women, organized in Boston in 1895, perceived "mutuality" between themselves and domestic servants of any hue. On middle class black women's organizations and the relationship to racism and sexism, see Hazel V. Carby, *Reconstructing Womanhood: The Emergence of the Afro-American Woman Novelist* (New York: Oxford University Press, 1987), 95–120; Willard B. Gatewood, *Aristocrats of Color: The Black Elite, 1880–1920* (Bloomington: Indiana University Press, 1990), 210–246.

22 Many African American working women attended northern or southern denominational schools. Violet Johnson, for example, was educated at an American Baptist Missionary school in Wilmington, North Carolina. *Indianapolis Freeman*, 31 July 1909, cited in Bettye Collier-Thomas, *Jesus, Jobs, and Justice: African American Women and Religion* (New York: Alfred A. Knopf, 2010), 281–282. On African American's communal valuation of education regardless of class status, see Heather Williams, *Self-Taught: African American Education in Slavery and Freedom* (Chapel Hill: University of North Carolina Press, 2005).

23 On the reperiodization of the civil rights movement, see Jacquelyn Dowd Hall, "The Long Civil Rights March and the Political Use of the Past," *Journal of American History* 91 (March 2005): 1233–1263; Glenda Elizabeth Gilmore, *Defying Dixie: The Radical Roots of Civil Rights, 1919–1950* (New York: W. W. Norton, 2008), 7–10; Thomas J. Sugrue, *Sweet Land of Liberty: The Forgotten Struggle for Civil Rights in the North* (New York: Random House, 2008), xviii, xix.

24 Glenda Elizabeth Gilmore, *Gender and Jim Crow: Women and the Politics of White Supremacy in North Carolina, 1896–1920* (Chapel Hill: University of North Carolina Press, 1996); Evelyn Brooks Higginbotham, *Righteous Discontent: The Women's Movement in the Black Baptist Church, 1880–1920* (Cambridge: Harvard University Press, 1993); Judith Weisenfeld, *African American Women and Christian Activism: New York's Black YWCA, 1905–1945* (Cambridge, Mass.: Harvard University Press, 1997); Nancy Marie Robertson, *Christian Sisterhood, Race Relations and the YWCA, 1906–46*

(Urbana: University of Illinois Press, 2007); Collier-Thomas, *Jesus, Jobs, and Justice*; Martha S. Jones, *All Bound Up Together: The Woman Question in African American Public Culture, 1830–1900* (Chapel Hill: University of North Carolina Press, 2007).

25 Thomas J. Sugrue, *Origins of the Urban Crisis: Race and Inequality in Postwar Detroit* (Princeton, N.J.: Princeton University Press, 1996); Kenneth T. Jackson, *Crabgrass Frontier: The Suburbanization of the United States* (New York: Oxford University Press, 1985); Robert Fishman, *Bourgeois Utopias: The Rise and Fall of Suburbia* (New York: Basic Books, 1987); John R. Stilgoe, *Borderland: Origins of the American Suburb, 1820–1939* (New Haven: Yale University Press, 1988); Margaret Marsh, *Suburban Lives* (New Brunswick: Rutgers University Press, 1990); Wiese, *Places of Their Own*; Becky M. Nicolaides, *My Blue Heaven: Life and Politics in the Working-Class Suburbs of Los Angeles, 1920–1965* (Chicago: University of Chicago Press, 2002).

CHAPTER 1. "PLEASE ALLOW ME SPACE"

1 U.S. Bureau of the Census, Manuscript Census, 1900, Summit, Union County, N.J.

2 *Summit Herald*, 15 May 1923.

3 L. J. Coppin, "Christian Endeavor Movement," *African Methodist Episcopal Church Review* 15 (January 1899): 677–688; Gaines M. Foster, *Moral Reconstruction: Christian Lobbyists and the Federal Legislation of Morality, 1865–1920* (Chapel Hill: University of North Carolina Press, 2002), 115.

4 F. W. Ricord, *History of Union County, N.J.* (Newark: East Jersey History Co., 1897), 593;

5 Fountain Baptist Church, *Seventy-Sixth Anniversary Journal, 1974*, Fountain Baptist Church Collection, Summit New Jersey (hereafter cited as FBC). The ordained minister and his family arrived in Summit a year before Violet Johnson. *Summit Herald*, 20 May 1905; *The Suburbanite*, September 1908, vol. 9, 1, http://www.archive.org/stream/suburbanitemonth04cent#page/n172/mode/1up.

6 FBC, *Seventy-Sixth Anniversary Journal*.

7 Ricord, *History of Union County*, 591–593.

8 David M. Katzman, *Seven Days a Week: Women and Domestic Service in Industrializing America* (New York: Oxford University Press, 1978); Phyllis M. Palmer, *Domesticity and Dirt: Housewives and Domestic Servants in the United States, 1920–1945* (Philadelphia: Temple University Press, 1989); Judith Rollins, *Between Women: Domestics and Their Employers* (Philadelphia: Temple University Press, 1985); Daniel Sutherland, *Americans and Their Servants: Domestic Service in the United States from 1800–1920* (Baton Rouge: Louisiana State University Press, 1985); Bonnie Dill, *Across the Boundaries of Race and Class: An Exploration of Work and Family among Black Female Domestic Servants* (New York: Garland, 1994); Elizabeth Clark-Lewis, *Living In, Living Out; African American Domestics and the Great Migration* (New York: Kodansha International, 1996); Susan Tucker, *Southern Women: Domestic Workers and Their Employers in the Segregated South* (New York: Schocken Books, 1988); Sharon Harley, "For the Good of the Family and Race: Gender, Work and Domestic Roles in the Black Community, 1890–1930," *Signs* 15:2 (Winter 1990): 336–349.

9 Myra B. Young Armstead, *"Lord, Please Don't Take Me in August": African Americans in Newport and Saratoga Springs, 1870–1930* (Urbana: University of Illinois Press, 1999), 35–61; Martin Paulsson, *The Social Anxieties of Progressive Reform: Atlantic City, 1854–1920* (New York: NYU Press, 1994), 14–41.

10 On religion as a site of negotiation for meaning and power, see James Melvin Washington, *Frustrated Fellowship: The Black Baptist Quest for Social Power* (Macon, Ga.: Mercer University Press, 1990), *xiii*; Thomas A. Tweed, ed., *Retelling U.S. Religious History* (Berkeley: University of California Press, 1997), 1–23.

11 First Baptist Church, Summit, New Jersey, Record Book, 1902, 218 and 1906, 263; *Summit Herald*, 3 May 1945.

12 Leroy Fitts, *A History of Black Baptists* (Nashville: Broadman Press, 1985), 46; New Jersey Historical Records Survey Project, *Inventory of the Church Archives of New Jersey; Prepared by the New Jersey Historical Records Survey Project, Division of Professional and Service Projects, Work Project Administration,* comp. Luther H. Evans and John A. Millington (Newark, N.J.: Historical Records Survey Project, 1938); Norman H. Maring, *Baptists in New Jersey: A Study in Transition* (Valley Forge: Judson Press, 1964), 259–261.

13 New England Baptist Missionary Convention, *Minutes of the Fourth Annual Session, Held in Brooklyn, New York, June 11 to 16, 1878,* 18–19, American Baptist Manuscript Collection, American Baptist Historical Society, Atlanta, Georgia (hereafter cited as NEBMC).

14 NEBMC, *Minutes of the Ninth Annual Session, Held in Brooklyn, New York, June 13 to 17, 1883,* 9.

15 NEBMC, *Minutes of the Third Annual Session, Held in Newport, Rhode Island, May 18 to May 23, 1877,* 3–4. African Americans in the Midwest formed independent associations in the 1840s. Fitts, *A History of Black Baptists,* 43–89. On denominationalism as an ecclesial and civic feature of American Protestantism, see Jon Butler, *Awash in a Sea of Faith: Christianizing the American People* (Cambridge, Mass.: Harvard University Press, 1992), 257–288.

16 New Jersey Afro-American Baptist State Convention, *Minutes of the First Annual Session, Held in Mont Clair, New Jersey, September 7 to 12, 1905,* 3, 20–21, Rutgers University Archives and Special Collections, New Brunswick, N.J. (hereafter cited as NJAABSC).

17 NJAABSC, *Minutes of the Third Annual Session, Held in Newark, New Jersey, September 5 to 10, 1907,* 3, 23–24.

18 NEBMC, *Minutes of the Thirteenth Annual Session, Held in Bedford, Massachusetts, June 15 to 20, 1887,* 17.

19 NEBMC, *Minutes of the Fifteenth Annual session, Held in Philadelphia, Pennsylvania, June 12 to 16, 1889,* 23.

20 NEBMC, *Minutes of the Twenty-Second Annual Session, Held in Cambridge, Massachusetts, June 17 to 22, 1896,* 19–21.

21 NEBMC, *Minutes of the Twenty-Sixth Annual Session, Held in Plainfield, New Jersey, June 14–18, 1900,* 12–14. Historian Willard Gatewood, Jr., concludes that by 1900

African American disappointment with the treatment of black soldiers, refusal of the War Department to commission black officers, use of black soldiers against Filipinos, and refusal to use those troops to protect black citizens at home led to general disaffection with American imperialism. Willard B. Gatewood, Jr., ed., *"Smoked Yankees" and the Struggle for Empire: Letters from Negro Soldiers, 1898–1902* (Champaign: University of Illinois Press, 1971), 6–10, 13, 64–101.

22 NEBMC, *Minutes of the Thirtieth Annual Session Held in Providence, Rhode Island, June 15-June 16 [1904]*, 32.

23 *Ibid.*

24 *Ibid.*

25 *Ibid.*, 33. On social equality as a mechanism for sexualizing the discussion of race, see Hazel V. Carby, "Policing the Black Woman's Body," *Critical Inquiry* 18 (Summer 1992): 738–755. On southern violence in the wake of disenfranchisement, see Glenda Elizabeth Gilmore, *Gender and Jim Crow: Women and the Politics of White Supremacy of North Carolina, 1896–1920* (Chapel Hill: University of North Carolina Press, 1996), 91–118; C. Vann Woodward, *Origins of the New South, 1877–1913* (Baton Rouge: Louisiana University Press, 1990), 350–353; on Northern Protestant rejection of racial equality, see Edward J. Blum, *Reforging the White Republic: Race, Religion, and American Nationalism, 1865–1898* (Baton Rouge: Louisiana State University Press, 2005).

26 NEBMC, *Minutes of the Eighteenth Annual Session, Held in New Haven, Connecticut, June 15 to 20, 1892*, 20–21. On race and citizenship, see Matthew Frye Jacobson, *Whiteness of a Different Color: European Immigration and the Alchemy of Race* (Cambridge, Mass.: Harvard University Press, 2001).

27 Gail Bederman, *Manliness and Civilization: A Cultural History of Gender and Race in the United States, 1880–1917* (Chicago: University of Chicago Press, 1995); Gilmore, *Gender and Jim Crow*, 62–76. For Martin Luther King's formulation, see James M. Washington, ed., *The Essential Writings and Speeches of Martin Luther King Jr.*(New York: HarperSanFrancisco, 1986), 217–220.

28 NEBMC, *Minutes of the Eighteenth Annual Session, 1892*, 18. On mainline Protestant churches as arbiters of Victorian behavior, see David B. Danbom, *"The World of Hope": Progressives and the Struggle for an Ethical Public Life* (Philadelphia: Temple University Press, 1987).

29 Evelyn Brooks Higginbotham, *Righteous Discontent: The Women's Movement in the Black Baptist Church* (Cambridge, Mass.: Harvard University Press, 1993), 16, 185–229; also Victoria W. Wolcott, *Remaking Respectability: African American Women in Interwar Detroit* (Chapel Hill: University of North Carolina Press, 2001). In contrast to Higginbotham and Wolcott who posit the politics of respectability as a female strategy, this study contends that, though the burden fell primarily on women, respectability was one element of a racial strategy based on Victorian conventions, republican political theory, and middle-class materiality. On the antebellum construction of the politics of respectability, see Eddie S. Glaude, Jr., *Exodus! Religion, Race, and Nation in Early Nineteenth-Century Black America* (Chicago: University of Chicago Press, 2000), 118–121; on respectability as a masculine construct, see Martin Summers, *Manliness and Its*

Discontents: The Black Middle Class and the Transformation of Masculinity, 1900–1930 (Chapel Hill: University of North Carolina Press, 2004).

30 NEBMC, *Minutes of the Ninth Annual Session, 1883*, 11; Kathy Lee Peiss, *Cheap Amusements: Working Women and Leisure in New York* (Philadelphia: Temple University Press, 1986); Tera W. Hunter, *To 'Joy My Freedom: Southern Black Women's Lives and Labor after the Civil War* (Cambridge: Harvard University Press, 2002), 145–167; on anxieties over desecration of the Sabbath, see Paulsson, *The Social Anxieties of Progressive Reform*, 38–39; Foster, *Moral Reconstruction*, 93–117.

31 NEBMC, *Minutes of the Eleventh Annual Session, Held in New York City, New York, June 17 to 21, 1885*, 7, 31. Originated on southern plantations, partners performed the cakewalk with exaggerated bodily movements and competed for a cake. Although the cakewalk had penetrated New York high society by the 1890s, the black middle class considered it a violation of the "genteel performance." Alessandra Lorini, *Rituals of Race: American Public Culture and the Search for Racial Democracy* (Charlottesville: University of Virginia Press, 1999), 161; Willard B. Gatewood, Jr., *Aristocrats of Color: The Black Elite, 1880–1920* (Bloomington: Indiana University Press, 1990), 192.

32 NEBMC, *Minutes of the Ninth Annual Session, 1883*, 11. On the Protestant missionary enterprise, see William R. Hutchinson, *Errand to the World: American Protestant Thought and Foreign Missions* (Chicago: University of Chicago Press, 1993); Walter L. Williams, *Black Americans and the Evangelization of Africa, 1877–1900* (Madison: University of Wisconsin Press, 1982); Sandy D. Martin, *Black Baptists and African Missions: The Origins of a Movement, 1880–1915* (Macon, Ga.: Mercer University Press, 1989); Mark Y. Hanley, "Revolution at Home and Abroad: Radical Implications of the Protestant Call to Missions, 1825–1870," in Daniel H. Bays and Grant Wacker, ed., *The Foreign Missionary Enterprise at Home: Explorations in North American Cultural History* (Tuscaloosa: University of Alabama Press, 2003),44–59; David W. Wills and Richard Newman, ed., *Black Apostles at Home and Abroad: Afro-Americans and the Christian Mission from the Revolution to Reconstruction* (Boston: G. K. Hall, 1982).

33 Maring, *Baptists in New Jersey*, 253–262; Giles R. Wright, *Afro-Americans in New Jersey: A Short History* (Trenton: New Jersey Historical Commission, Department of State, 1988), Appendix 2, 80.

34 NEBMC, *Minutes of the Fourth Annual Session, 1878*, 18; and *Minutes of the Fifteenth Annual Session, 1889*, 24.

35 NEBMC, *Minutes of the Thirteenth Annual Session, 1887*, 13.

36 NEBMC, *Minutes of the Thirty-Sixth Annual Session, Held in New York City, New York, June 2 to 6, 1910*, 13–14. Of Dixon (1833–1909), one contemporary wrote, "Though he lived for all these years in the far North, away from the great mass of his people, he espoused their cause throughout the country." N. H. Pius, *An Outline of Baptist History: A Splendid Reference Work for Busy Workers: A Record of the Struggles and Triumphs of Baptist Pioneers and Builders* (Nashville: National Baptist Publishing Board, 1911), 116.

37 *Summit Herald*, 23 May 1908.

38 *New Jersey* (Montclair*) Observer*, 20 January 1917, FBC Collection. The black Baptist church was, as Evelyn Brooks Higginbotham concludes, the "product and process of male and female interaction." Higginbotham, *Righteous Discontent*, 2.

39 FBC, *Seventy-Sixth Anniversary Journal*, 1974. On Nora Taylor, see Bettye Collier-Thomas, *Daughters of Thunder: Black Women Preachers and Their Sermons* (San Francisco: Jossey-Bass, 1998), 32; Julius F. Nimmons, "Social Reform and Moral Uplift in the Black Community, 1890–1910: Social Settlements, Temperance and Social Purity" (Ph. D. diss., Harvard University, 1981), 106.

40 NEMBC, *Minutes of the Seventeenth Annual Meeting, Held New York City, N.Y., June 17–23, 1891*, 21.

41 Peiss, *Cheap Amusements*, 62–63.

42 Eileen Southern, *The Music of Black Americans: A History*, 2d ed. (New York: W. W. Norton, 1983), 247–252.

43 *Summit Herald*, 19 January 1901 and 3 January 1903.

44 *Summit Herald*, 6 October 1906. Baston (1864–1906) died within months of her Summit concert. Southern, *Music of Black Americans*, 242.

45 *Summit Herald*, 13 December 1912.

46 Participation in a shared popular culture contrasted with the experience of European workers who were often separated by language, religion, and culture. Irish girls in Boston refused to work in the suburbs because of the absence of companions and the Catholic Church. Sarah Deutsch, *Women and the City: Gender, Space, and Power in Boston, 1870–1940* (New York: Oxford University Press, 2000), 18.

47 *Summit Herald*, 20 August 1929. Most pastors remained for less than three years. FBC, *One-Hundredth Anniversary Souvenir Journal*, 21, FBC Collection.

48 Erected in 1894, the building was variously known as Temperance Hall, Willard Hall, the Summit Opera House, and the Van Cise Building. Edward S. Olcott, *20th Century Summit, 1899–1999* (Summit, N.J.: Howell & Williams, 1998), 4.

49 NEBMC, *Minutes of the Thirty-First Annual Session, Held in Brooklyn, New York, June 15 to 18, 1905*, 25.

50 NJAABSC, *Minutes of the Third Annual Session, 1907*, 39.

51 "A Short History of Coming and Foundering of the Fountain Baptist Church[,] Summit[,] New Jersey. Compiled by the Pastor Rev. Daniel W. Wisher[,] D. D. & Sister Violi [sic] Johnson," MS, [c.1916], FBC Collection.

52 *Summit Herald*, 9 September 1905. Born in South Carolina in 1864, McDaniels had previously led churches in New York and was a signatory to a 1904 pastoral circular advocating that northern voters use their political power to defeat Southern disenfranchisement. Charles William Anderson to Booker T. Washington, 10 July 1904, *Booker T. Washington Papers*, Vol. 8, 24–25.

53 *Summit Herald*, 20 January 1906. On muscular Christianity and feminization of the church, see Gail Bederman, "'The Women Have Had Charge of the Church Work Long Enough': The Men and Religion Forward Movement of 1911–1912 and the Masculinization of Middle-Class Protestantism," *American Quarterly* 41 (September 1989):

432–465; David G. Hackett, "Gender and Religion in American Culture, 1870–1930," *Religion and American Culture* 5 (Summer 1995): 127–157.

54 Deutsch, *Women and the City*, 54–55; also Ellen Fitzpatrick, *Endless Crusade: Women Social Scientists and Progressive Reform* (New York: Oxford University Press, 1990); Cheryl D. Hicks, *Talk with You Like a Woman: African American Women, Justice, and Reform in New York, 1890–1935* (Chapel Hill: University of North Carolina Press, 2010); Frances Alice Kellor, "Sex in Crime," *International Journal of Ethics* 9 (October 1898): 74–85; Frances A. Kellor, "Southern Colored Girls in the North: The Problem of Their Protection," *Charities* 13 (18 March 1905): 584–585.

55 Bederman, *Manliness and Civilization*, 134–150; Hunter, *To 'Joy My Freedom*, 166. On the antebellum trope of the black woman as the intractable slave woman and the licentious Jezebel, see Deborah Gray White, *Ar'n't I a Woman? Female Slaves in the Plantation South* (New York: W. W. Norton, 1987), 27–61.

56 NEBMC, *Minutes of the Eighteenth Annual Session, 1892*, 16.

57 Chestnut Avenue was the most densely settled area with numerous boarding houses and businesses that catered to Italian and Polish immigrants. *The* (Morristown) *Jerseyman*, 17 June 1898.

58 *Summit Herald*, 26 May 1906.

59 *Summit Herald*, 20 June 1907.

60 *Ibid.* Signaling the relationship he would pursue with the suburb's white men, McDaniels included the suburb's white pastors in his formal installation service and recruited a white Methodist layman and New York City businessman to head the building fund and four white laymen as church trustees. *Summit Herald*, 21 June 1905.

61 Mimeographed flyer, August 1908, FBC Collection.

62 *Ibid.* Son of a renowned abolitionist and Methodist bishop, Haven was Corresponding Secretary of the American Bible Society and a founder of the Federal Council of Churches. Eric M. North, "William Ingraham Haven," in *The Encyclopedia of World Methodism*, Vol. I (Nashville: United Methodist Publishing House, 1974), 1094–1095; William Gravely, *Gilbert Haven Methodist Abolitionist: A Study in Race, Religion, and Reform, 1850–1880* (Nashville: Abingdon Press, 1973).

63 *Summit Herald*, 16 January 1909.

64 *Summit Herald*, 31 May 1912 and 19 December 1913.

65 *Summit Herald*, 19 March 1915. Jackson had previously led churches in Norwich and Hartford, Connecticut; New York City; and Montclair and Plainfield, New Jersey.

66 *Summit Herald*, 14 February 1912 and 8 November 1912.

67 *Newark Star*, 22 March 1915, 2.

68 *Summit Herald*, 26 March 1915.

69 Wiese, *Places of Their Own*, 25–27, 34–66.

70 *Summit Herald*, 26 March 1915.

71 Robert A. Orsi, "The Religious Boundaries of an In-Between People: Street *Feste* and the Problem of the Dark-Skinned Other in Italian Harlem, 1920–1990," in *Gods of the City: Religion and the American Urban Landscape*, ed. Robert A. Orsi (Bloomington: Indiana University Press, 1999), 264.

72 According to historian Robert Fishman, the Anglo-American middle class suburb was "built on a foundation of fear as well as hope" where the home was "more sacred to the bourgeoisie than any place of worship" and imaginary lines created the illusion of a "protected place where the true American family could . . . ward off the alien invasion." Robert Fishman, *Bourgeois Utopias: The Rise and Fall of Suburbia* (New York: Basic Books, 1987), 142.

73 *Summit Herald*, 26 March 1915.

74 *Summit Herald*, 9 April 1915.

75 On the interconnectedness between identity and space, Orsi argues, "The individual subjectivity is defined with reference to space, its qualities disclosed in the public theater of the neighborhood and pressed into the landscape. This means that the boundary-marking and meaning-making work . . . is always both an inner process and a . . . performance, a psychological struggle as well as a neighborhood contest." Orsi, "The Religious Boundaries of an In-Between People," 278.

76 Benedict Anderson, *Imagined Communities: Reflections on the Origin and Spread of Nationalism* (London: Verso, 1991), 4–6. Kenneth Jackson identifies the post office and village hall as the leading symbols of white middle class suburban identity. Jackson, *Crabgrass Frontier*, 120.

77 *Summit Herald*, 8 August 1911; Michael H. Ebner, "Mrs. Miller and 'The Paterson Show': A 1911 Defeat for Racial Discrimination," *New Jersey History* 86 (Summer 1968): 88–91. Under the 1884 New Jersey Civil Rights Act, the court assigned Miller's $500 award to charitable institutions rather than the aggrieved party. Marion Thompson Wright, "Extending Civil Rights in New Jersey through the Division against Discrimination," *Journal of Negro History* 38 (January 1953): 94.

78 *Summit Herald*, 26 February 1915.

79 *Ibid.* According to James C. Scott, the linguistic deference of the public apology is an admission of the violation of the norms of domination, an attempt at dissociation from a perceived offense, and acceptance of the judgment and censure of superiors rather than a sincere "retraction and disavowal, since what the apology repairs is the public transcript of apparent compliance." James C. Scott, *Domination and the Arts of Resistance: Hidden Transcripts* (New Haven, Conn.: Yale University Press, 1990), 57–59.

80 Nancy J. Weiss, "The Negro and the New Freedom: Fighting Wilsonian Segregation," *Political Science Quarterly* 84 (March 1969): 67–79; Arthur Link, *Woodrow Wilson and the Progressive Era, 1900–1920* (New York: Harper & Row; Harper Torchbooks, 1963), 63–66; *Jersey* (Jersey City) *Journal*, 12 February 1914, newspaper clipping collection, Jersey City Public Library, Jersey City, New Jersey. In 1914 NEBMC formed an alumni committee to investigate Newton Theological Seminary and in 1915 created a committee to lobby Congress. NEBMC, *Minutes of the Fortieth Annual Session Held in Bridgeton, Connecticut, June 18 to 23, 1914*, 16; and *Minutes of the Forty-Second Annual Session Held in Philadelphia, 15–19 June 1916*, 52.

81 American National Baptist Convention, *Journal, Sermons and Lectures*, 1888, 27, 47, quoted in Washington, *Frustrated Fellowship*, 145. The 1888 meeting was an attempt

to rationalize leadership and financial support for domestic missions between black and white Baptists. *Baptist Home Mission Monthly* 10 (August 1888): 201, 229.

82 Until able to secure lodging in Summit, Wisher (1853–1925) commuted from Philadelphia. In the 1890s, the native Virginian owned several valuable houses in Harlem, property on Long Island, and a home in Jersey City where he employed a number of Swedish servants and owned carriages and livery among the most stylish in town. *New York Times*, 14 July 1895, 21.

83 *Summit Herald*, 21 January 1916.

84 *Ibid.*

85 "A Short History of Coming and Foundering."

86 At the same meeting in which the white Methodists voted against the black church, the congregation decided to build a separate church for white working-class Methodists less than a mile distant in East Summit. *Summit Herald*, 28 January 1916.

87 *Summit Herald*, 11 February 1916; "A Short History of Coming and Foundering." According to church lore, Johnson also held veto power over pastoral appointments. On the complicated position of women as narrators of the past and their exclusion from public discourse, see Laurie F. Maffly-Kipp, *Setting Down the Sacred Past: African-American Race Histories* (Cambridge: Belknap Press of Harvard University Press, 2010).

88 "A Short History of Coming and Foundering."

89 *Summit Herald*, 20 October 1916 and 27 October 1916.

90 "An Important Matter to the Citizens of Summit," 24 October 1916, mimeographed flyer, FBC Collection.

91 *Summit Herald*, 27 October 1916.

92 "An Important Matter."

93 Where no clearly demarcated "Negro section" existed, one had to be created, first on the mental map and then on the landscape. Historian Margaret Marsh argues that early twentieth-century middle class suburbanites privileged the symbolic meaning of place over property ownership. Margaret Marsh, *Suburban Lives* (New Brunswick: Rutgers University Press, 1990), xiv, 68. As this book demonstrates, ownership became paramount in the World War I era.

94 "Cornerstone Laying Ceremony," [1917], mimeographed copy, FBC Collection.

95 "A Short History of Coming and Foundering."

CHAPTER 2. "A GREAT WORK FOR GOD AND HUMANITY"

1 New England Baptist Missionary Convention, *Minutes of the Third Annual Meeting, Held in Newport, R.I., May 18–23, 1877*, 9, American Baptist Manuscript Collection, American Baptist Historical Library, Atlanta, Georgia (hereafter cited as NEBMC).

2 Third Annual President's Address, 26 July 1918. Florence Randolph Collection, MG1321, Folder 2, New Jersey Historical Society, Newark, N.J. (hereafter cited as FRC).

3 In 1892 Anna Julia Cooper (1858–1964) voiced black women's anguish as they confronted the structural and ideological spaces that ignored their intersecting identities of race and gender: "I see two dingy little rooms with, "FOR LADIES"

swinging over one and "FOR COLORED PEOPLE" over the other; while wondering under which head I come." Anna Julia Cooper, *The Voice of Anna Julia Cooper, including a Voice from the South and Other Important Essays, Papers, and Letters*, ed. Charles Lemert and Esme Bhan (Lanham, Md.: Rowman & Littlefield, 1998), 95. Historian Martha S. Jones foregrounds gender as the primary force leading women to create alternative sites. Martha S. Jones, *All Bound Up Together: The Woman Question in African American Public Culture, 1830–1900* (Chapel Hill: University of North Carolina Press, 2007), especially 151–171. As this book shows, race and gender factored into black women's organizational choices. On the complex nature of black women's subjectivity and attitudes toward them, see Beverly Guy-Sheftall, *Daughters of Sorrow: Attitudes toward Black Women, 1880–1920* (Brooklyn, N.Y.: Carlson Publishing, 1990).

4 In established congregations only men sat on the powerful discipline committee that judged private and public behavior on matters ranging from the promulgation of false doctrine to immoral conduct or arrogant deportment. Edward T. Hiscox, *Principles and Practices for Baptist Churches: A Guide to the Administration of Baptist Churches,1894*; reprint (Grand Rapids, Mich.: Kregel Publications, 1984), 160–191; Norman H. Maring, *Baptists in New Jersey: A Study in Transition* (Valley Forge, Pa.: Judson Press, 1964), 29–31.

5 *Summit Herald*, 11 February 1909.

6 NEBMC, *Minutes of the Twenty-Second Annual Meeting, Held in Cambridge, Ma., June 17–22, 1896*.

7 NEBMC, *Minutes of the Thirty-Fourth Annual Meeting, Held in Philadelphia, Pa., June 18–22, 1908*, 23, 44.

8 NEBMC, *Minutes of the Fifteenth Annual Meeting, Held in Philadelphia, Pa., June 12–17, 1889*, 14. In 1880 the white New Jersey Baptist Association permitted women to read their own reports. Maring, *Baptists in New Jersey*, 232–233.

9 NEBMC, Appendix, "Meeting of the Fourth Annual Meeting of the Women's Missionary Bible Band, Held with the Union Baptist Church, Cambridge, Mass., June 16, 1896." See Evelyn Brooks Higginbotham, *Righteous Discontent: The Women's Movement in the Black Baptist Church, 1880–1920* (Cambridge: Harvard University Press, 1993) on the church's "inherent gender conflict." For studies that emphasize gender equality in church relations, see Julyanne E. Dodson, *Engendering Church: Women, Power, and the A.M.E. Church*. (Lanham, Md.: Rowman & Littlefield, 2002); Elsa Barkley Brown, "Negotiating and Transforming the Public Square: African American Political Life in the Transition from Slavery to Freedom," *Public Culture* 7 (1994): 107–146; and Cheryl Townsend Gilkes, *If It Weren't for the Women: Black Women's Experience and Womanist Culture in Church and Community* (Marynoll, N.Y.: Orbis Books, 2001). As this book argues, the church valorized differently individual women's work and women's organized work, which church men perceived as a threat to the church's mission and governance.

10 NEBMC, *Minutes of the Twentieth Annual Meeting, Held in Brooklyn, N.Y., June 14–19, 1894*, 15.

11 Afro-American Baptist Association of New Jersey, *Minutes of the Fifth Anniversary, Held in Princeton, N.J., September 3–4, 1897*, 16–17, Rutgers University Archives and Special Collections, New Brunswick, N.J.

12 *Ibid.*, 9.

13 *Ibid.*, 17.

14 NEBMC, *Minutes of the Twenty-Fifth Annual Meeting, Held in Providence, R.I.*, June 15 -19, 1899, 16. On the importance of foreign missions to the Protestant enterprise, see William R. Hutchinson, *Errand to the World: American Protestant Thought and Foreign Missions* (Chicago: University of Chicago Press, 1993); Sandy Dwayne Martin, *Black Baptists and African Missions: The Origins of a Movement, 1880–1915* (Macon, Ga: Mercer University Press, 1989); B. Adams, "African American Baptist Identity and the Idea of Missions to Africa, 1880–1900," MS in author's possession.

15 *Ibid.*, 62–64. In 1901 the National Baptist Woman's Convention refused a proposed name change. Higginbotham, *Righteous Discontent*, 160. A former teacher and daughter of a prominent Philadelphia minister and NEBMC officer, Layten (1863–1950) was secretary of the New York-Philadelphia Association for the Protection of Colored Women. Bettye Collier-Thomas, *Jesus, Jobs, and Justice: African American Women and Religion* (New York: Alfred A. Knopf, 2010), 127–130; Higginbotham, *Righteous Discontent*, 157–158.

16 NEBMC, *Minutes of the Twenty-Fifth Annual Meeting, 1899*, 41. Emphasis added.

17 *Ibid.*, 64. Some pastors locked church doors against Bible Bands. Higginbotham, *Righteous Discontent*, 71.

18 Afro-American Baptist State Convention of New Jersey, *Minutes of the Eighth Annual Session of the Afro-American [Baptist] Association of New Jersey and the Woman's Missionary Union Held in Asbury Park, N J., 19–23 September, 1900*, 9, Rutgers University Archives and Special Collections, New Brunswick, N.J. (hereafter cited as NJAABSC).

19 On women's resource mobilization and voluntary organizations as political behavior, see Louise A. Tilly and Patricia Gurin, ed., *Women, Politics, and Change* (New York: Russell Sage Foundation, 1990), 4–24; Michael McGerr, "Political Style and Women's Power, 1830–1930," *Journal of American History* 77 (December 1990): 864–865.

20 Higginbotham, *Righteous Discontent*, 151. As historian Anthea D. Butler argues, Higginbotham understates the significant role Bible Bands played in establishing the framework for the organization of the Woman's Convention. Anthea D. Butler, "'Only a Woman Would Do': Bible Reading and African American Women's Organizing Work," in *Women and Religion in the African Diaspora: Knowledge, Power, and Performance*, ed. R. Marie Griffith and Barbara Dianne Savage (Baltimore, Md.: Johns Hopkins University Press, 2006), 155–178.

21 Higginbotham, *Righteous Discontent*, 180.

22 *Ibid.*, 161, 176; Opal V. Easter, *Nannie Helen Burroughs* (New York: Garland, 1995), 36–37.

23 Nannie H. Burroughs, "The Colored Woman and Her Relation to the Domestic Problem," in *The United Negro: His Problems and His Progress; Containing the Ad-*

dresses and Proceedings of the Negro Young People's Christian and Educational Congress, Held August 6–11, 1902, ed. I. Garland Penn and J. W. E. Bowen (Atlanta: D. E. Luther Publishing Co., 1902), 325, 239.

24 NJAABSC, *Minutes of the Second Annual Session, Held in Jersey City, N.J., September 6 to 10, 1906*, 12, 56; and *Minutes of the Third Annual Session, Held in Newark, N.J., September 5–10, 1907*, 51, 56.

25 NJAABSC, *Minutes of the First Annual Session, Held Mont Clair, N.J., September 7–12, 1905*, 47–48. On middle-class claims to women's moral superiority, see Deborah Gray White, *Too Heavy a Load: Black Women in Defense of Themselves, 1894–1994* (New York: W. W. Norton, 1999), 39.

26 *Summit Herald*, 20 June 1924; NJAABSC, *Minutes of the Fifth Annual Session, Held in Atlantic City, N.J., September 8–13, 1909*, 34, 55–57. On Burroughs, see Collier-Thomas, *Jesus, Jobs, and Justice*, 123, 131–133, 282; Victoria W. Wolcott, "'Bible, Bath, and Broom': Nannie Helen Burroughs's National Training School and African-American Racial Uplift," *Journal of Women's History* 9 (Spring 1997): 88–110.

27 *Summit Herald*, 4 December 1909.

28 NEBMC, *Minutes of the Thirty-Fourth Annual Session . . . 1908*, 12, 13.

29 *Union Signal*, 4 October 1883, 11; Margaret Smith Crocco, "Women of New Jersey: Charting a Path to Full Citizenship, 1870–1920," *New Jersey History* 115 (Fall/Winter 1997): 39.

30 *Union Signal*, 25 October 1883, 11. Ann-Marie Szymanski, *Pathways to Prohibition: Radicals, Moderates, and Social Movement Outcomes* (Durham: Duke University Press, 2003).

31 *Union Signal*, 23 August 1883, 10.

32 *Union Signal*, 3 April 1884, 1; Delight W. Dodyk, "Education and Agitation: The Woman Suffrage Movement in New Jersey" (Ph. D. Diss., Rutgers University, 1977), 204–205.

33 *Union Signal*, 4 June 1885, 11; 9 July 1885, 10; and 17 December 1885, 10–11.

34 *Union Signal*, 9 July 1885, 10. Southern white women bemoaned working with black women: "This work among the colored people is a trial to we [*sic*] women of the south . . . . [H]owever, natural because right, it may seem to you, it is certainly a marvel to me that some of our most timid shrinking ladies have consented to address the colored meeting." *Union Signal*, 7 May 1885, 9.

35 *Union Signal*, 9 July 1885, 10.

36 Ruth Bordin, *Women and Temperance: The Quest for Power and Liberty 1873–1900* (Philadelphia: Temple University Press, 1981), 76; Carolyn De Swarte Gifford, "Frances W. Willard and the Woman's Christian Temperance Union's Conversion to Woman's Suffrage," in *One Woman, One Vote: Rediscovering the Woman Suffrage Movement*, ed. Marjorie Spruill Wheeler (Troutdale, Oreg.: NewSage Press, 1996), 117–133; Janet Zollinger Giele, *Two Paths to Women's Equality: Temperance, Suffrage, and the Origins of Modern Feminism* (New York: Twayne, 1995).

37 *Union Signal*, 8 November 1883, 8; Carol Mattingly, *Well-Tempered Women: Nineteenth-Century Temperance Rhetoric* (Carbondale: Southern Illinois University

Press, 1998), 85–86. In 1900 the Michigan Federation of Colored Women "heartily endors[ed]" the WCTU for having "shown the absence of prejudice against us" by appointing to "positions of honor and trust" Lucy Thurman and Frances Harper. *Union Signal*, 11 October 1900, 1. For national club women active in the WCTU, see Elizabeth Lindsay Davis, *Lifting as They Climb: The National Association of Colored Women* (Washington: National Association of Colored Women, 1933).

38 *Union Signal*, 28 May 1885, 12. Mattingly, *Well-Tempered Women*, 85–86; Bettye Collier-Thomas, "Frances Ellen Watkins Harper: Abolitionist and Feminist Reformer 1825–1911," in *African American Women and the Vote, 1837–1965*, ed. Ann D. Gordon *et al.* (Amherst: University of Massachusetts Press, 1997), 41–65.

39 *Union Signal*, 28 May 1885, 12.

40 *Union Signal*, 2 October 1890, 12.

41 *Union Signal*, 25 April 1889, 11; and 25 July 1889, 4. In 1888 the New Jersey State Supreme Court upheld the local option law, ensuring continuation of local option battles and the recruitment of black women. Szymanski, *Pathways to Prohibition*, 111.

42 *Union Signal*, 4 July 1889, 11. On white women's distrust of black and foreign women's support in local option elections, see Felice D. Gordon, *After Winning: The Legacy of New Jersey Suffragists, 1920–1947* (New Brunswick: Rutgers University Press, 1986), 10; Glenda Elizabeth Gilmore, *Gender and Jim Crow: Women and the Politics of White Supremacy in North Carolina, 1896–1920* (Chapel Hill: University of North Carolina Press, 1996), 55.

43 *Union Signal*, 4 April 1889, 10; and 6 March 1890, 9; William Edgar Sackett, *Modern Battles of Trenton, Being a History of New Jersey's Politics and Legislation from the Year 1868 to the Year 1894* (Trenton, N.J.: John L. Murphy, 1895), 284–293.

44 *Union Signal*, 14 August 1890, 5; J. B. Graw, ed., *Life of Mrs. S. J. C. Downs; or, Ten Years at the Head of the Woman's Christian Temperance Union of New Jersey* (Camden, N.J.: Gazette Printing and Publishing House, 1892), 79.

45 *Union Signal*, 4 May 1899, 4; and 21 March 1895, 11, 12. Following southern white women's objection to being designated a missionary field along with "colored" and "foreign" women, the WCTU dissolved the Southern Department, elevated the Department of Work among Colored People, and granted national officer status to black state presidents. *Union Signal*, 21 May 1891, 12; Mattingly, *Well-Tempered Women*, 90.

46 *Union Signal*, 2 June 1898, 12.

47 Szymanski, *Pathways to Prohibition*, 68. Bordin highlights learning the art of politics by lobbying for compulsory scientific instruction and petitioning various levels of government as the WCTU's most lasting legacy. Bordin, *Women and Temperance*, 136–139. On middle class black women's WCTU activities, see Gilmore, *Gender and Jim Crow*; Stephanie J. Shaw, *What a Woman Ought to Be and to Do: Black Professional Women Workers during the Jim Crow Era* (Chicago: University of Chicago Press, 1996); Mattingly, *Well-Tempered Women*, 92–94; Tullia Kay Brown Hamilton, "The National Association of Colored Women, 1896–1920" (Ph.D. diss., Emory University, 1978).

48 The "genius" of the organizational culture of women's nineteenth-century voluntary associations, sociologist Elisabeth S. Clemens argues, was the "cultivation of trans-

portable routines for collective action . . . grounded in the sociability of communities and friendship networks" where women learned in "the most intimate associations" of women's space. Elisabeth S. Clemens, "Securing Political Returns to Social Capital: Women's Associations in the United States, 1880s–1920s," *Journal of Interdisciplinary History* 29 (Spring 1999): 615.

49 Emma J. Ray, *Twice Sold, Twice Ransomed: Autobiography of Mr. and Mrs. L. Ray*, 1926; reprint (Freeport, N.Y.: Books for Libraries Press, 1971), 68, 115, 171. Another example is New Orleans prison reformer Frances Joseph Gaudet, whose pastor criticized her for transgressing the bounds of womanhood by visiting prisons and courts. White women of the upper class New Orleans Era Club adopted Gaudet's prison reform work and helped establish her industrial school for African American orphans. Frances Joseph Gaudet, *"He Leadeth Me,"* 1913; reprint (New York: G. K. Hall, 1996), 20, 126–128. More research is needed on the impact of African American women on the reform agenda of white women. For one example, see Mary E. Frederickson, "'Each One Is Dependent on the Other': Southern Churchwomen, Racial Reform, and the Process of Transformation, 1880–1940," in *Visible Women: New Essays on American Activism*, ed. Nancy A. Hewitt and Suzanne Lebsock (Urbana: University of Illinois Press, 1993), 296–324.

50 African American women in Evanston, Illinois, a middle-class Chicago suburb, declined the invitation to join a white union in which black women would serve as vice presidents. Instead, the working women organized their own union and managed white women's involvement. *Union Signal*, 3 April 1890, 12.

51 Arthur S. Link, *Woodrow Wilson and the Progressive Era, 1910–1917* (New York: Harper & Row, 1954; Harper Torchbooks, 1963), 9–10, 64; Floyd W. Parsons, *New Jersey: Life, Industries, and Resources of a Great State* (Newark: New Jersey State Chamber of Commerce, 1928), 37; Nancy J. Weiss, "The Negro and the New Freedom: Fighting Wilsonian Segregation," *Political Science Quarterly* 84 (March 1969): 61–79.

52 *Union Signal*, 28 March 1912, 14.

53 *Union Signal*, 20 April 1911, 11.

54 *Union Signal*, 27 June 1912, 14. President of the Texas State Thurman Union and Lucy Thurman's successor, Peterson's itinerary from February to November 1911 indicates African American women's organizational activity. Peterson traveled to Chicago; Spokane, Washington; Pasadena and Long Beach, California; Portland, Oregon; Washington, D.C.; and Milwaukee, Wisconsin. January 1912 found her in Cheyenne, Wyoming. *Union Signal*, 9 February 1911, 9 and *passim*. For a visual representation of Peterson's activities to stir black women's political consciousness and leverage their support in prohibition elections, see "A White Map and the Colored People," *Union Signal*, 22 January 1914, 14.

55 *Union Signal*, 1 January 1914, 11.

56 *Union Signal*, 15 July 1915, 2.

57 *Union Signal*, 11 February 1915, 3.

58 Joseph F. Mahoney, "Woman Suffrage and the Urban Masses," *New Jersey History* 87 (Autumn 1969): 152. The New Jersey constitution stipulated that a constitutional

referendum pass two successive legislative sessions before being presented to the electorate. Defeat delayed another suffrage vote by at least two years.

59 *New York Times,* 12 October 1915, 4; *Newark Evening News,* 15 October 1915, 5.

60 *Newark Evening News,* 9 October 1915, 9. On the persistence of discrimination in
the suffrage movement, see Nancy F. Cott, "Feminist Politics in the 1920s: The National
Woman's Party," *Journal of American History* 71 (June 1984): 43–68; Rosalyn Terborg-
Penn, *African American Women in the Struggle for the Vote, 1850–1920* (Bloomington:
Indiana University Press, 1998).

61 *New York Times,* 20 October 1915, 2. Violet Johnson served without incident
as a poll watcher in Summit with the Equal Suffrage League. *Summit Herald,* 22
October 1915.

62 *Union Signal,* 11 November 1915, 2; Terborg-Penn, *African American Women in
the Struggle for the Vote,*121. Susan E. Marshall attributes the defeat to the strength of
the anti-suffrage coalition. Susan E. Marshall, *Splintered Sisterhood: Gender and Class
in the Campaign against Woman Suffrage* (Madison: University of Wisconsin Press,
1997), 153–160. For an exoneration of foreign-born men accused of being under the
influence of the liquor industry and urban machine bosses, see Mahoney, "Woman
Suffrage and the Urban Masses," 151–172.

63 New Jersey State Federation of Colored Women's Clubs, *Proceedings of the New
Jersey State Federation of Colored Women's Clubs Conference and First, Second and
Third Annual Meetings, July 1915–1918,1920,* 7, FRC, MG 1321, Folder 2 (hereafter cited
as NJSFCWC).

64 NJSFCWC, *Proceedings,* 1916, 7.

65 *Ibid.,* 7.

66 "Votes for Women: A Symposium," *Crisis* 10 (August 1915), 187.

67 NJSFCWC, *Proceedings,* 1917, 23; *Star of Zion,* 20 January 1916, 2.

68 Willard B. Gatewood, Jr., *Aristocrats of Color: The Black Elite, 1880–1920* (Bloom-
ington: Indiana University Press, 1990), 237, 246; Davis, *Lifting as They Climb,* 357.
On black women's experience with limited suffrage, see Wanda Hendricks, "Ida B.
Wells-Barnett and the Alpha Suffrage Club of Chicago," in *One Woman, One Vote:
Rediscovering the Woman Suffrage Movement,* ed. Marjorie Spruill Wheeler (Troutdale,
Oreg.: New Sage Press, 1996), 263–275; Wanda Hendricks, "African American Women
as Political Constituents in Chicago, 1913–1915," in *We Have Come to Stay: American
Women and Political Parties, 1880–1960,* ed. Melanie Gustafson, Kristie Miller, and
Elisabeth I. Perry (Albuquerque: University of New Mexico Press, 1999), 55–64; Patri-
cia A. Schechter, *Ida B. Wells-Barnett and American Reform, 1880–1930* (Chapel Hill:
University of North Carolina Press, 2001); Mia Bay, *To Tell the Truth Freely: The Life of
Ida B. Wells* (New York: Hill and Wang, 2009).

69 NJSFCWC, *Proceedings,* 1917, 23. Mobilization theory provides insight into the
process by which groups increase their readiness to act collectively through creation
of social capital, "the generative power of social ties . . . to produce social good." In her
study of women's associations, Elisabeth S. Clemens identifies three levels: trusting relationships, "the web of ties among individuals"; a formal organization that transforms

the network into a system of roles and routines that enable integrating new members; and organizations that allow structured discourse about civic life. Clemens, "Securing Political Returns to Social Capital," 613–615.

70 NJSFCWC, *Proceedings, 1916*, 12–15; *New Jersey State Federation News, 1* (September 1927), 2.

71 The Oregon Federation of Colored Women illustrates the contingency and agency in black women's organizational choices. Following Lucy Thurman's visit to Portland in 1899, the women contemplated organizing an eponymous temperance union in her honor. Because some objected to taking the abstinence pledge, they formed an independent women's club and joined the NACW. Davis, *Lifting as They Climb*, 118–120, 373. On the contingency and subjectivity in women's organizational strategies, see Nan Enstad, "Urban Spaces and Popular Cultures, 1890–1930," in *A Companion to American Women's History*, ed. Nancy A. Hewitt (Oxford: Blackwell, 2002), 308–309; Gilmore, *Gender and Jim Crow*, 93.

72 Thirtieth Anniversary Dinner of the New Jersey State Federation of Colored Women's Clubs with Florence Randolph, D. D., Founder, Honored Guest, 18 October 1945, FRC, MG1321, Folder 2.

CHAPTER 3. "THE HOME AWAY FROM HOME"

1 New Jersey State Federation of Colored Women's Clubs, *Constitution of the New Jersey State Federation of Women's Clubs*, 1928, Florence Randolph Collection, MG 1321, Folder 2, New Jersey Historical Society, Newark, New Jersey (hereafter cited as NJSFCWC and FRC).

2 Between 1910 and 1920 the state's black population increased from 89,760 to 117,132, 3.7 percent of the 1920 population. Giles R. Wright, *Afro-Americans in New Jersey, A Short History* (Trenton: New Jersey Historical Commission, Department of State, 1988), Appendixes 1 and 2, 79–80.

3 *Summit Herald*, 2 July 1942. Department stores and the mail order industry increased opportunities for seamstresses. Sarah Deutsch, *Women and the City: Gender, Space, and Power in Boston, 1870–1940* (Oxford: Oxford University Press, 2000), 132; Tera W. Hunter, *To 'Joy My Freedom: Southern Black Women's Lives and Labor after the Civil War* (Cambridge: Harvard University Press, 2002); Mamie Garvin Fields, with Karen Fields, *Lemon Swamp and Other Places: A Carolina Memoir* (New York: Free Press, 1983), 148. Like many African American women, Randolph worked after marriage, though Hugh Randolph's job with the Pullman Company placed the young family in the black middle class. Hugh Randolph died in 1913. Stephanie J. Shaw, *What a Woman Ought to Be and to Do: Black Professional Women Workers during the Jim Crow Era* (Chicago: University of Chicago Press, 1996), 115–133; Sharon Harley, "When Your Work Is Not Who You Are: The Development of a Working-Class Consciousness among Afro-American Women," in *Gender, Class, Race, and Reform in the Progressive Era*, ed. Noralee Frankel and Nancy S. Dye (Lexington: University Press of Kentucky, 1991), 44–45.

4 *Summit Herald*, 2 July 1942. On Randolph's life and preaching career, see Bettye Collier-Thomas, "Minister and Feminist Reformer: The Life of Florence Spearing

Randolph," in *This Far by Faith: Readings in African-American Women's Religious Biography*, ed. Judith Weisenfeld and Richard Newman (New York: Routledge, 1996), 177–185; idem, *Daughters of Thunder: Black Women Preachers and Their Sermons*. (San Francisco: Jossey-Bass, 1998), 103; idem, *Jesus, Jobs, and Justice: African American Women and Religion* (New York: Alfred A. Knopf, 2010), 23, 300. Randolph completed a Moody Bible Institute course and after moving to Summit in 1925 audited courses at Drew Theological Seminary. Collier-Thomas, *Daughters of Thunder*, 57–68.

5 William J. Walls, *The African Methodist Episcopal Zion Church: Reality of the Black Church* (Charlotte: A. M. E. Zion Publishing House, 1974), 365.

6 Randolph considered White Rose Mission founder Victoria Earle Matthews her model in women's work. *Summit Herald*, 2 July 1942; Collier-Thomas, *Daughters of Thunder*, 104; Judith Weisenfeld, *African American Women and Christian Activism: New York's Black YWCA, 1905–1945* (Cambridge, Mass.: Harvard University Press, 1997), 44–48; Steve Kramer, "Uplifting Our 'Downtrodden Sisterhood': Victoria Earle Matthews and New York City's White Rose Mission, 1897–1907," *Journal of African American History* 91 (Summer 2006): 243–266.

7 "Founders' Address to the Members of the African Methodist Episcopal Church in America," 1820, quoted in Walls, *The African Methodist Episcopal Zion Church*, 49–50.

8 Collier-Thomas, "Minister and Feminist Reformer," 179. On the evangelist role as a "means of control," see Jualynne E. Dodson, "Nineteenth-Century A. M. E. Preaching Women," in *Women in New Worlds*, Vol. 1, ed. Hilah G. Thomas and Rosemary Skinner Keller (Nashville, Tenn.: Abingdon Press, 1981), 286.

9 *Summit Herald*, 2 July 1942; Collier-Thomas, *Daughters of Thunder*, 104–105. The press extolled Randolph's "modest womanly manner." *Jersey Journal*, 7 December 1903, n.p. Clipping Collection, Jersey City Library, Jersey City, New Jersey. Alexander Walters was president of the Afro-American Council, a trustee of the Christian Endeavor Society and the Federal Council of Churches, and NAACP director until his resignation in 1913 over a *Crisis* article critical of President Wilson. Rufus E. Clement, "Alexander Walters," *Phylon* 7 (First Quarter 1946): 15–19; Ronald C. White, Jr., *Liberty and Justice for All: Racial Reform and the Social Gospel (1877–1925)* (San Francisco: Harper & Row, 1990), 178–180.

10 Collier-Thomas, *Daughters of Thunder*, 105.

11 Idonia Elizabeth Rogerson, comp., *Historical Synopsis of the Woman's Home and Foreign Mission Society, African Methodist Episcopal Zion Church* (Charlotte, N.C.: A. M. E. Zion Publishing House, 1967), 45; Walls, *The African Methodist Episcopal Zion Church*, 397; Glenda Elizabeth Gilmore, *Gender and Jim Crow: Women and the Politics of White Supremacy in North Carolina, 1896–1920* (Chapel Hill: University of North Carolina Press, 1996), 154.

12 Alexander Walters, *My Life and Work* (New York: Fleming H. Revell Company, 1917), 145.

13 Rogerson, *Historical Synopsis*, 45–46; Collier-Thomas, "Minister and Feminist Reformer," 181. As chairman of the Foreign Missions Board Randolph's mentor, Bishop Alexander, aided the expansion of women's authority.

14 Quoted in Collier-Thomas, "Minister and Feminist Reformer," 179.

15 *Union Signal*, 8 June 1899, 13.

16 Lawson attended a parlor meeting "at the beautiful, spacious residence of Bishop and Mrs. Alexander Walters (both of whom espoused the white ribbon during our meetings)." *Union Signal*, 1 November 1900, 13.

17 *Union Signal*, 29 March 1900, 12.

18 *Union Signal*, 16 August 1900, 12. Randolph's "colored union" hosted the County WCTU Spring School of Methods the following year. *Union Signal*, 28 March 1901, 11.

19 NJSFCWC, *Proceedings of the NJSFCWC Conference and First and Second and Third Annual Meetings, July 1915–1918*, 23, FRC, MG 1321, Folder 2 (hereafter cited as *Proceedings*).

20 Other organizations included the Woman's Home and Foreign Missionary Society of the New England Baptist Missionary Convention, New York State Federation of Women's Clubs, the Bureau of Associated Charities, and the Women's Auxiliary of the Fifteenth Colored Regiment of New York National Guard. NJSFCWC, *Proceedings, 1917*, 12–13.

21 NJFCWC, *Proceedings, 1917*, 12.

22 *Ibid.* Suburban Orange resident Lucy Stone formed the first state suffrage organization in 1867. Following Stone's move to Massachusetts, Mary Hussey revived the organization and became president in 1890. Ida Husted Harper, ed., *History of Woman Suffrage, 1900–1920*, Volume 6, 1922; reprint (New York: Arno Press, 1969), 416–418.

23 Committee members included the Equal Franchise League, the middle- and upper-class women's NJWSA, the professional and wage-earning women's Equal Suffrage League, and the Men's League for Woman Suffrage. Delight W. Dodyk, "Education and Agitation: The Woman Suffrage Movement in New Jersey" (Ph.D. Diss., Rutgers University, 1977), 321.

24 *New York Times*, 20 October 1915, 2; *Union Signal*, 11 November 1915, 2; Rosalyn Terborg-Penn, *African American Women in the Struggle for the Vote, 1850–1920* (Bloomington: Indiana University Press, 1998), 121; chapter 2 above.

25 NJSFCWC, *Proceedings, 1917*, 12–13.

26 Lillian F. Feickert to Dear Fellow-Worker, 31 July 1917, Lena Anthony Robbins Papers, Rutgers University Archives and Special Collections, New Brunswick, New Jersey (hereafter cited as LARP).

27 *Ibid.*

28 Sylvia Strauss, "The Passage of Woman Suffrage in New Jersey, 1911–1920," *New Jersey History* 111 (Fall/Winter 1993): 29; Felice D. Gordon, *After Winning: The Legacy of New Jersey Suffragists, 1920–194* (New Brunswick: Rutgers University Press, 1986), 8–39.

29 Alice Dunbar-Nelson, "Negro Women in War Work," in *Scott's Official History of the American Negro in the World War*, ed. Emmett J. Scott, 1919; reprint (New York: Arno Press, 1969), 395; *Chicago Defender*, 31 August 1918, 2; *National Baptist Union Review*, 3 June 1916, quoted in Milton Sernett, *Bound for the Promised Land: African American Religion and the Great Migration* (Durham: Duke University Press, 1997), 40.

30 Ida Clyde Clarke, *American Women and the World War* (New York: D. Appleton and Company, 1918), 27–32.

31 Lillian Feickert to [Mrs. Sarah B. Bolmer] Dear Madam President, 25 June 1917, LARP; Dodyk, "Education and Agitation," 453. Intended to stem the high infant mortality rate and respond to women's shifting employment responsibilities, the work of the Woman's Committees often fell short as reform and war objectives in poor black and white communities. Robyn Muncy, *Creating a Female Reform Dominion in American Reform, 1890–1935* (New York: Oxford University Press, 1991), 97.

32 Clarke, *American Women and the World War*, 189–211, 515–523. NACW reaction to the oversight is unclear, although the women seemed to use it as a wedge for future interaction.

33 Maria C. Libby, "Women's Activities during World War I," MS, Summit Historical Society; "Illustrated Supplement," *Summit Herald*, 4 July 919.

34 Libbby, "Women's Activities"; Dodyk, "Education and Agitation," 479–480.

35 NJSFCWC, *Proceedings, 1917*, 32. Historian Nikki Brown concludes that tolerating the indignities of Jim Crow was the most challenging task facing black club women and their war work. Nikki Brown, *Private Politics and Public Voices: Black Women's Activism from World War I to the New Deal* (Bloomington: Indiana University Press, 2006), 14.

36 Jane L. Scheiber and Harry N. Scheiber, "The Wilson Administration and the Wartime Mobilization of Black Americans, 1917–18," *Labor History* X (Summer 1969): 438, 440; Mark Ellis, "'Closing Ranks' and 'Seeking Honors': W. E. B. Du Bois in World War I," *Journal of American History* 79 (June 1992): 96–124; Mark Ellis, "W. E. B. Du Bois and the Formation of Black Opinion in World War I: A Commentary on 'The Damnable Dilemma,'" *Journal of American History* 81 (March 1995): 1584–1590; Adriane Lentz-Smith, *Freedom Struggles: African Americans and World War I* (Cambridge, Mass.: Harvard University Press, 2009), 43–79; Elliot M. Rudwick, *Race Riot in East Saint Louis, July 2, 1917* (Cleveland: World Publishing Company, 1970); David Levering Lewis, *W. E. B. Du Bois: Biography of a Race, 1868–1919* (New York: Henry Holt and Company, 1993); Mark Ellis, *Race, War, and Surveillance: African Americans and the United States Government during World War I* (Bloomington: Indiana University Press, 2001).

37 Emmett J. Scott, ed., *Scott's Official History of the American Negro in the World War*, 1919; reprint (New York: Arno Press, 1969), 423–424; Scheiber and Scheiber, "The Wilson Administration and the Wartime Mobilization of Black Americans," 446; William J. Breen, "Black Women and the Great War: Mobilization and Reform in the South," *Journal of Southern History* 44 (August 1978): 424.

38 National suffrage leader Carrie Chapman Catt had earlier advised, "Demand Justice NOW. . . . We should take the mote from the American eye before we go after the Prussian eye." The NJWSA legislative chair emphasized "the absurdity of fighting to make the world safe for democracy, while denying democracy to American women." Clippings, LARP.

39 Dunbar-Nelson, "Negro Women in War Work," 387–390; Brown, *Private Politics*, 37–40; Dorothy C. Salem, *To Better Our World: Black Women in Organized Reform, 1890–1920* (Brooklyn, N.Y.: Carlson Publishing, 1990), 207–208.

40 NJSFCWC, *Proceedings, 1918*, 24.

41 Opened in 1917 with a segregated black section lacking recreational and social facilities, Camp Merritt's black soldiers rarely received leave to enter nearby towns; nonetheless, white residents resented their presence and harassed soldiers and civilians. E. Frederic Morrow, *Way Down South Up North* (Philadelphia: Pilgrim Press, 1973), 76–79; Michael J. Birkner, *A Country Place No More: The Transformation of Bergenfield, New Jersey, 1894–1994* (Rutherford, N.J.: Fairleigh Dickinson University Press, 1994), 54–56. On the August 1918 "race riot," see NAACP Administrative File, Box IC 363, Folder 4, Manuscript Division, Library of Congress (hereafter cited as LOC).

42 Morrow, *Way Down South Up North*, 76; Salem, *To Better Our World*, 206. In Alabama and Mississippi, the Red Cross prohibited black women from doing canteen work at railroad stations. Breen, "Black Women and the Great War," 436.

43 NJSFCWC, *Proceedings, 1918*, 24–25.

44 Dunbar-Nelson, "Negro Women in War Work," 377. On efforts to ameliorate discriminatory treatment of black soldiers in Europe, see Addie W. Hunton and Kathryn M. Johnson, *Two Colored Women in the American Expeditionary Forces*, 1920; reprint (New York: G. K. Hall, 1997).

45 Nancy K. Bristow, *Making Men Moral: Social Engineering during the Great War* (New York: NYU Press, 1996), 91–136; Sarah Mercer Judson, "'Solving the Girl Problem': Race, Womanhood, and Leisure in Atlanta during World War I," in *Women Shaping the South: Creating and Confronting Change*, ed. Angela Boswell and Judith N. McArthur (Columbia: University of Missouri Press, 2006), 152–173; John F. McClymer, *War and Welfare: Social Engineering in America, 1890–1925* (Westport, Conn.: Greenwood Press, 1980); David M. Kennedy, *Over Here: The First World War and American Society* (New York: Oxford University Press, 1980), 185–187; Weisenfeld, *African American Women and Christian Activism*, 134–141.

46 Funds allocated for YWCA Colored Work were not commensurate with the expanded program and not appropriated until January 1918. Weisenfeld, *African American Women and Christian Activism*, 138; Dunbar-Nelson, "Negro Women in War Work," 379–380; Salem, *To Better Our World*, 208.

47 Dunbar-Nelson, "Negro Women in War Work," 380–381; Jacqueline Anne Rouse, *Lugenia Burns Hope: Black Southern Reformer* (Athens: University of Georgia Press, 1989), 95–96.

48 Scott, ed., *Scott's Official History*, 404; also Bristow, *Making Men Moral*, 150.

49 NJSFCWC, *Proceedings, 1918*, 24.

50 Libby, "Women's Activities during World War I"; *Summit Herald*, 18 March 1932.

51 Maurine Weiner Greenwald, *Women, War, and Work: The Impact of World War I on Women Workers in the United States* (Westport, Conn.: Greenwood Press, 1980), 4, 22–23, 114–115; Jacqueline Jones, *Labor of Love, Labor of Sorrow: Black Women, Work, and the Family From Slavery to the Present* (New York: Vintage Books, 1986), 161–179; Mary Church Terrell, *A Colored Woman in a White World* (Washington: Ransdell Publishing, 1940), 250–259.

52 Greenwald, *Women, War, and Work*, 60.

53 Walter K. Hickel, "War, Region, and Social Welfare: Federal Aid to Servicemen's Dependents in the South, 1917–1921," *Journal of American History* 87 (March 2001): 1362–1391.

54 Gordon, *After Winning*, 26.

55 Salem, *To Better Our World*, 214–215. Black women organized YWCAs in Newark, Jersey City, Plainfield, Montclair, Princeton, Orange, Trenton, Atlantic City, and Camden. New Jersey Conference of Social Work, Interracial Committee, *The Negro in New Jersey: Report of a Survey by the Interracial Committee of the New Jersey Conference of Social Work in Cooperation with the State Department of Institutions and Agencies* (Newark: The Conference,1932), 49. Prior to the war, only YWCA industrial clubs at Thomas Edison's plant in Orange and domestic clubs in Montclair and Burlington included black women. Nationally, the YWCA recognized only thirteen black branches before the war. Weisenfeld, *African American Women and Christian Activism*, 133; Jane Olcott, comp., *The Work of the Colored Women* (New York: Colored Work Committee War Work Council, National Board Young Women's Christian Association, 1919), 135–136.

56 Breen, "Black Women and the Great War," 440.

57 Randolph announced the reversal at the Federation's annual session. NJSFCWC, *Proceedings, 1918*, 20.

58 Dunbar-Nelson, "Women in War Work," 383; Breen, "Black Women and the Great War," 425–428. The Woman's Committee did not initially inform the NACW of Dunbar-Nelson's appointment. Brown, *Private Politics*, 42.

59 NJSFCWC, *Proceedings, 1918*, 33.

60 *Jersey Journal*, 6 October 1917, n.p.

61 Salem, *To Better Our World*, 214; Dunbar-Nelson, "Negro Women in the War," 391–392.

62 *Asbury Park Evening Press*, 30 April 1918, 8; Emmett J. Scott, *Negro Migration during the War* (New York: Oxford University Press, 1920), 139–140.

63 NJSFCWC, *Proceedings, 1918*, 33. The War Department's commendation of the white State Federation of Women's Clubs for the Liberty Bond Drive must have added insult to injury. Summit also recognized only white women's contributions. Ada A. Fuller, *A History of the New Jersey State Federation of Women's Clubs. From 1894 to 1927* (Newark, N.J.: Ada D. Fuller, 1927), 33–35; *Summit Herald*, 15 March 1918.

64 Dunbar-Nelson, "Negro Women in War Work," 377.

65 Penelope B. P. Huse, *The Mercy Committee of New Jersey* (New Jersey: Prepared & Issued for the Board of Trustees by Penelope B. P. Huse, Secretary, 1919).

66 NJSFCWC, *Proceedings, 1917*, 13; *Summit Herald*, 22 February 1918; 6 August 1920; and 27 August 1920.

67 Scott, *Negro Migration*, 139–140.

68 NJSFCWC, *Proceedings, 1918*, 24–26.

69 *Ibid.*, 17–20.

70 *Ibid.*, 23–24.

71 *Ibid.*, 23–24. Randolph's emphasis on an inclusive black womanhood suggests concern over the increasing class diversity within the State Federation. On internal differences that limited elite black women's reform agenda and marginalized the NACW, see Deborah Gray White, *Too Heavy a Load: Black Women in Defense of Themselves, 1894–1994* (New York: W. W. Norton, 1999); *idem*, "The Cost of Club Work, the Price of Black Feminism," in *Visible Women: New Essays on American Activism*, ed. Nancy Hewitt and Suzanne Lebsock (Urbana: University of Illinois Press, 1993), 247–269. On the effect of Christian culture on diversity within the black women's club movement, see Cheryl Townsend Gilkes, "Exploring the Religious Connection: Black Women Community Workers, Religious Agency and the Force of Faith," in *Women and Religion in the African Diaspora: Knowledge, Power, and Performance*, ed. R. Marie Griffith and Barbara Dianne Savage (Baltimore: Johns Hopkins University Press, 2006), 184–185.

72 NJSFCWC, *Proceedings, 1918*, 26.

73 *Ibid.*, *1918*, 26.

74 *Ibid.*, 29.

75 On civic righteousness and American political culture, see Douglas M. Strong, *Perfectionist Politics: Abolitionism and the Religious Tensions of American Democracy* (Syracuse, N.Y.: Syracuse University Press, 1999); Jonathan D. Sassi, *A Republic of Righteousness: The Public Christianity of the Post-Revolutionary New England Clergy* (Oxford: Oxford University Press, 2001); Daniel Walker Howe, "The Evangelical Movement and Political Culture in the North during the Second Party System," *Journal of American History* 77 (March 1991): 1216–1239; Donald K. Gorrell, *The Age of Social Responsibility: The Social Gospel in the Progressive Era, 1900–1920* (Macon, Ga.: Mercer University Press, 1988); Jon Difenthaler, "America's Democratic Society and the Authority of the Church," *Currents in Theology and Mission* 7 (August 1980): 230–238; also "The Relation of the Public School Teacher to Civic Righteousness," "Relation of the Public School Teachers to Civic Righteousness," and "The Relation of the Teacher to Civic Righteousness," in *The United Negro: His Problems and His Progress*, ed. I. Garland Penn and J. E. Bowen (Atlanta, Ga.: D. E. Luther Publishing Co., 1902), 395–398.

76 NJSFCWC, *Proceedings, 1918*, 27.

77 *Ibid.*

78 Evelyn Brooks Higginbotham, *Righteous Discontent: The Women's Movement in the Black Baptist Church, 1880–1920* (Cambridge: Harvard University Press, 1993), 203.

79 NJSFCWC, *Proceedings, 1918*, 27.

80 "Prominent Women to Speak at Suffrage War Conference," Press Release, 5 June 1918, LARP.

81 Lillian F. Feickert to My Dear Mrs. Basset, 19 August 1918, LARP; *Summit Herald*, 26 August 1918. Basset compared the "problem" of black voters to the "more serious problem" of foreign voters. *New York Times* 24 July 1920, 15. On the national anti-suffrage campaign, see Susan E. Marshall, *Splintered Sisterhood: Gender and Class in the Campaign against Woman Suffrage* (Madison: University of Wisconsin Press, 1997).

82 Appointed to fill the unexpired term of deceased pro-suffrage Senator William Hughes, Baird, the Republican "boss" of South Jersey, based his opposition on states'

rights. *Summit Herald*, 14 June 1918; Strauss, "The Passage of Woman Suffrage in New Jersey," 32.

83 Terborg-Penn, *African American Women in the Struggle for the Vote*, 123–134; Kenneth R. Johnson, "White Racial Attitudes as a Factor in the Arguments against the Nineteenth Amendment," *Phylon* 31 (Spring 1970): 31–37; Marjorie Julian Spruill, "Race, Reform, and Reaction at the Turn of the Century: Southern Suffragists, the NAWSA, and the 'Southern Strategy' in Context," in *Votes for Women: The Struggle for Suffrage Revisited*, ed. Jean H. Baker (New York: Oxford University Press, 2002), 102–117; Louise M. Newman, *White Women's Rights: The Racial Origins of Feminism in the United States* (New York: Oxford University Press, 1999); Marshall, *Splintered Sisterhood*, 214; Elna C. Green, *Southern Strategies: Southern Women and the Woman Suffrage Question* (Chapel Hill: University of North Carolina Press, 1997).

84 Ida Husted-Harper to Mary Church Terrell, 18 March 1919; Ida Husted-Harper to Elizabeth C. Carter, 18 March 1919; Walter White to Mary Church Terrell, 14 March 1919; Mary Church Terrell Papers, Box 3, Manuscript Division, LOC; Terborg-Penn, *African American Women in the Struggle for the Vote*, 130–131, 263–264; Rosalyn Terborg-Penn, "Discontented Black Feminists: Prelude and Postscript to the Passage of the Nineteenth Amendment," in *Decades of Discontent: The Women's Movement, 1920–1940*, ed. Lois Scharf and Joan M. Jensen (Westport, Conn.: Greenwood Press, 1983), 263–264.

85 *Asbury Park Evening Press*, 14 August, 1919, 1; Strauss, "The Passage of Woman Suffrage in New Jersey," 32.

86 Newspaper Clipping, 26 July 1919, LARP; Harper, *History of Woman Suffrage*, 428; Gordon, *After Winning*, 29. For a southern biracial suffrage alliance, see Anita Shafer Goodstein, "A Rare Alliance: African American and White Women in Tennessee Elections of 1919 and 1920," *Journal of Southern History* 64 (May 1998): 219–246.

87 NJWSA Press Release, 4 August 1919, LARP; *Asbury Park Evening Press*, 7 August 1919, 1; 13 August 1919, 1; and 14 August 1919, 1; Nancy F. Cott, *The Grounding of Modern Feminism* (New Haven, Conn.: Yale University Press, 1987), 61–62.

88 Strauss, "The Passage of Woman Suffrage in New Jersey," 31–34.

89 Rudolph J. Vecoli, *The People of New Jersey* (Princeton, N.J.: D. Van Nostrand Inc., 1965), 157; Warren E. Stickle, III, "The Applejack Campaign of 1919: 'As "Wet" as the Atlantic Ocean,'" *New Jersey History* 89 (Spring 1971): 5–22.

90 Stickle, "The Applejack Campaign of 1919," 6.

91 *Ibid.*, 6, 17–22; Warren E. Stickle, III, "Edward I. Edwards and the Urban Coalition of 1919," *New Jersey History* 90 (Summer 1972): 83–96.

92 Harper, *History of Woman Suffrage*, 429.

93 Strauss, "The Passage of Woman Suffrage in New Jersey," 34–36; John D. Buenker, "Urban, New-Stock Liberalism and Progressive Reform in New Jersey," *New Jersey History* 87 (Summer 1969): 101.

94 Florence Randolph served on the State LWV board. Harper, *History of Woman Suffrage*, 431; Gordon, *After Winning*, 30, 36.

95 Gordon, *After Winning*, 78. The Democratic and Republican parties distanced women from the center of political power by creating separate women's committees or

appointing women as alternate delegates to decision-making bodies. In 1921 the New Jersey legislature granted women the right to serve equally on regular party committees.

96 Gordon, *After Winning*, 36; Richard P. McCormick and Katheryne C. McCormick, *Equality Deferred: Women Candidates for the New Jersey Assembly, 1920–1993* (New Brunswick, N.J.: Center for the American Woman and Politics, Eagleton Institute of Politics, Rutgers the State University, 1994), 11.

97 *New York Times*, 3 November 1920, 3; "In the Political Arena: Women's Work in Essex County, N.J.," *Competitor* 3 (June 1921), 34.

98 Republicans won fifty-nine of sixty open assembly seats. John F. Reynolds, *Testing Democracy: Electoral Behavior and Progressive Reform in New Jersey, 1880–1920* (Chapel Hill: University of North Carolina Press, 1988), 166; also Brown, *Private Politics*; Lisa G. Materson, *For the Freedom of Her Race: Black Women and Electoral Politics in Illinois, 1877–1932* (Chapel Hill: University of North Carolina Press, 2009); Wanda A. Hendricks, *Gender, Race, and Politics in the Midwest: Black Club Women in Illinois* (Bloomington: Indiana University Press, 1998); Nancy A. Hewitt, "From Seneca Falls to Suffrage? Reimagining a 'Master' Narrative in U. S. Women's History," in *No Permanent Waves: Recasting Histories of U. S. Feminism*, ed. Nancy A. Hewitt (New Brunswick, N.J.: Rutgers University Press, 2010), 31.

99 Alice Dunbar-Nelson, "A Profile of Violet Johnson," MS, Alice Dunbar-Nelson Papers, Folder F441, Special Collections, University of Delaware Library, Newark, Delaware.

100 *Ibid.*

101 On power struggles between white and black women in the YWCA, see Weisenfeld, *African American Women and Christian Activism*; Nancy Marie Robertson, *Christian Sisterhood, Race Relations and the YWCA, 1906–46* (Urbana: University of Illinois Press, 2007); Adrienne Lash Jones, "Struggle among Saints: African American Women and the YWCA, 1870–1920," in *Men and Women Adrift: The YMCA and the YWCA in the City*, ed. Nina Mjagkij and Margaret Spratt (New York: NYU Press, 1997), 160–187.

102 Dunbar-Nelson, "A Profile of Violet Johnson"; Davis, *Lifting as They Climb*, 360.

103 *Summit Herald*, 24 November 1939.

104 Dunbar-Nelson, "A Profile of Violet Johnson."

105 Calvin Coolidge, "Better Homes," in *Better Homes in America Plan Book for Demonstration Week, October 9 to 14, 1922* (New York: *Delineator*, 1922), 4–6. Calvin Coolidge chaired and Herbert Hoover served as president of the politically conservative Better Homes in America organization founded in 1922 to boost home ownership and consumption. Dolores Hayden, *Redesigning the American Dream: The Future of Housing, Work, and Family Life* (New York: W. W. Norton, 1984), 34; John F. Bauman, *Public Housing, Race, and Renewal: Urban Planning in Philadelphia, 1920–1974* (Philadelphia: Temple University Press, 1987), 15–16.

106 Herbert Hoover, "The Home as an Investment," in *Better Homes in America Plan Book for Demonstration Week, October 9 to 14 1922* (New York: *Delineator*, 1922), 7–8.

107 Kim E. Nielsen concludes, "Clearly, the home was more than a simple physical space in these arguments. It was the metaphorical, and vulnerable, source of national well-being. It was the embodiment of the patriarchal family." Kim E. Nielsen, *Un-American Womanhood: Antiradicalism, Antifeminism, and the First Red Scare* (Columbus: Ohio State University Press, 2001), 99. Between 1922 and 1929, half of the new homes Americans built were single-family dwellings. On the ideological shift from renting to home ownership, see Margaret Marsh, *Suburban Lives* (New Brunswick: Rutgers University Press, 1990), 129–155; Paul H. Mattingly, *Suburban Landscapes: Culture and Politics in a New York Metropolitan Community* (Baltimore: Johns Hopkins University Press, 2001), 154; Harlan Hahn, "Ethnic Minorities: Politics and the Family in Suburbia," in *The Urbanization of the Suburbs*, ed. Louis Masotti and Jeffrey K. Hadden (Beverly Hills: Sage Publications, 1973), 186; Rosalyn Baxnall and Elizabeth Ewen, *Picture Windows: How the Suburbs Happened* (New York: Basic Books, 2000), 29.

108 *Summit Herald*, 15 May 1923.

109 *Ibid.*

110 *Ibid.* On the politics of maternalism, see Molly Ladd-Taylor, *Mother-Work: Women, Child Welfare, and the State, 1890–1930* (Urbana: University of Illinois Press, 1994), 44; Susan Lynn, *Progressive Women in Conservative Times: Racial Justice, Peace, and Feminism, 1945 to the 1960s* (New Brunswick, N.J.: Rutgers University Press, 1992), 4.

111 *Summit Herald*, 15 May 1923.

112 *Ibid.*; NJSFCWC, *Yearbook, 1923*, 30. Organized in 1897, the elite women's civic agency lobbied on municipal health and environmental issues at the city, county, and state levels.

113 *Summit Herald*, 15 May 1923. On "city beautiful" planning for New York City and suburbs, see *New York Times*, 11 May 1922, 1.

114 Dunbar-Nelson, "Negro Women in War Work," 376.

CHAPTER 4. "UNHOLY AND UNCHRISTIAN ATTITUDE"

1 W. E. B. Du Bois, "Returning Soldiers," *Crisis* XVIII (May 1919), 13.

2 "The Glorious Task of Lifting as We Climb," *Competitor* 3:1 (1920), 40.

3 New Jersey State Federation of Colored Women's Clubs, *Proceedings of the New Jersey State Federation of Colored Women's Clubs Conference and First and Second and Third Annual Meetings, July 1915–1918*, 31, Florence Randolph Collection, MG 1321, Folder 2. New Jersey Historical Society (hereafter cited as NJSFCWC, *Proceedings*, FRC).

4 William B. Tuttle, *Race Riot: Chicago in the Red Summer of 1919* (New York: Atheneum, 1970); Theodore Kornweibel, Jr., *"Seeing Red": Federal Campaigns against Black Militancy, 1919–1925* (Bloomington: Indiana University Press, 1998); Robert K. Murray, *Red Scare: A Study of National Hysteria, 1919–1920* (New York: McGraw-Hill, 1955); Nan Elizabeth Woodruff, "The New Negro in the American Congo: World War I and the Elaine, Arkansas Massacre of 1919," in *Time Longer than Rope: A Century of African American Activism, 1850–1950*, ed. Charles M. Payne and Adam Green (New York: NYU Press, 2003), 150–178.

5 Violet Johnson to His Excellency Woodrow Wilson, 5 August 1919, Woodrow Wilson Papers Project, Order No. 141, File VI, Boxes 191–196, Reel No. 1, Princeton University, Princeton, N.J.; *Summit Herald*, 8 August 1919.

6 Violet Johnson to His Excellency Woodrow Wilson, 5 August 1919. On the linkage between sexual violence and racial domination, historian Danielle L. McGuire writes, "Rape like lynching and murder, served as a tool of psychological and physical intimidation that expressed white male domination and buttressed white supremacy." Danielle L. McGuire, "'It Was Like All of Us Had Been Raped': Sexual Violence, Community Mobilization, and the African American Freedom Struggle," *Journal of American History* 91 (December 2004): 907. Ida B. Wells made the same connection in the 1890s. Patricia A. Schechter, *Ida B. Wells-Barnett and American Reform, 1880–1930* (Chapel Hill: University of North Carolina Press, 2001); Paula J. Giddings, *Ida: A Sword among Lions: Ida B. Wells and the Campaign against Lynching* (New York: Amistad, 2008); Mia Bay, *To Tell the Truth Freely: The Life of Ida B. Wells* (New York: Hill and Wang, 2009); Gail Bederman, *Manliness and Civilization: A Cultural History of Gender and Race in the United States, 1880–1917* (Chicago: University of Chicago Press, 1995), 45–76 .

7 Violet Johnson to His Excellency Woodrow Wilson, 5 August 1919. During the "Red Summer" of labor and racial unrest, several African American religious groups called for government intervention. See *Asbury Park Evening Press*, 19 August 1919, 2; New England Missionary Baptist Convention, *Minutes of the Forty-Fifth Annual Session, Held in New York City, June 10–17, 1919*, 27, American Baptist Manuscript Collection, American Baptist Historical Society. On the postwar intersection of race and labor that stoked the "red scare," see Glenda Elizabeth Gilmore, *Defying Dixie: The Radical Roots of Civil Rights, 1919–1950* (New York: W. W. Norton, 2008), 15–66; Tuttle, *Race Riot*; Kornweibel, *"Seeing Red."*

8 NJSFCWC, *Proceedings, Minutes of the Fifth Annual Session, Held in Jersey City, New Jersey, July 7–9, 1920*, 6.

9 *Ibid.*, 6. Emphasis added.

10 *Ibid.*, 5.

11 NJSFCWC, *Yearbook, Minutes, 30 March 1921*, 9, FRC, MG1321; William Pickens, "The Woman Voter Hits the Color Line," *Nation* 3 (6 October 1920), 372–373; Rosalyn Terborg-Penn, *African American Women in the Struggle for the Vote, 1850–1920* (Bloomington: Indiana University Press, 1998), 155.

12 NJSFCWC, *Yearbook, Minutes, July 28–29, 1921*, 10, 19; and *October 20, 1921*, 12. The Tulsa Riot lasted from 30 May to 1 June 1921. Alfred L. Brophy, *Reconstructing the Dreamland: The Tulsa Riot of 1921: Race, Reparations and Reconciliation* (New York: Oxford University Press, 2002); Scott Ellsworth, *Death in a Promised Land: The Tulsa Race Riot of 1921* (Baton Rouge: Louisiana State University Press, 1982).

13 "Meet Me at the Annual Convention in Newark, N.J. June 18 to 23, 1922," NAACP Papers, Group 1, Series G, Reel 8, Microfilm Collection, Rutgers University, New Brunswick, New Jersey.

14 The Senate would defeat the bill in December. *Chicago Defender*, 9 December 1922, 8; Robert L. Zangrando, *The NAACP Crusade against Lynching, 1909–1950* (Philadelphia: Temple University Press, 1980), 42–43; Richard B. Sherman, "The Harding

Administration and the Negro: An Opportunity Lost," *Journal of Negro History* 49 (July 1964): 160–162.

15 NJSFCWC, *Yearbook, Minutes, October 5, 1922,* 16; Press Service of the NAACP, June 1922, NAACP Papers, Group 1, Series, G, Reel 8.

16 "N.A.A.C.P. Newark Conference Opens with Anti-Lynching Parade," NAACP Papers, Group 1, Series G, Reel, 8; *Newark Evening News,* 19 June 1922, 10; NJSFCWC, *Proceedings,* 1922, 6; Mary Jane Brown, *Eradicating Evil: Women in the American Anti-Lynching Movement, 1892–1940* (New York: Garland, 2000), 144.

17 *Newark Evening News,* 21 June 1922, 10.

18 Press Release, 21 June 1922, NAACP Papers, Group 1, Series G, Reel 8.

19 *Newark Evening News,* 21 June 1922, 10.

20 National Convention of the National Woman's Party, February 15–18, 1921, National Woman's Party Papers, Series II, Part L, No. 1B, Reel, 115, Microfilm Collection, Rutgers University; Nancy F. Cott, "Feminist Politics in the 1920s: The National Woman's Party," *Journal of American History* 71 (June 1984), 51; Rosalyn Terborg-Penn, "African American Women and the Woman Suffrage Movement," in *One Woman, One Vote: Rediscovering the Woman Suffrage Movement,* ed. Marjorie Spruill Wheeler (Troutdale, Oreg.: NewSage Press, 1996), 153.

21 Ella Rush Murray to the Editor of *The Suffragist,* 15 November 1920; Mary White Ovington to Mrs. Harriet Stanton Blatch, 3 December 1920; Mary White Ovington to Miss Lucy Burns, 17 December 1920; Headquarters Secretary to Mrs. Harriot Stanton Blatch, 29 December 1920, NAACP Papers, Group 1 Series, Rutgers University Library, Microfilm Series; Freda Kirchwey, "Alice Paul Pulls the Strings," *Nation* 112 (2 March 1921), 332–333; Cott, "Feminist Politics in the 1920s," 43–68.

22 Mary B. Talbert to James Weldon Johnson, 28 June 1922, *Agreement between the Anti-Lynching Crusaders and the N.A.A.C.P.,* NAACP Papers, Anti-Lynching Campaign, 1912–1955, Series B, Manuscript Division, LOC; Rosalyn Terborg-Penn, "African American Women's Networks in the Anti-Lynching Crusade," in *Gender, Class, Race, Reform in the Progressive Era,* ed. Noralee Frankel and Nancy S. Dye (Lexington: University of Kentucky Press, 1991), 148–161; Brown, *Eradicating Evil,* 144–145. Brown incorrectly identifies Helen Curtis, a member of Talbert's organizational team, as NJSF-CWC president.

23 Brown, *Eradicating Evil,* 127–169; Lisa G. Materson, *For the Freedom of Her Race: Black Women and Electoral Politics in Illinois, 1877–1932* (Chapel Hill: University of North Carolina Press, 2009), 136–137.

24 Rosalyn Terborg-Penn, "Discontented Black Feminists: Prelude and Postscript to the Passage of the Nineteenth Amendment," in *Decades of Discontent: The Women's Movement, 1920–1940,* ed. Lois Scharf and Joan M. Jensen (Westport, Conn.: Greenwood Press, 1983), 272.

25 Nancy Marie Robertson, *Christian Sisterhood, Race Relations and the YWCA, 1906–46* (Urbana: University of Illinois Press, 2007), 96.

26 Estelle Freedman, "Separatism as Strategy: Female Institution Building and American Feminism, 1870–1930," *Feminism Studies* 5 (Fall 1979): 522–524.

27 Jacquelyn Dowd Hall, *Revolt against Chivalry: Jessie Daniel Ames and the Women's Campaign against Lynching* (New York: Columbia University Press, 1979), 166; Nancy Cott, *The Grounding of Modern Feminism* (New Haven: Yale University Press, 1987).

28 *Summit Herald*, 5 January 1923; NAACP Papers, January 18, 1931, Series B. The Northeast, Part 12: Selected Branch Files 1913–1939, Reel 1; Mark R. Schneider, *"We Return Fighting": The Civil Rights Movement in the Jazz Age* (Boston: Northeastern University Press, 2002).

29 NJSFCWC, *Yearbook, Minutes October 5–9, 1922*, 20–21.

30 NJSFCWC, *Yearbook, Minutes October 26, 1923*, 30; Brown, *Eradicating Evil*, 152; Elizabeth Lindsey Davis, *Lifting As They Climb: The National Association of Colored Women* (Washington: National Association of Colored Women, 1933), 172.

31 NJSFCWC, *Yearbook, Minutes October 5–9, 1922*, 21.

32 David M. Chalmers, *Hooded Americanism: The History of the Ku Klux Klan, 1865–1965* (Garden City, N.Y.: Doubleday, 1965), 3, 243–247; Shawn Lay, *Hooded Knights on the Niagara: The Ku Klux Klan in Buffalo, New York* (New York: NYU Press, 1995), 39.

33 *New York Times*, 30 August 1921, 24; Alma White, *Heroes of the Fiery Cross* (Zarepath, N.J.: Good Citizen, 1928). Membership estimates range from a low of 12,000 to a high of 65,000. *New York Times*, 1 September 1923, S8; Kenneth T. Jackson, *The Ku Klux Klan in the City 1915–1930* (New York: Oxford University Press, 1967), 236.

34 *New York Times*, 30 August 1921, 24; (daylight parades with Protestant ministers and elected officials) *New York Times*, 2 June 1923, 13 and 4 June 1923, S8; (rally to protest the hiring of an African American woman public school teacher) E. Frederic Morrow, *Way Down South Up North* (Philadelphia: Pilgrim Press, 1973), 95.

35 *Summit Herald*, 6 October 1922 and 5 August 1924; *New York Times*, 28 May 1923, 1. Women and girls joined the "Loties" (Ladies of the Invisible Empire) and the "Tri-K." *New York Times*, 3 June 1923, S8 and 19 August 1923, 2; Chalmers, *Hooded Americanism*, 245–246; Kathleen M. Blee, *Women of the Klan: Racism and Gender in the 1920s* (Berkeley: University of California Press, 1991); Nancy MacLean, *Behind the Mask of Chivalry: The Making of the Second Ku Klux Klan* (New York: Oxford University Press, 1994); MacLean, "White Women, Klan Violence in the 1920s: Agency, Complicity, and the Politics of Women's History," *Gender and History* 3 (1991): 285–303; Paul Murphy, "Sources and Natures of Intolerance in the 1920's," *Journal of American History* 51 (June 1964): 60–76.

36 *New York Times*, 26 November 1923, 14.

37 *Summit Herald*, 19 April 1935. On the Klan's demise, see *New York Times*, 5 April, 1924, 17; Michael J. Birkner, *A Country Place No More: The Transformation of Bergenfield, New Jersey, 1894–1994* (Rutherford, N.J.: Fairleigh Dickinson University Press, 1994), 86; Rudolph J. Vecoli, *The People of New Jersey* (Princeton, N.J.: D. Van Nostrand Inc., 1965), 211, 213.

38 NJSFCWC, *Yearbook, Minutes October 5–9, 1922*, 21.

NOTES | 191

39 *Summit Herald*, 25 January 1924.

40 *Ibid.*

41 Molly Ladd-Taylor, *Mother-Work: Women, Child Welfare, and the State, 1890–1930* (Urbana: University of Illinois Press, 1994), 63.

42 The verse is from James Russell Lowell's "Stanzas on Freedom." The women added that they joined "in spirit" with the more than two thousand protesters mobilized against the statue in Washington, D.C. *Summit Herald*, 30 March 1923. On the Daughters of the Confederacy and the "Mammy" statue, see Deborah Gray White, *Too Heavy a Load: Black Women in Defense of Themselves, 1894–1994* (New York: W. W. Norton, 1999), 134.

43 *Summit Herald*, 17 June 1924.

44 Richard B. Sherman, *The Republican Party and Black America from McKinley to Hoover, 1896–1933* (Charlottesville: University Press of Virginia, 1973), 206; Jackson, *The Ku Klux Klan in the City*, 248; Robert Allen, *Reluctant Reformers: Racism and Social Reform Movements in the United States* (Washington: Howard University Press, 1983), 98.

45 *Special Committee of the Council of Women for Home Missions*, 19 January 1923, National Council of Churches Papers, RG 18, Box 56, Folder 11, Presbyterian Historical Society, Philadelphia, Pa. (hereafter cited as NCCP).

46 *Newark Evening News*, 9 February 1920, 14.

47 *New York Times* 31 January 1923, 2. The FCC hoped "gradually to shift the motive" for Race Relations Sunday "from one for Lincoln's sake to one for Jesus." George Edmund Haynes, "Changing Racial Attitudes and Customs," *Phylon* 2 (1st Qtr. 1941): 28; David M. Reimers, *White Protestantism and the Negro* (New York: Oxford University Press, 1963), 84–92; Ronald C. White, Jr., *Liberty and Justice for All: Racial Reform and the Social Gospel, 1877–1925* (San Francisco: Harper & Row, 1990), 245–260; Nina Mjagkij, *Light in the Darkness: African Americans and the YMCA, 1852–1946* (Lexington: University Press of Kentucky, 1994), 101–106.

48 *New Jersey Baptist Bulletin*, March 1921; Norman H. Maring, *Baptists in New Jersey: A Study in Transition* (Valley Forge, Pa.: Judson Press, 1964), 341.

49 On post-war militancy, see Adriane Lentz-Smith, *Freedom Struggles: African Americans and World War I* (Cambridge, Mass.: Harvard University Press, 2009); Nikki Brown, *Private Politics and Public Voices: Black Women's Activism from World War I to the New Deal* (Bloomington: Indiana University Press, 2006); Barbara Foley, *Spectres of 1919: Class and Nation in the Making of the New Negro* (Urbana: University of Illinois Press, 2003); Mark Whalen, *The Great War and the Culture of the New Negro* (Gainesville: University Press of Florida, 2008); Beth Tompkins Bates, *Pullman Porters and the Rise of Protest Politics in Black America, 1925–1945* (Chapel Hill: University of North Carolina Press, 2001).

50 Gail Bederman, "'The Women Have Had Charge of the Church Work Long Enough': The Men and Religion Forward Movement of 1911–1912 and the Masculinization of Middle-Class Protestantism," *American Quarterly* 41 (September 1989): 454. Nancy Marie Robertson argues that Christian women's socially radical stance

provided one reason for male subordination. Nancy Marie Robertson, *Christian Sisterhood, Race Relations and the YWCA, 1906–46* (Urbana: University of Illinois Press, 2007), 108, 115.

51 On gender conflicts in middle-class African American fraternal societies and lodges, see Martin Summers, *Manliness and Its Discontents: The Black Middle Class and the Transformation of Masculinity, 1900–1930* (Chapel Hill: University of North Carolina Press, 2004).

52 NJSFCWC, *Yearbook, Minutes,* October 25–26, 1923, 40; Violet A. Johnson to "My dear friend," 17 November 1936, Nannie H. Burroughs Papers, Box 15, General Correspondence, Manuscript Division, LOC (hereafter cited as NHBP). For a different model of gender relations in the interwar period, see Anthea D. Butler, *Women in the Church of God in Christ: Making a Sanctified World* (Chapel Hill: University of North Carolina Press, 2007).

53 On these well-documented meetings, see Terborg-Penn, "African-American Women's Networks in the Anti-Lynching Crusade," 156; Brown, *Eradicating Evil*, 133–134; Jacquelyn Dowd Hall, *Revolt against Chivalry: Jessie Daniel Ames and the Women's Campaign against Lynching* (New York: Columbia University Press, 1979), 87–94; Dorothy C. Salem, *To Better Our World: Black Women in Organized Reform, 1890–1920* (Brooklyn, N.Y.: Carlson Publishing, 1990), 238; Adrienne Lash Jones, "Struggle among Saints: African American Women and the YWCA, 1870–1920," in *Men and Women Adrift: The YMCA and YWCA in the City,* ed. Nina Mjagkij and Margaret Spratt (New York: NYU Press, 1997), 160–187.

54 *Church Women in Interracial Cooperation, Prepared by the Continuation Committee of the Interracial Conference of Church Women Held at Eagles Mere, Pa., September 21–22, 1926, Pamphlet Number Seven, December, 1926,* 1, NCCP, RG 18, Box 56, Folder 13; also Bettye Collier-Thomas, *Jesus, Jobs, and Justice: African American Women and Religion* (New York: Alfred Knopf, 2010), 312–325; Betty Livingston Adams, "'The Best Hotel on the Boardwalk': Church Women, Negro Art, and the Construction of Interracial Space in the Interwar Years," in Sally Promey, ed., *Sensational Religion: Sensory Cultures in Material Practice* (New Haven: Yale University Press, 2014), 275–296; Janine Marie Denomme, "'To End This Day of Strife': Churchwomen and the Campaign for Integration, 1920–1970" (Ph.D. diss. University of Pennsylvania, 2001), 65–70.

55 *Church Women in Interracial Cooperation, Pamphlet Number Seven, December, 1926,* 1–2.

56 *Ibid.,* 3–4.

57 Gilmore, *Defying Dixie,* 203.

58 Haynes, "Changing Racial Attitudes and Customs," 28. For Haynes, "race" was a sociological construct produced by shared experiences rather than fixed biology. Though race consciousness, like class or caste consciousness, resulted in social distance, as a "phenomenon," like public opinion, it was amenable to education. George Edmund Haynes, *The Trend of the Races* (New York: Council of Women for Home Missions and Missionary Education of the United States and Canada, 1922), 13 n1, 67;

also Robert E. Park, "The Nature of Race Relations," in *Race Relations and the Race Problem: A Definition and an Analysis*, ed. Edgar T. Thompson (Durham, N.C.: Duke University Press, 1939), 3.

59 Haynes, *The Trend of the Races*, 86. Haynes differentiated "the rising tide of race consciousness, the manifestation of a people becoming aware of its intrinsic worth" from the "rising tide of color" rhetoric of eugenicist Lothrop Stoddard who "failed to adhere to good science in facts and argument." Haynes, *The Trend of the Races*, 151; Lothrop Stoddard, *The Rising Tide of Color against White World-Supremacy*, 1921; reprint (Westport, Conn.: Negro Universities Press, 1971); Lothrop Stoddard, *Clashing Tides of Color* (New York: Charles Scribner's Sons, 1935).

60 *Church Women in Interracial Cooperation, Pamphlet Number Seven, December, 1926*, 5. Emphasis in original.

61 *Ibid.*, 5–7.

62 *Ibid.*, 6. Emphasis added.

63 White southerners included Jessie Daniel Ames, a Methodist member of the CIC's Women's Committee and future president of the Association of Southern Women for the Prevention of Lynching. As Paul Allen Carter concluded, from 1920 to 1940 American ecumenism never extended beyond the separate but equal doctrine. Paul Allen Carter, *The Decline and Revival of the Social Gospel: Social and Political Liberalism in American Protestant Churches, 1920–1940* (Ithaca, N.Y.: Cornell University Press, 1954), 195–196. On the racial divide in Protestant churches, see James B. Bennett, *Religion and the Rise of Jim Crow in New Orleans* (Princeton, N.J.: Princeton University Press, 2005); Morris Davis, *The Methodist Unification: Christianity and the Politics of Race in the Jim Crow Era* (New York: NYU Press, 2008); Donald K. Gorrell, *The Age of Social Responsibility: The Social Gospel in the Progressive Era, 1900–1920* (Macon, Ga.: Mercer University Press, 1988); John F. Piper, *The American Churches in World War I* (Athens: Ohio University Press, 1985). On Protestant women's ecumenism, see Gladys Gilkey Calkins, *Follow Those Women: Church Women in the Ecumenical Movement, a History of the Development of United Work among Women of the Protestant Churches in the United States* (New York: National Council of Churches, 1961); Kendal P. Mobley, "The Ecumenical Woman's Missionary Movement: Helen Barrett Montgomery and *The Baptist*, 1920–30," in *Gender and the Social Gospel*, ed. Wendy J. Deichmann Edwards and Carolyn DeSwarte Gifford (Urbana: University of Illinois Press, 2003), 167–181.

64 *Minutes of the Meeting of the Church Women's Committee on Race Relations, Held Monday, February 28, 1927, Federal Council Conference Room*, NCC Papers, RG 18, Box 56, Folder 11; Collier-Thomas, *Jesus, Justice, Jobs*, 339.

65 *Findings of the Interracial Conference of Church Women of Philadelphia and Adjacent Territory Held at the Woolman School, Wyncote, Pa., May 13–15, 1927*, NCCP, RG 18, Box 56, Folder 13; "Church Women Plan for Better Race Relations," *Federal Council Bulletin* (June 1927), 13, NCCP, RG 18, Box 56, Folder 13.

66 Gloria T. Hull, ed., *The Works of Alice Dunbar-Nelson*, Vol. 2 (New York: Oxford University Press, 1988), 230.

67 Press Release Federal Council of Churches, 1928, NCCP, RG 18, Box 56, Folder 13; *Summit Herald*, 14 September 1928; *Chicago Defender*, 29 September 1928, 5.

68 *Second General Interracial Conference of Church Women, Eagles Mere, Pa., September 18–19, 1928*, 5, NCCP, RG 18, Box 56, Folder 13; "Church Women in Interracial Conference," *Federal Council Bulletin* XI (September 1928), 21; and XI (October 1928), 13–14.

69 Gloria T. Hull, ed., *Give Us Each Day: The Diary of Alice Dunbar-Nelson* (New York: W. W. Norton, 1984), 265.

70 Hull, ed., *The Works of Alice Dunbar-Nelson*, 230–231.

71 *Ibid.*.

72 *New Jersey Interracial Conference of Church Women, Stacy-Trent Hotel, Trenton, N.J. and New Jersey Training School, Bordentown, N.J., May 8–9, 1929*; Katherine Gardner to Dear Friends, 1 June 1929, NCCP, RG 18, Box 56, Folder 13.

73 Katherine Gardner to Dear Friends, 1 June 1929, NCCP.

74 *Ibid.*; Marion Thompson Wright, *The Education of Negroes in New Jersey*, 1941; reprint (AMS Press, 1972), 183–194. For examples of school segregation in other northern locations, see Kimberly L. Phillips, *Alabama North: African-American Migrants, Community, and Working-Class Activism in Cleveland, 1915–1945* (Chicago: University of Illinois Press, 1999), 159; William B. Thomas, "Schooling as a Political Instrument of Social Control: Social Response to Black Migrant Youth in Buffalo, New York, 1917–1940," in *The Great Migration and After, 1917–1930*, ed. Kenneth L. Kusmer (New York: Garland, 1991), 217–230.

75 Katherine Gardner to Dear Friends, 1 June 1929, NCCP.

76 *Report of the New Jersey Interracial Conference of Church Women held in Trenton, N.J., May 8, 9, and 10, 1930*, NCCP, RG 18, Box 56, Folder 13. Liberal Protestants believed in the transformative effect of fine art, personally and nationally. Sally Promey, "Taste Cultures: The Visual Practice of Liberal Protestantism, 1940–1965," in Laurie F. Maffly-Kipp, Leigh E. Schmidt, and Mark Valeri, ed., *Practicing Protestants: Histories of Christian Life in America, 1630–1965* (Baltimore: Johns Hopkins University Press, 2006), 250–293; David Morgan, *The Sacred Gaze: Religious Visual Culture in Theory and Practice* (Berkeley: University of California Press, 2005); Adams, "'The Best Hotel on the Boardwalk.'"

77 *Report of the New Jersey Interracial Conference of Church Women, May 8, 9, 10, 1930.*

78 The New Jersey Church Women's Interracial Conference sites included Trenton (April 1932), Newark YWCA (March 1933), Bethany Baptist Church, Newark (February 1934), Camden (May 1934), and Wallace Chapel AME Zion Church, Summit (May 1937).

79 *Summit Herald*, 29 January 1929; *Sixtieth Anniversary Souvenir Journal of the Wallace Chapel African Methodist Episcopal Zion Church, 1983*, copy in author's possession; Collier-Thomas, *Jesus, Jobs, Justice*, 341.

80 *Summit Herald*, 25 September 1931.

81 *Ibid.* On competition for domestic service jobs and the exploitation of black women, see Anna Arnold Hedgeman, *The Trumpet Sounds: A Memoir of Negro Leadership* (New York: Holt, Rinehart and Winston, 1964), 68–69; Lois Scharf, *To Work and*

to Wed: Female Employment, Feminism, and the Great Depression (Wesport, Conn.: Greenwood Press, 1980), 43–45, 95, 114; Julia Kirk Blackwelder, *Women of the Depression: Caste and Culture in San Antonio, 1939–1949* (College Station: Texas A & M Press, 1984), 76–87, 109, 122; Jacqueline Jones, *Labor of Love, Labor of Sorrow: Black Women, Work, and the Family from Slavery to the Present* (New York: Vintage Books, 1986), 205–208; Deborah Gray White, *Too Heavy a Load: Black Women in Defense of Themselves, 1894–1994* (New York: W. W. Norton, 1998), 145; Nancy J. Weiss, *The National Urban League, 1910–1940* (New York: Oxford University Press, 1974), 253.

82 *Summit Herald*, 25 September 1931.

83 Walter White, Assistant Secretary, to Dr. George E. Cannon, 29 January 1923; and George E. Cannon to Miss Mary White Ovington, 14 February, 1923, NAACP Papers, Part 1, Box C 275, Folder 2.

84 *New York Herald Tribune*, 29 April 1926, n.p., clipping, NAACP Papers, Administrative File, Box IC 362, Folder 5.

85 *Sunday Call*, 2 May 1926, n.p., clipping, NAACP Papers, Administrative File, Box IC363, Folder 7.

86 *Newark Evening News*, 3 May 1926, n.p., clipping, NAACP Papers, Administrative File, Box IC 362, Folder 5; Maring, *Baptists in New Jersey*, 341.

87 Rev. George Sayre Miller to Gentlemen, 15 May, 192[6], Walter White to Rev. George Sayre Miller, 24 May, 1926, NAACP Papers, Administrative File, Box IC 362, Folder 5; *New York Herald Tribune*, 29 April 1926, clippings, NAACP Papers, Administrative File, Box IC 363, Folder 7.

88 *Summit Herald*, 25 September 1928.

89 *Ibid.*

90 On public school gerrymandering, see Wright, *The Education of Negroes in New Jersey*, 194; Morrow, *Way Down South Up North*, 16. Though Summit's black population doubled between 1920 and 1930, increasing to 8.7 percent of the total population of 14,457, growth alone does not explain the hysteria that turned northern classrooms into segregated space. As early as 1914 Northwestern University in Evanston, Illinois, excluded African American women from dormitories; Harvard University closed its dormitories to black men in 1923. Andrew Wiese, *Places of Their Own: African American Suburbanization in the Twentieth Century* (Chicago: University of Chicago Press, 2005), 63; Willard B. Gatewood, Jr., *Aristocrats of Color: The Black Elite, 1880–1920* (Bloomington: Indiana University Press, 1990), 147; David Levering Lewis, *W. E. B. Du Bois: The Fight for Equality and the American Century, 1919–1963* (New York: Henry Holt, 2000), 88–90.

91 *Summit Herald*, 17 January 1928. Of his suburban school experience, Morrow wrote, "There were so many Negroes in the special class that one who wasn't stood out in bold relief." Morrow, *Way Down South Up North*, 13.

92 *Summit Herald*, 18 March 1932; 22 April 1932; and 13 May 1932; Davis, *Lifting as They Climb*, 364.

93 *Summit Herald*, 22 December 1931.

94 *Summit Herald*, 6 August 1929 and 27 August 1929.

95 *Summit Herald*, 24 September 1929.

96 James C. Scott, *Domination and the Arts of Resistance: Hidden Transcripts* (New Haven, Conn.: Yale University Press, 1990).

97 *Summit Herald*, 20 September 1929. On the Episcopalian rector, see *New York Times*, 17 September 1929, 20; and 18 September 1929, 64; David M. Reimers, *White Protestantism and the Negro* (New York: Oxford University Press, 1963), 101–102; Robert Moats Miller, "The Attitude of American Protestantism toward the Negro, 1919–1939," *Journal of Negro History* 41 (July 1956): 219.

98 *Summit Herald*, 27 September 1929.

99 *Summit Herald*, 5 November 1929.

100 *Summit Herald*, 29 September 1936. Black men formed a car pool to transport boys for two hours of swimming at the segregated Orange YMCA, about fifteen miles away. On the controversy surrounding the construction of the segregated pool, see Robertson, *Christian Sisterhood*, 117.

101 *Summit Herald*, 30 April 1935. The white board offered to assist in forming an "independent Colored Y.M.C.A. if they desire such an organization."

102 *Summit Herald*, 7 May 1935. Though the Lincoln YMCA elected its own board of managers, Summit's white elite exerted influence through control of the suburb's resources.

103 The Women's Auxiliary sponsored a range of activities that fused the sacred and secular, including teen and adult dances, a Negro Life and History club, and a coed choral group. *Summit Herald*, 25 January 1935; 4 August 1941; and 30 March 1944, *passim*. On the fusion of the secular and sacred in the production of an African American mass culture, see Evelyn Brooks Higginbotham, "Rethinking Vernacular Culture: Black Religion and Race Records in the 1920s and 1930s," in *The House that Race Built: Black Americans, U.S. Terrain*, ed. Lubiano Wahneema (New York: Pantheon Books, 1997), 157–177.

104 *Summit Herald*, 19 June 1936.

105 Luncheon Conference of the New Jersey Interracial Conference of Church Women, May 13, 1937, Summit, New Jersey, NCCP, RG 18, Box 56, Folder 13; *Summit Herald*, 18 May 1937.

CHAPTER 5. "PUTTING REAL AMERICAN IDEALS IN AMERICAN LIFE"

1 New Jersey State Federation Colored Women's Clubs, *Proceedings of the New Jersey State Federation of Colored Women's Clubs Conference and First, Second, and Third Annual Meetings, Trenton, Englewood, Plainfield, Bordentown, July 1915–1918, 1920*, 9, Florence Randolph Collection, MG 1321, New Jersey Historical Society (hereafter cited as NJSFCWC, *Proceedings*, and FRC).

2 NJSFCWC, *Yearbook, Eighth Annual Convention, Atlantic City, New Jersey, October 24–26, 1923*, 30, FRC, MG 1321.

3 NJSFCWC, *Yearbook, Seventh Annual Convention, Paterson, New Jersey, October 5, 1922*, 17. The politics of home was not the sole province of middle-class women.

Black working women formulated an understanding of respectability and home that extended beyond the nuclear family to the entire community.

4 Elizabeth Lindsay Davis, *Lifting as They Climb: The National Association of Colored Women* (Washington: National Association of Colored Women, 1933), 358.

5 *Chicago Defender*, 1 November 1924, A5.

6 NJSFCWC, *Proceedings*, 1917, 14.

7 NJSFCWC, *Yearbook*, 1922, 19.

8 *Ibid.*, 18.

9 *Ibid.*, 19.

10 *Ibid.*, 19.

11 *Ibid.*, 19–22.

12 Davis, *Lifting as They Climb*, 200.

13 "In the Political Arena: Women's Work in Essex County, N.J.," *Competitor*, 3:4 (1921), 34.

14 NJSFCWC, *Yearbook, 1922*, 20. The legislation updated the state's 1884 civil rights statute, but failed to provide an effective mechanism for prosecuting violations.

15 NJSFCWC, *Yearbook*, 1923, 34–35.

16 NJSFCWC, *Yearbook, 1923*, 25, 34–35; Felice D. Gordon, *After Winning: The Legacy of New Jersey Suffragists, 1920–1947* (New Brunswick: Rutgers University Press, 1986), 81. Molly Ladd-Taylor sees the maternalist ideology of white middle-class women as "racial politics" that emerged in the context of white alarm over "race suicide." Molly Ladd-Taylor, *Mother-Work: Women, Child Welfare, and the State, 1890–1930* (Urbana: University of Illinois Press, 1994), 4–5, 49.

17 *New York Times*, 28 September 1921, 3.

18 Davis, *Lifting as They Climb*, 200.

19 NJSFCWC, *Yearbook, 1922*, 21.

20 "The Glorious Task of 'Lifting as We Climb,'" *Competitor*, 3:1 (1921), 40.

21 NJSFCWC, *Yearbook, 1921*, 9; Davis, *Lifting as They Climb*, 358.

22 "In the Political Arena," 34.

23 Gordon, *After Winning*, 79; Gordon, "After Winning: The New Jersey Suffragists in the Political Parties, 1920–30," *New Jersey History* 101 (Fall/Winter 1983): 21, 24. On women's subordinate position nationally, see Kristi Andersen, *After Suffrage: Women and Partisan and Electoral Politics before the New Deal* (Chicago: University of Chicago Press, 1996), 83–84, 142; Nancy F. Cott, "Across the Great Divide: Women in Politics before and after 1920," in *Women, Politics and Change*, ed. Louise A. Tilly and Patricia Gurin (New York: Russell Sage Foundation, 1990), 161; Melanie Susan Gustafson, *Women and the Republican Party, 1854–1924* (Urbana: University of Illinois Press, 2001), 191; Lorraine Gates Schuyler, *The Weight of Their Votes: Southern Women and Political Leverage in the 1920s* (Chapel Hill: University of North Carolina Press, 2006), 27; Jan Doolittle Wilson, *The Women's Joint Congressional Committee and the Politics in Illinois, 1877–1932* (Chapel Hill: University of North Carolina Press, 2009), 18.

24 For an exception, see Priscilla A. Dowden-White, "To See Past the Difference to the Fundamentals: Racial Coalition within the League of Women Voters of St.

Louis, 1920–1946," in *Women Shaping the South: Creating and Confronting Change,* ed. Angela Boswell and Judith N. McArthur (Columbia: University of Missouri Press, 2006), 174–203.

25 NJSFCWC, *Yearbook,1922,* 13.

26 *New York Times,* 14 May 1922, 14.

27 The special train car allowed the women to avoid transferring to Jim Crow cars upon reaching the nation's capital. NJSFCWC, *Yearbook, 1921,* 9.

28 *Chicago Defender,* 26 August 1922, 5; *New York Times,* 15 August 1922, 10; Davis, *Lifting as They Climb,* 67; Rosalyn Terborg-Penn, "African American Women's Networks in the Anti-Lynching Crusade," in *Gender, Class, Race, Reform in the Progressive Era,* ed. Noralee Frankel and Nancy S. Dye (Lexington: University of Kentucky Press, 1991), 153. Terborg-Penn mistakes New Jersey's Ida Brown for spokespersons NACW President Hallie Q. Brown and anti-lynching activist Ida Wells.

29 *Summit Herald,* 22 September 1922.

30 Davis, *Lifting as They Climb,* 358.

31 NJSFCWC, *Yearbook, 1923,* 30.

32 *Ibid.,* 40–41. Randolph's comments suggest that internal distinctions based on class and complexion had surfaced within the increasingly diverse membership.

33 *Newark Evening News,* 20 June 1922, 10.

34 *Ibid.*

35 NJSFCWC, *Yearbook, 1922,* 17. They also endorsed the "dry" Republican gubernatorial candidate who lost to the "wet" Democrat. Congressional candidates targeted by the NAACP lost seats in Michigan and Delaware. Robert L. Zangrando, *The NAACP Crusade against Lynching, 1909–1950* (Philadelphia: Temple University Press, 1980), 74.

36 Davis, *Lifting as They Climb,* 67–69; *Minutes of the National League of Republican Colored Women, Chicago, Ill., August 7–11, 1924,* Nannie Helen Burroughs Papers, Box 309, Division of Manuscript Collection, Library of Congress, Washington, D.C. (hereafter cited as NHBP); Evelyn Brooks Higginbotham, "In Politics to Stay: Black Women Leaders and Party Politics in the 1920s," in *Women, Politics, and Change,* ed. Louise A. Tilly and Patricia Gurin (New York: Russell Sage Foundation, 1990), 199–220; Evelyn Brooks Higginbotham, "Clubwomen and Electoral Politics in the 1920s," in *African American Women and the Vote, 1837–1967,* ed. Ann D. Gordon *et al.* (Amherst: University of Massachusetts, 1997), 134–155; Deborah Gray White, *Too Heavy a Load: Black Women in Defense of Themselves, 1894–1994* (New York: W. W. Norton, 1999), 134–135; Andersen, *After Suffrage,* 84; Nikki Brown, *Private Politics and Public Voices: Black Women's Activism from World War I to the New Deal* (Bloomington: Indiana University Press, 2006), 151–152.

37 Higginbotham, "In Politics to Stay," 206–207.

38 *Chicago Defender,* 12 April 1924, A8.

39 Higginbotham, "Clubwomen and Electoral Politics in the 1920s," 141–144; New Jersey National League of Republican Colored Women (NLRCW) groups, NHB Papers.

40 *Washington Post,* 18 August 1924, 3; and 21 September 1924, 6; *Chicago Defender,* 6 September 1924, A10.

41 *Newark Evening News,* 20 June 1922, 10; *Chicago Defender,* 23 August 1924, 17; and 6 September 1924, A10; Dennis C. Dickerson, "Walter G. Alexander: A Physician in Civil Rights and Public Service," *New Jersey History* 101 (Fall/Winter 1983): 47–48.

42 *Washington Post,* 21 September 1924, 6.

43 *Ibid.; Chicago Defender,* 23 August 1924, 17. Gordon, *After Winning,* 88; Rosalyn Terborg-Penn, *African American Women in the Struggle for the Vote, 1850–1920* (Bloomington: Indiana University Press, 1998), 156.

44 NJSFCWC, *Yearbook, 1923,* 35, 41.

45 *Ibid.,* 35.

46 *Chicago Defender,* 20 October 1928, 4.

47 "Step-by-Step Plans for Organizing Hoover-Curtis Clubs," Issued by Colored Voters Division Republican National Committee" (ca. 1928), Box 309, NHBP; *Summit Herald,* 25 September 1928 and 2 November 1928.

48 "Step-by-Step Plans for Hoover-Curtis Clubs," NHBP.

49 Nannie H. Burroughs, "What the Negro Wants Politically," MS, Box 46, NHBP. On women and the pivotal 1928 election, see Terborg-Penn, *African American Women in the Struggle for the Vote*; Lisa G. Materson, *For the Freedom of Her Race: Black Women and Electoral Politics in Illinois, 1877–1932* (Chapel Hill: University of North Carolina Press, 2009); Higginbotham, "Clubwomen and Electoral Politics in the 1920s," 134–155; Schuyler, *The Weight of Their Votes; Kristi* Andersen, "Women and Citizenship in the 1920s," in *Women, Politics and Change,* ed. Louise A. Tilly and Patricia Gurin (New York: Russell Sage Foundation, 1990), 177–198; Kristi Andersen, *The Creation of a Democratic Majority, 1928–36* (Chicago: University of Chicago Press, 1979); Nancy J. Weiss, *Farewell to the Party of Lincoln: Black Politics in the Age of FDR* (Princeton, N.J.: Princeton University Press, 1983); Ruth C. Silva, *Rum, Religion, and Votes: 1928 Re-Examined* (University Park: Pennsylvania State University Press, 1962); Allan J. Lichtman, *Prejudice and the Old Order: The Presidential Election of 1928* (Chapel Hill: University of North Carolina Press, 1979); Edmund A. Moore, *A Catholic Runs for President: The Campaign of 1928* (New York: Ronald Press Company, 1956); Robert Moats Miller, "A Footnote to the Role of the Protestant Churches in the Election of 1928," *Church History* 25 (June 1956): 145–159; Paul Allen Carter, *The Decline and Revival of the Social Gospel: Social and Political Liberalism in American Protestant Churches, 1920–1940* (Ithaca, N.Y.: Cornell University Press, 1954).

50 Burroughs, "What the Negro Wants Politically." On moral issues as a factor in women's mobilization across political lines, see Andersen, *After Suffrage.*

51 Gordon, *After Winning,* 68–70.

52 Burroughs, "What the Negro Wants Politically." On the recommendation to Hoover to appoint an African American woman to the Children's Bureau, see Kenneth W. Goings, *"The NAACP Comes of Age": The Defeat of Judge John J. Parker* (Bloomington: Indiana University Press, 1990), 44–45. On privileged white women's domination of the Children's Bureau leadership, see Linda Gordon, *Pitied but Not Entitled: Single*

Mothers and the History of Welfare, 1890–1935 (New York: Maxwell Macmillan International, 1994), 71; Linda Gordon, "Black and White Visions of Welfare: Women's Welfare Activism, 1890–1945," *Journal of American History* 70 (September 1991): 559–590; Ladd-Taylor, *Mother-Work*; Gwendolyn Mink, *The Wages of Motherhood: Inequality in the Welfare State, 1917–1942* (Ithaca, N.Y.: Cornell University Press, 1995); Susan Ware, *Beyond Suffrage: Women in the New Deal* (Cambridge, Mass.: Harvard University Press, 1981).

53 *Summit Herald*, 7 December 1928.

54 *Summit Herald*, 14 December 1928.

55 *Summit Herald*, 1 January 1929. On the 1916 celebration, see chapter 1 above.

56 Federal Writers' Project, comp., *The WPA Guide to 1930s New Jersey*, 1939; reprint (New Brunswick, N.J.: Rutgers University Press, 1986), 74.

57 Paul A. Stellhorn, "Boom, Bust and Boosterisms: Attitudes, Residency and the Newark Chamber of Commerce, 1920–1941," in *Urban New Jersey since 1870, Papers Presented at the Sixth Annual New Jersey Historical Symposium*, ed. William C. Wright (Trenton: New Jersey Historical Commission, 1975), 60; David M. Kennedy, *Freedom from Fear: The American People in Depression and War, 1929–1945* (New York: Oxford University Press, 1999), 18, 44; Steve Fraser, "The 'Labor Question,'" in *The Rise and Fall of the New Deal Order, 1930–1980*, ed. Steve Fraser and Gary Gerstle (Princeton, N.J.: Princeton University Press, 1989), 55–84.

58 *Summit Herald*, 15 September 1931.

59 *Summit Herald*, 28 February 1930 and 23 September 1930.

60 *Summit Herald*, 28 February 1930 and 16 January 1931.

61 Violet A. Johnson to "My dear friend," 14 November 1930, Box 15, NHBP.

62 *Summit Herald*, 17 July 1931 and 28 July 1931.

63 *Summit Herald*, 17 July, 1931.

64 *Summit Herald*, 21 July 1931.

65 *Summit Herald*, 4 September 1931.

66 *New York Times*, 2 September 1931, 3; *Summit Herald*, 11 September 1931. The State Emergency Relief Administration met only the last of its objectives: encourage hiring by private enterprises, stimulate new public works projects by dollar-for-dollar match of local funds, and supplement local direct relief funds as necessary. On the disorganization of state and local relief, see Paul Tutt Stafford, *Government and the Needy: A Study of Public Assistance in New Jersey* (Princeton, N.J.: Princeton University Press, 1942), 96–101. For an excellent treatment of the state's response to the Great Depression and New Deal, see Michael J. Birkner, *A Country Place No More: The Transformation of Bergenfield, New Jersey, 1894–1994* (Rutherford, N.J.: Fairleigh Dickinson University Press, 1994).

67 *Summit Herald*, 9 October 1931.

68 *Summit Herald*, 6 November 1931.

69 *Summit Herald*, 1 December 1931.

70 *Summit Herald*, 20 October 1931 and 6 November 1931.

71 *Summit Herald*, 29 March 1932 and 5 April 1932.

72 *Summit Herald*, 25 September 1931.

73 *Summit Herald*, 31 July 1931 and 7 August 1931.

74 *New York Times*, 26 May 1931, 22; and 2 June 1931, 14; *Camden Courier Post*, 29 October 1931. Democrats were "wet" and Republicans, by proposing to repeal the Eighteenth Amendment and leave enforcement of the liquor trade to states, declared themselves "sufficiently moist." *Washington Post*, 21 September 1924, 6.

75 *Summit Herald*, 7 August 1931.

76 *Ibid.*; *New York Times*, 10 June 1931, 2.

77 *Summit Herald*, 11 August 1931. On Oscar DePriest's election, see Wanda A. Hendricks, *Gender, Race, and Politics in the Midwest: Black Club Women in Illinois* (Bloomington: Indiana University Press, 1998).

78 *Summit Herald*, 9 October 1931.

79 *Chicago Defender*, 10 October 1931, 2. White Women's Republican Club leader Lillian Feickert opposed Baird because of his "shabby treatment" of women and his "vicious political machine." *New York Times*, 9 June 1931, 20.

80 The NAACP and the American Federation of Labor opposed the nomination. *New York Times*, 23 July 1931, 6; Kenneth W. Goings, *"The NAACP Comes of Age": The Defeat of Judge John J. Parker* (Bloomington: Indiana University Press, 1990), 19–36.

81 Draft New Jersey State Conference for the National Association for the Advancement of Colored People, 13 April 1931 and David Baird Jr. to Dr. Vernon F. Bunce, 7 May 1931, NAACP Papers, Papers, Group 1, Series B, Reel 8; *Chicago Defender*, 19 September 1931, 13; and 17 October 1931, 14; Goings, *"The NAACP Comes of Age,"* 67–68; Richard L. Watson, "The Defeat of Judge Parker: A Study in Pressure Groups and Politics," *Mississippi Valley Historical Review* 50 (September 1963): 213–234; Richard B. Sherman, *The Republican Party and Black America from McKinley to Hoover, 1896–1933* (Charlottesville: University Press of Virginia, 1973), 239–246; Harvard Sitkoff, *A New Deal for Blacks: The Emergence of Civil Rights as a National Issue: The Depression Decade* (Oxford: Oxford University Press, 1978), 86.

82 *Camden Courier*, 29 October 1931.

83 *Ibid.*

84 *Summit Herald*, 14 October 1932.

85 *Summit Herald*, October 25, 1932 and 4 November 1932.

86 *Summit Herald*, 25 September 1931.

87 *Summit Herald*, 3 November, 1931.

88 *New York Times*, 5 November 1931, 3; and 6 November 1931; *Chicago Defender*, 14 November 1931, 14; and 21 November 1931, 4. Of the 90,000 African American votes cast statewide, 75,000 were against Baird. Goings, *"The NAACP Comes of Age,"* 73; Sherman, *The Republican Party and Black America*, 246.

89 *Summit Herald*, 6 November, 1931.

90 *Summit Herald*, 18 October 1932.

91 *Ibid.*

92 Violet Johnson to "My very dear friend," 5 November, 1932, NHBP, Box 15.

93 *Summit Herald*, 14 October 1932.

94 *Ibid.*

95 Violet Johnson to "My very dear friend," 5 November, 1932.

96 *Ibid.* There are no extant copies of Johnson's speeches or articles in the Burroughs collection. On women's diverse campaign activities, see Paula Baker, "'She is the Best Man on the Ward Committee': Women in Grassroots Party Organizations, 1930s–1950s," in *We Have Come to Stay: American Women and Political Parties, 1880–1960*, ed. Melanie Gustafson, Kristie Miller, and Elisabeth I. Perry (Albuquerque: University of New Mexico Press, 1999), 151–160.

97 *Summit Herald*, 18 October 1932.

98 Violet A. Johnson to "My very dear friend," 5 November 1932.

99 *Summit Herald*, 11 November 1932.

100 Nannie H. Burroughs to "My dear Miss Johnson," 15 November 1932, NHBP, Box 39.

101 *Summit Herald*, 30 December 1932. On black women's use of public prayer to transmit messages to white audiences, see Mary E. Frederickson, "'Each One Is Dependent on the Other': Southern Churchwomen, Racial Reform, and the Process of Transformation, 1880–1940," in *Visible Women: New Essays on American Activism*, ed. Nancy A. Hewitt and Suzanne Lebsock (Urbana: University of Illinois Press, 1993), 311.

102 *Summit Herald*, 30 December 1932.

103 The conference elected Mary Burrell as one of the vice presidents. *New York Times*, 22 July, 1923, E7; NJSFCWC, *Yearbook, 1923*, 35; Zangrando, *The NAACP Crusade against Lynching*, 79; Sherman, *The Republican Party and Black America*, 209; Richard B. Sherman, "The Harding Administration and the Negro: An Opportunity Lost," *Journal of Negro History* 49 (July 1964): 165 n53.

104 *Chicago Defender*, 9 May 1931, 4. White Republican women demanded more leadership positions for themselves in the party and government. *New York Times*, 28 April, 1931, 3.

105 Glenda Elizabeth Gilmore, "False Friends and Avowed Enemies: Southern African Americans and Party Allegiances in the 1920s," in *Jumpin' Jim Crow: Southern Politics from Civil War to Civil Rights*, ed. Jane Dailey, Glenda Elizabeth Gilmore, and Bryant Simon (Princeton, N.J.: Princeton University Press, 2000), 220.

106 Nannie H. Burroughs, "From a Woman's Point of View": "Vote for Justice and Jobs," MS, NHBP, Box 46.

107 *New York Times*, 4 November 1936, 1 and 17; 5 November 1936, 17; *Chicago Defender*, 28 November 1936, 23.

108 Gilmore, "False Friends and Avowed Enemies," 219; Higginbotham, "Clubwomen and Electoral Politics in the 1920s," 134–155; Weiss, *Farewell to the Party of Lincoln*, 192–218; Sitkoff, *A New Deal for Blacks*, 96; Patricia Sullivan, *Days of Hope: Race and Democracy in the New Deal Era* (Chapel Hill: University of North Carolina Press, 1996), 93.

109 Gilmore posits as central to understanding the realignment of 1936 the new political culture created by passage of the Nineteenth Amendment and incremental events that led to changes in political style, evident in black women's agency and politi-

cal aspirations. Gilmore, "False Friends and Avowed Enemies," 219–238. In her analysis of middle-class black women's political mobilization in Chicago, Materson locates the early stages of a major realignment in the 1928 election and the gendered politics of enforcement of federal amendments. Materson, *For the Freedom of Her Race*, 150, 156–160; see also Christopher Robert Reed, "Black Chicago Political Realignment during the Great Depression and New Deal," in *Depression, War, and the New Migration, 1930–1960*, ed. Kenneth L. Kusmer (New York: General Publishing, 1991), 82–96.

110 *Summit Herald*, 14 October 1932.

111 African American intellectual Kelly Miller attributed black women's Republican partisanship to "woman's emotion" and, in the North, to the "serious aim and purpose" with which they entered the political arena through their political clubs and organizations. They would be the last, he suggested, to desert the burning Republican ship and "take the risk" in the uncertain Democratic sea. Kelly Miller, "Negro Vote a Puzzle in the North," *Chicago Defender*, 24 August 1924, XX6.

CHAPTER 6. "CARTHAGE MUST BE DESTROYED"

1 *Summit Herald*, 30 December 1932.

2 U.S. 15th Federal Census, 1930; *New York Times*, 18 June 1931, 17; and 3 July 1931, 10.

3 By 1937 New Jersey ranked second among states in acquisition of government-backed financing for middle-class homes and subdivisions. *New York Times*, 28 March 1937, 178; and 18 April 1937, 192, *passim*.

4 David M. Freund, "Marketing the Free Market: State Intervention and the Politics of Prosperity in Metropolitan America," in *The New Suburban History*, ed. Kevin M. Kruse and Thomas J. Sugrue (Chicago: University of Chicago Press, 2006), 11–32; Philip C. Dolce, ed., *Suburbia: The American Dream and Dilemma* (Garden City: Anchor Books/Doubleday, 1976), vii.

5 Ira De. A. Reid, "The Negro Riddance Act," *Social Work Today* 1:1 (March 1934): 13–14.

6 *Summit Herald*, 4 October 1932.

7 *Ibid.*

8 Twenty-five percent of Summit residents were Italian, many second or third generation. New Jersey Conference of Social Work, Interracial Committee, *Survey of Negro Life in New Jersey: Community Reports, Vol.1* (Newark, N.J.: Interracial Committee, New Jersey Conference of Social Work [1932]), 7–8 (hereafter cited as NJCSW).

9 *Summit Herald*, 4 October 1932.

10 *Ibid.*

11 *Ibid.*

12 NJCSW, *The Negro in New Jersey: Report of a Survey by the Interracial Committee of the New Jersey Conference of Social Work in Cooperation with the State Department of Institutions and Agencies* (Newark: The Conference, 1932). National Urban League Director of Research from 1928–1934, Reid conducted studies in New York, Colorado, Minnesota, Michigan, and Massachusetts. Nancy J. Weiss, *The National Urban League, 1910–1940* (New York: Oxford University Press, 1974), 217–219.

13 See chapter 4 above.

14 *Summit Herald*, 4 October 1932.

15 *Ibid.*; NJCSW, *The Negro in New Jersey*, 13. Following World War I, many women used their war work to self-identify as social workers. Linda Gordon, *Pitied but Not Entitled: Single Mothers and the History of Welfare, 1890–1935* (New York: Maxwell Macmillan International, 1994), 100.

16 Restrictive covenants ranged from a covenant executed in the deed by a land company or subdivision developer to separate restrictive agreements among property owners. FHA requirements included restrictive covenants along with building codes until 1950. Charles Abrams, *Forbidden Neighbors: A Study of Prejudice in Housing* (New York: Harper, 1955), 224; Clement Vose, *Caucasians Only: The Supreme Court, the NAACP, and the Restrictive Covenant Cases* (Berkeley: University of California Press, 1973), 7–8. For examples of housing developments "where the deed restrictions . . . give assurances that this and other communities will always maintain their suburban atmosphere," see *New York Times*, 9 June 1929, RE1; and 29 November 1936, RE1. While much of the analysis on the politics of race and property focuses on post–World War II, most historians locate the genesis in New Deal policies and practices. David M. Freund, *Colored Property: State Policy and White Racial Politics in Suburban America* (Chicago: University of Chicago Press, 2007); Andrew Wiese, *Places of Their Own: African American Suburbanization in the Twentieth Century* (Chicago: University of Chicago Press, 2005); Thomas Sugrue, *The Origins of the Urban Crisis: Race and Inequality in Postwar Detroit* (Princeton, N.J.: Princeton University Press, 1996).

17 Susan L. Smith, *Sick and Tired of Being Sick and Tired: Black Women's Health Activism in America, 1890–1950* (Philadelphia: University of Pennsylvania Press, 1995), 47, 65–66; Dennis C. Dickerson, "Walter G. Alexander: A Physician in Civil Rights and Public Service," *New Jersey History* 101 (Fall/Winter 1983): 37–59.

18 Smith, *Sick and Tired*, 58–75, quotation on 70; also David McBride, *From TB to AIDS: Epidemics among Urban Blacks since 1900* (Albany: SUNY Press, 1991), 109.

19 *Summit Herald*, 26 April 1935; *Chicago Defender*, 6 July 1935, 6.

20 *Summit Herald*, 4 October 1932. Reid presented his findings to twenty-three communities, the State Church Women's Interracial Conference, and the State Federation of Colored Women's Clubs. *Chicago Defender*, 5 November 1932, 6.

21 *Summit Herald*, 6 December 1932; and 3 January 1933.

22 *Summit Herald*, 10 January 1933; 17 January 1933; 7 February 1933; and 4 July 1933.

23 Allan M. Brandt, *No Magic Bullet: A Social History of Venereal Disease in the United States since 1880* (New York: Oxford University Press, 1985), 13; Suzanne Poirier, *Chicago's War on Syphilis, 1937–1940: The Times, the Trib, and the Clap Doctor* (Urbana: University of Illinois Press, 1995); McBride, *From TB to AIDS*, 113, 114.

24 Prior to 1932, Summit's ordinance applied only to food handlers; Newark expanded its ordinance to include domestic servants in 1931. Vanessa H. May, *Unprotected Labor: Household Workers, Politics, and Middle Class Reform in New York, 1870–1940* (Chapel Hill: University of North Carolina Press, 2011), 127–128. On Texas's

unsuccessful attempt to legislate health examinations for food handlers and garment workers, see Julia Kirk Blackwelder, *Women of the Depression: Caste and Culture in San Antonio, 1939–1949* (College Station: Texas A & M Press, 1984), 107.

25 Natalia Molina, *Fit to Be Citizens? Public Health and Race in Los Angeles, 1879–1939* (Berkeley: University of California Press, 2006), 3.

26 *Summit Herald*, 10 January 1933; 25 January 1935; and 13 August 1937. On the culture of dissemblance, see Darlene Clark Hine, "Rape and the Inner Lives of Black Women in the Middle West," *Signs* 14 (Summer 1989): 912, 920; Rosalyn Terborg-Penn, *African American Women in the Struggle for the Vote, 1850–1920* (Bloomington: Indiana University Press, 1998), 71; also Elizabeth Clark-Lewis, *Living In, Living Out: African American Domestics and the Great Migration* (New York: Kodansha International, 1996).

27 *Summit Herald*, 25 January 1935. Historian Tera W. Hunter concludes that white female employers' refusal to surrender power to male municipal authorities led to the demise of the policing of black women's bodies in Atlanta. Tera W. Hunter, *To 'Joy My Freedom: Southern Black Women's Lives and Labor after the Civil War* (Cambridge: Harvard University Press, 2002), 209.

28 *Summit Herald*, 7 February 1933; *New York Times*, 3 January 1937, D6. PTAs in Westchester County, New York, also endorsed compulsory examinations. May, *Unprotected Labor*, 132.

29 Montclair organizers expected one hundred women to participate in the next demonstration. *New York Times*, 10 November 1937, 9. Montclair refused to enact the LWV's compulsory testing proposal. Patricia Hampson Eget, "Challenging Containment: African Americans and Racial Politics in Montclair, New Jersey, 1920–1940," *New Jersey History* 126:1 (2011): 1–17.

30 *New York Times*, 16 May 1938, 34.

31 Poirier, *Chicago's War on Syphilis*; *Summit Herald*, 15 June 1937. Plainfield, Englewood, East Orange, Orange, and Asbury Park received awards. *New York Times*, 15 April 1940, 12.

32 *Chicago Defender*, 11 November 1938, 8.

33 Marsha Ritzdorf, "Sex, Lies, and Urban Life: How Municipal Planning Marginalizes African American Women and Their Families," in *Gendering the City: Women, Boundaries, and Visions of Urban Life*, ed. Kristina B. Miranne and Alma H. Young (Lanham, Md.: Rowman & Littlefield, 2000), 179.

34 Hunter, *To 'Joy My Freedom*, 212; Brandt, *No Magic Bullet*, 14, 158. Estelle B. Freedman connects the disruption of family life during the Great Depression with concerns about masculinity and male preoccupation with female hypersexuality. Estelle B. Freedman, "'Uncontrollable Desires': The Response to the Sexual Psychopath, 1920–1960," *Journal of American History* 74 (June 1987): 83–106.

35 *Summit Herald*, 4 May, 1937; 14 May 1937; and 14 September 1937. Ader remained with the Summit Health Board for ten years, eventually resigning to relocate to Kentucky with her third husband, a former Summit physician and Dartmouth College and Howard University Medical School graduate. *Summit Herald*, 5 February 1948.

36 In 1937 and 1938 the USPHS funded local anti-syphilis health programs. Brandt argues that the programs remained grounded in a racialist approach to health in the black community, despite the growing strength of environmentalism. Brandt, *No Magic Bullet*, 107.

37 *Summit Herald*, 28 May 1937; 9 July 1937; and 14 September 1937. On Ader's community-wide reception, see *Summit Herald*, 8 June 1937. Decades later one woman angrily recalled Ader's intrusion into her bedroom following the birth of her first child; another gratefully remembered the nurse's diagnosis of her childhood polio infection. Arlie Andrews and Lorraine Young, interview by author, 23 June 2003, Summit, New Jersey, tape recording in possession of author, Summit.

38 Dr. Norman S. Hill, interview by author, 15 November 1997, Maplewood, N.J., tape recording in possession of author, Summit.

39 *Summit Herald*, 28 December 1934.

40 The *New York Times* covered events in White Plains from mid-April through July. *New York Times*, 17 April 1930, 22; 1 May 1930, 24; and 24 July 1930, 4, *passim*. Contemporary sociologists noted the "hazardous and frequently humiliating" phenomenon of black physicians as targets of mob violence in cities and suburbs. John M. Griese and James Ford, ed., *Negro Housing: Report of the Committee on Negro Housing; Prepared for the Committee by Charles S. Johnson* (Washington, D.C.: President's Conference on Home Building and Home Ownership, 1932), 47; Charles S. Johnson, *The Negro in American Civilization: A Study of Negro Life and Race Relations in the Light of Social Research* (New York: Henry Holt and Company, 1930), 360–361.

41 The real estate industry adopted a restrictive code regarding home sales to racial groups that it codified in textbooks and encoded in New Deal policies. Kenneth T. Jackson, *Crabgrass Frontier: The Suburbanization of the United States* (New York: Oxford University Press, 1985), 190–218; Stephen Grant Meyer, *As Long as They Don't Move Next Door: Segregation and Racial Conflict in American Neighborhoods* (Lanham, Md.: Rowman & Littlefield, 2000); Abrams, *Forbidden Neighbors*, 150–168. On the terror white neighborhood associations perpetrated, see Abrams, *Forbidden Neighbors*, 182; Vose, *Caucasians Only*, 77; Victoria W. Wolcott, *Remaking Respectability: African American Women in Interwar Detroit* (Chapel Hill: University of North Carolina Press, 2001), 131–165; Thomas J. Sugrue, "Crabgrass-Roots Politics: Race, Rights and the Reaction against Liberalism in the Urban North, 1940–1964," *Journal of American History* 82 (September 1995): 561, 562. For a black physician's attempt to protect his home, see Kevin Boyle, *Arc of Justice: A Saga of Race, Civil Rights, and Murder in the Jazz Age* (New York: Henry Holt, 2004).

42 *Summit Herald*, 14 September 1937.

43 *Summit Herald*, 21 October 1938.

44 Spencer Logan, *A Negro's Faith in America* (New York: Macmillan, 1946), 3–8; *Summit Herald*, 21 October 1938.

45 See chapter 1 above.

46 *Summit Herald*, 15 November 1938. In 1930s Los Angeles businessmen used public health ordinances to eliminate competition from Chinese launderers. Molina, *Fit to Be Citizens?* 14.

47 *Summit Herald*, 18 November 1938.

48 *Ibid.*

49 *Ibid.*

50 *Summit Herald*, 9 December 1938.

51 *Summit Herald*, 23 December 1938. Logan attributed the successful outcome to the support of black "church activists" and "influential white Christians." He operated the "sweet shop" until drafted into the army in 1942. Logan, *A Negro's Faith*, 6–7.

52 Historian Victoria Wolcott argues that the rhetorical defense of "a colored man's rights" is a masculine discourse of citizenship and rights that emerged in the late 1930s and 1940s and marked a shift in the discourse of respectability, leading ultimately to the decline of black women in visible leadership positions. Wolcott, *Remaking Respectability*, 148–150. Though suggestive, Wolcott's premise requires further analysis. As this study shows, black working women employed the discourse of rights to claim the economic, social, and legal rights due them as enfranchised citizens.

53 Ella Handen, "Social Service Stations: New Jersey Settlement Houses Founded in the Progressive Era," *New Jersey History* 108 (Spring/Summer 1990): 1–29. On African Americans and the settlement movement, see Floris Bennett Cash, *African American Women and Social Action: The Clubwomen and Volunteerism from Jim Crow to the New Deal, 1896–1936* (Westport, Conn.: Greenwood Press, 2001); Elisabeth Lasch-Quinn, *Black Neighbors: Race and the Limits of Reform in the American Settlement House Movement, 1890–1945* (Chapel Hill: University of North Carolina Press, 1993).

54 *Summit Herald*, 11 February 1930.

55 Emmett J. Scott, *Negro Migration during the War*, 1920; reprint (New York: Arno Press, 1969), 139.

56 *Ibid.*

57 *New Jersey* (Montclair) *Observer*, 10 January 1917, Fountain Baptist Church Collection; *Asbury Park Evening Press*, 30 April 1918; *Jersey Journal*, 24 April 1919, Clipping Collection, Jersey City Library; Scott, *Negro Migration*, 139–140; Kenneth T. Jackson and Barbara B. Jackson, "The Black Experience in Newark: The Growth of the Ghetto, 1870–1970," in *New Jersey since 1860: New Findings and Interpretations*, ed. William C. Wright (Trenton: New Jersey Historical Commission, 1972), 44.

58 African American women established settlement houses in Newark and suburban Bloomfield and East Orange and shared community houses in New Brunswick and suburban Madison, Englewood, Montclair, and Silver Lake. NJCSW, *The Negro in New Jersey*, 50. Historian Clement Price concludes that for post–World War I black migrants in Newark, housing discrimination was more problematic than employment. Clement Price, "The Beleaguered City as Promised Land: Blacks in Newark, 1917–1947," in *Urban New Jersey since 1870*, ed. William C. Wright (Trenton: New Jersey Historical Society, 1975), 19–23.

59 *Summit Herald*, 14 October 1932.

60 *Summit Herald*, 3 November 1936.

61 *Summit Herald*, 12 February 1937.

62 *Summit Herald*, 14 September 1937.

63 *Summit Herald*, 26 January 1937.

64 *Summit Herald*, 29 January 1937.

65 *Summit Herald*, 9 March 1937.

66 Historian John F. Bauman argues that Wagner-Steagall removed the moral obligation for housing by not positioning decent housing as a right. John F. Bauman, *Public Housing, Race, and Renewal: Urban Planning in Philadelphia, 1920–1974* (Philadelphia: Temple University Press, 1987), 441. In 1931, Nannie Helen Burroughs, chair of the President's Conference on Home Building and Home Ownership, called for "community responsibility" over "individual responsibility" as a solution to the "distinct problem" of housing for African Americans. Gries and Ford, ed., *Negro Housing*, viii, 2.

67 Suzanne Mettler, *Dividing Citizens: Gender and Federalism in New Deal Public Policy* (Ithaca, N.Y.: Cornell University Press, 1998); also Mary Poole, *The Segregated Origins of Social Security: African Americans and the Welfare State* (Chapel Hill: University of North Carolina Press, 2006); Ira Katznelson, *When Affirmative Action Was White: An Untold History of Racial Inequality* (New York: W. W. Norton, 2005); Arnold R. Hirsch, "Less than *Plessy*: The Inner City, Suburbs, and the State-Sanctioned Residential Segregation in the Age of *Brown*," in *The New Suburban History*, ed. Kruse and Sugrue, 33–56.

68 *Summit City Directory*, 1930.

69 *Summit Herald*, 4 March 1938; and 5 April 1938.

70 *Summit Herald*, 9 March 1937.

71 *Summit Herald*, 19 April 1938.

72 *Summit Herald*, 23 July 1937.

73 Sugrue, "Crabgrass-Roots Politics," 551–578, quotation on 557.

74 *New York Times*, 21 April 1930, 21.

75 Sugrue, "Crabgrass-Roots Politics," 557–558.

76 *Summit Herald*, 13 May 1938.

77 Historian Andrew Wiese uses the term to refer to the myriad of regulatory and discretionary powers used by suburban municipalities to racialize space after World War II. Wiese, *Places of Their Own*.

78 *Summit Herald*, 13 May 1938.

79 *Ibid.*

80 *Ibid.*

81 *Ibid.* The health board periodically announced the discovery of infected black and white migratory workers "found in communities like Summit wandering around seeking employment." *Summit Herald*, 12 September 1939.

82 *Summit Herald*, 10 June 1938.

83 *Summit Herald*, 12 August 1938; 2 June 1939; and 23 February 1940.

84 *Summit Herald*, 23 September 1938.

85 *Summit Herald*, 28 June 1938. Montclair was the first New Jersey municipality to apply for federal funds under Wagner-Steagall. *New York Times*, 16 November 1938, 25.

86 *Summit Herald*, 28 June 1938.

87 Abrams, *Forbidden Neighbors*, 229; Bauman, *Public Housing*, 44–47.

88 *Summit Herald*, 17 October 1939.

89 *Summit Herald*, 29 September 1939.

90 *Summit Herald*, 17 October 1939.

91 *Summit Herald*, 24 October 1939. Since public housing tenants had to meet an income qualification or means test and overall returns had to be sufficient to repay the federal investment, the lowest income groups would not qualify for public housing. Without legislation that mandated razing unsuitable structures, landlords could opt to bring unsightly buildings up to code, board them up, or rent them. Christopher Wye, "The New Deal and the Negro Community: Toward a Broader Conceptualization," *Journal of American History 59* (December 1972): 628.

92 *Summit Herald*, 17 October 1939.

93 *Ibid.* The 1931 housing conference similarly concluded, "Instead of assuming that Negroes must live in habitations rather than homes because of their poverty, the new approach must be based upon the assumption that Negroes must be given the opportunity to earn more [so] that they may pay economic rent." Gries and Ford, ed., *Negro Housing*, 77. On domestic servants' "disgracefully low wages," see Weiss, *National Urban League*, 253.

94 *Summit Herald*, 24 October 1939. The 1931 housing conference cited home ownership as an "index of social stability and good citizenship." Gries and Ford, ed., *Negro Housing*, 77.

95 *Summit Herald*, 27 October 1939. Living out allowed white employers to reduce wages and domestic servants to gain greater control over their lives and terms of employment. Clark-Lewis, *Living In, Living Out*, 146–172; Kimberley L. Phillips, *Alabama North: African-American Migrants, Community, and Working-Class Activism in Cleveland, 1915–1945* (Chicago: University of Illinois Press, 1999), 90.

96 *Summit Herald*, 24 October 1939. As Bauman notes, for a brief period prior to World War II, public housing tenants "represented a cross-section of the white and black working class, not an underclass." Bauman, *Public Housing*, 52–53.

97 *Summit Herald*, 8 September 1939.

98 *Summit Herald*, 13 January 1928; 12 May 1941; 15 May 1941; 23 October 1941; and 20 November 1941.

99 Gladys Gilkey Calkins, *Follow Those Women; Church Women in the Ecumenical Movement; A History of the Development of United Work among Women of the Protestant Churches in the United States* (New York: National Council of Churches, 1961), 38. According to historian Robert Moats Miller, Protestant "liberalism gave way before the crashing ascendancy of neo-orthodoxy" and the Social Gospel succumbed to a "theology of crisis." Robert Moats Miller, *American Protestantism and Social Issues, 1919–1939* (Chapel Hill: University of North Carolina Press, 1958), 63; see also Richard Wightman Fox, *Reinhold Niebuhr: A Biography* (New York: Pantheon Books, 1985).

100 *Summit Herald*, 24 October 1939.

101 *Summit Herald*, 31 October 1939.

102 *Summit Herald*, 3 November 1939.

103 Suburban Plainfield and Montclair also rejected public housing proposals. Montclair's real estate board, chamber of commerce, and homeowners' associations raised the specter of falling property values caused by an influx of domestic workers. *New York Times*, 16 November 1938, 25; Eget, "Challenging Containment," 1–17.

104 On post–World War II urban renewal, see Freund, *Colored Property*; Hirsch, "Less than *Plessy*," 33–56; Arnold R. Hirsch, "'Containment' on the Home Front: Race and Federal Housing Policy from the New Deal to the Cold War," *Journal of Urban History* 26 (January 2000): 158–190; Arnold R. Hirsch, *Making the Second Ghetto: Race and Housing in Chicago, 1940–1960* (New York: Cambridge University Press, 1983); Sugrue, *Origins of the Urban Crisis*; Henry Louis Taylor, "Creating the Metropolis in Black and White: Black Suburbanization and the Planning Movement in Cincinnati, 1900–1950," in *Historical Roots of the Urban Crisis: African Americans in the Industrial City, 1900–1950*, ed. Henry Louis Taylor, Jr., and Walter Hill (New York: Garland, 2000), 51–71; Ronald H. Bayor, "Urban Renewal, Public Housing and the Racial Shaping of Atlanta," in *Depression, War and the New Migration, 1930–1960*, ed. Kenneth L. Kusmer (New York: Garland, 1991), 235–255; Ronald H. Bayor, *Race and the Shaping of Twentieth-Century Atlanta* (Chapel Hill: University of North Carolina Press, 1996); Weise, *Places of Their Own*.

105 Gordon, *Pitied but Not Entitled*, 198.

106 Using private funds, Summit replaced the Weaver Court tenements with two-family homes in 1960 and upgraded housing on Glenwood Place in 1972. *Summit Independent Press*, 21 December 2005.

107 *Summit Herald*, 24 November 1939 and 5 December 1939. On the Easter recital before an audience of 75,000, see *Washington Post*, 10 April 1939, 1; *Chicago Defender*, 15 April 1939, 2.

CONCLUSION

1 *Summit Herald*, 27 November 1941.

2 *Ibid.*

3 *Ibid.*

4 *Ibid.* Randolph read 1 John 4:24 and 1 John 2:11.

5 *Summit Herald*, 18 March 1941 and 18 November 1943. On women's work during World War II, see Karen Anderson, *Wartime Women: Sex Roles, Family Relations, and the Status of Women during World War II* (Westport, Conn.: Greenwood Press, 1981); Karen Tucker Anderson, "Last Hired, First Fired: Black Women Workers during World War II," *Journal of American History* 69 (June 1982): 82–99.

6 *Summit Herald*, 28 February 1941.

7 *Ibid.*

8 *Summit Herald*, 15 May 1941.

9 *Summit Herald*, 4 June 1942 and 9 July 1942.

10 *Summit Herald*, 15 April 1943 and 4 May 1944.

11 *Summit Herald*, 20 April 1944.

12 *Summit Herald*, 22 June 1944.

13 *Ibid.*

14 *Summit Herald*, 4 May 1944. On the Red Cross, see Kevin Mumford, *Newark: A History of Race, Rights, and Riots in America* (New York: NYU Press, 2007), 40–44.

15 *Summit Herald*, 11 February 1943. Bettye Collier-Thomas notes that Randolph originally wrote "If I Were White" as a 1941 Race Relations sermon. Bettye Collier-Thomas, *Daughters of Thunder: Black Women Preachers and Their Sermons, 1850–1979* (San Francisco: Jossey-Bass, 1998), 111–112.

16 *Summit Herald*, 11 February 1943; 18 February 1943; 25 February 1943; and 4 March 1943.

17 *Summit Herald*, 2 November 1944; *Chicago Defender*, 23 December 1944, 11. East Orange and Burlington also issued cancellations. *Chicago Defender*, 18 November 1944, 13. Wendy L. Wall, *Inventing the "American Way": The Politics of Consensus from the New Deal to the Civil Rights Movement* (Oxford: Oxford University Press, 2008), 262. See also Glenda Elizabeth Gilmore, *Defying Dixie: The Radical Roots of Civil Rights, 1919–1950* (New York: W. W. Norton, 2008); John B. Kirby, *Black Americans in the Roosevelt Era: Liberalism and Race* (Knoxville: University of Tennessee Press, 1980).

18 *Chicago Defender*, 12 May 1945, 11; *Summit Herald*, 31 May 1945 and 7 June 1945.

19 *Summit Herald*, 29 March 1945.

20 *PM Daily*, 30 March 1945, 12; *Summit Herald*, 12 April 1945.

21 Thirtieth Anniversary Dinner of the New Jersey Federation of Colored Women's Clubs with Florence Randolph, D. D., Founder, Honored Guest, 18 October 1945, Florence Randolph Collection, MG1321, Folder 2.

22 Evelyn Brooks Higginbotham, *Righteous Discontent: The Women's Movement in the Black Baptist Church, 1880–1920* (Cambridge: Harvard University Press, 1993); Glenda Elizabeth Gilmore, *Gender and Jim Crow: Women and the Politics of White Supremacy in North Carolina, 1896–1920* (Chapel Hill: University of North Carolina Press, 1996); Anne Firor Scott, "Most Invisible of All: Black Women's Voluntary Associations," *Journal of Southern History*, 56 (1990): 3–22.

SELECTED BIBLIOGRAPHY

PRIMARY SOURCES
Manuscript Collections
Alice Dunbar-Nelson Papers. Special Collections. University of Delaware. Newark, Delaware.
Florence Randolph Collection. New Jersey Historical Society. Newark, New Jersey.
Fountain Baptist Church (FBC) Collection. Summit New Jersey.
Lena Anthony Robbins Papers, Rutgers University Archives and Special Collections. New Brunswick, New Jersey.
Mary Church Terrell Papers, Manuscript Division, Library of Congress, Washington, D. C.
Nannie Helen Burroughs Papers. Manuscript Division, Library of Congress. Washington, D.C.
National Association for the Advancement of Colored People (NAACP) Papers, Manuscript Division, Library of Congress, Washington, D.C.
National Council of Churches Papers. Presbyterian Historical Society. Philadelphia, Pennsylvania.
New England Baptist Missionary Convention Minutes. American Baptist Manuscript Collection. American Baptist Historical Library, Atlanta, Georgia.
New Jersey Afro-American Baptist State Convention. Rutgers University Archives and Special Collections. New Brunswick, New Jersey.
Woodrow Wilson Papers Project. Princeton University, Princeton, New Jersey.

Interviews
Arlie Andrews and Lorraine Young. Interview by author, 23 June 2003, Summit, New Jersey. Tape recording. Summit, New Jersey.
Dr. Norman S. Hill, Summit Dentist. Interview by author, 15 November 1997, Maplewood, New Jersey. Tape recording. Summit, New Jersey.

Newspapers
Asbury Park Evening Press
Camden Courier Post
Chicago Defender
Jersey City Journal

Jersey City Observer
Jerseyman (Morristown)
New Jersey Baptist Bulletin
New Jersey Observer (Montclair)
New York Times
Newark Evening News
Newark Star
PM Daily
Star of Zion
The Suburbanite
Summit Herald
Union Signal
Washington Post

Published Works

Buhle, Mari Jo, and Paul Buhle. *The Concise History of Woman Suffrage: Selections from the Classic Work of Stanton, Anthony, Gage and Harper*. Urbana: University of Illinois Press, 1979.

Burroughs, Nannie Helen. "The Colored Woman and Her Relationship to the Domestic Problem." In *The United Negro: His Problems and His Progress: Containing the Addresses and Proceedings of the Negro Young People's Christian Educational Congress, Held August 6–11, 1902*. Edited by I. Garland Penn and J. W. E. Bowen. Atlanta: D. E. Luther Publishing Co., 1902, 328–329.

Calkins, Gladys Gilkey. *Follow Those Women; Church Women in the Ecumenical Movement, A History of the Development of United Work among Women of the Protestant Churches in the United States*. New York: National Council of Churches, 1961.

"Church Women in Interracial Conference," *Federal Council Bulletin* XI (September 1928), 21.

"Church Women in Interracial Conference," *Federal Council Bulletin* XI (October 1928), 13–14.

Clarke, Ida Clyde. *American Women and the World War*. New York: D. Appleton and Company, 1918.

Coolidge, Calvin. "Better Homes." In *Better Homes in America Plan Book for Demonstration Week, October 9 to 14 1922*. New York: *Delineator*, 1922, 4–6.

Coppin, L. J. "Christian Endeavor Movement." *African Methodist Episcopal Church Review* 15 (January 1899): 677–688.

Davis, Elizabeth Lindsay. *Lifting as They Climb: The National Association of Colored Women*. Washington: National Association of Colored Women, 1933.

Du Bois, W. E. B. "Returning Soldiers." *Crisis* XVII (May 1919): 13.

Dunbar-Nelson, Alice. "Negro Women in War Work." In *Scott's Official History of the American Negro in the World War*. Edited by Emmett J. J. Scott. Chicago: Homewood Press, 1919. Reprint, New York: Arno Press, 1969.

Federal Writers' Project, comp. *The WPA Guide to 1930s New Jersey*. New York: Viking Press, 1939. Reprint, New Brunswick, N.J.: Rutgers University Press, 1986.

Fields, Mamie Garvin, with Karen Fields. *Lemon Swamp and Other Places: A Carolina Memoir*. New York: Free Press, 1983.

Fuller, Ada D. *A History of the New Jersey State Federation of Women's Clubs. From 1894 to 1927*. Newark, N.J.: Ada D. Fuller, 1927.

Gaudet, Frances Joseph. *"He Leadeth Me,"* 1913. Reprint, New York: G. K. Hall & Co., 1996.

"The Glorious Task of Lifting as We Climb." *Competitor* 3:1(1920): 40.

Gordon, Elizabeth Putnam. *Women Torch-Bearers: The Story of the Woman's Christian Temperance Union*. Evanston, Ill.: National Woman's Christian Temperance Union Publishing House, 1924.

Graw, J. B., ed. *Life of Mrs. S. J. C. Downs; or, Ten Years at the Head of the Woman's Christian Temperance Union of New Jersey*. Camden, N.J.: Gazette Printing and Publishing House, 1892.

Griese, John M., and James Ford, ed. *Negro Housing: Report of the Committee on Negro Housing; Prepared for the Committee by Charles S. Johnson*. Washington, D.C.: President's Conference on Home Building and Home Ownership, 1932.

Harper, Ida Husted, ed. *History of Woman Suffrage, 1900–1920*, Volume 6. New York: National American Woman Suffrage Association, 1922. Reprint, New York: Arno Press, 1969.

Haynes, George Edmund. "Changing Racial Attitudes and Customs." *Phylon* 2 (1st Qtr. 1941): 28–43.

——. *The Trend of the Races*. New York: Council of Women for Home Missions and Missionary Education of the United States and Canada, 1922.

Hedgeman, Anna Arnold. *The Trumpet Sounds: A Memoir of Negro Leadership*. New York: Holt, Rinehart and Winston, 1964.

Hiscox, Edward T. *Principles and Practices for Baptist Churches: A Guide to the Administration of Baptist Churches*.1894. Reprint, Grand Rapids, Mich.: Kregel Publications, 1980.

Hoover, Herbert. "The Home as an Investment." In *Better Homes in America Plan Book for Demonstration Week, October 9 to 14 1922*. New York: *Delineator*, 1922, 7–8.

Hull, Gloria, ed. *Give Us Each Day: The Diary of Alice Dunbar-Nelson*. New York: W. W. Norton, 1984.

——, ed. *The Works of Alice Dunbar-Nelson*, Vol. 2. New York: Oxford University Press, 1988.

Hunton, Addie W., and Kathryn M. Johnson. *Two Colored Women in the American Expeditionary Forces*. Brooklyn, N.Y.: Brooklyn Eagle Press, 1920. Reprint, New York: G. K. Hall, 1997.

Huse, Penelope B. P. *The Mercy Committee of New Jersey*. New Jersey: Prepared & Issued for the Board of Trustees by Penelope B. P. Huse, Secretary, 1919.

"In the Political Arena: Women's Work in Essex County, NJ." *Competitor*, 3:4 (1921): 34.

Johnson, Charles S. *The Negro in American Civilization: A Study of Negro Life and Race Relations in the Light of Social Research*. New York: Henry Holt and Company, 1930.

Kellor, Frances A., "Sex in Crime." *International Journal of Ethics* 9 (October 1898): 74–85.

———. "Southern Colored Girls in the North: The Problem of Their Protection." *Charities* 13 (18 March 1905): 584–585.

Kirchwey, Freda. "Alice Paul Pulls the Strings." *Nation* (2 March 1921): 332–333.

Logan, Spencer. *A Negro's Faith in America*. New York: Macmillan, 1946.

Miller, Kelly. "Negro Vote a Puzzle in the North." *Chicago Defender*, 24 August 1924, XX6.

Morrow, E. Frederic. *Way Down South Up North*. Philadelphia: Pilgrim Press, 1973.

New Jersey Conference of Social Work. Interracial Committee. *The Negro in New Jersey: Report of a Survey by the Interracial Committee of the New Jersey Conference of Social Work in Cooperation with the State Department of Institutions and Agencies*. [Newark, N.J.] The Conference, 1932.

New Jersey Conference of Social Work, Interracial Committee. *Survey of Negro Life in New Jersey: Community Reports, Volume 1, North Jersey*. Newark: Interracial Committee, New Jersey Conference of Social Work [1932].

New Jersey Historical Records Survey Project. *Inventory of the Church Archives of New Jersey: Prepared by the New Jersey Historical Records Survey Project, Division of Professional and Service Projects, Work Project Administration*. Compiled by Luther H. Evans and John A. Millington. Newark, N.J.: Historical Records Survey Project, 1938.

Olcott, Jane, comp. *The Work of the Colored Women*. New York: Colored Work Committee War Work Council, National Board, Young Women's Christian Association, 1919.

Ovington, Mary White. *Half a Man: The Status of the Negro in New York*, 1911. Reprint, New York: American Century Series, 1969.

Park, Robert E. "The Nature of Race Relations." In *Race Relations and the Race Problem: A Definition and an Analysis*. Edited by Edgar T. Thompson. Durham, N.C.: Duke University Press, 1939, 3–45.

Parsons, Floyd W. *New Jersey: Life, Industries and Resources of a Great State*. Newark: New Jersey State Chamber of Commerce, 1928.

Pawley, James A., comp. *The Negro Church in New Jersey*. Hackensack, N.J., 1938.

Penn, I. Garland, and J. W. E. Bowen, ed. *The United Negro: His Problems and His Progress: Containing the Addresses and Proceedings of the Negro Young People's Christian Educational Congress, Held August 6–11, 1902*. Atlanta: D. E. Luther Publishing Co., 1902.

Pickens, William. "The Woman Voter Hits the Color Line." *Nation* 3 (October 1920): 372–373.

Pius, N. H., *An Outline of Baptist History: A Splendid Reference Work for Busy Workers: A Record of the Struggles and Triumphs of Baptist Pioneers and Builders*. Nashville: National Baptist Publishing Board, 1911.

Ray, Mrs. Emma J. *Twice Sold, Twice Ransomed: Autobiography of Mr. and Mrs. L. Ray*. Chicago: Free Methodist Publishing House, 1926. Reprint, Freeport, N.Y.: Books for Libraries Press, 1971.

Reid, Ira De Augustine. "The Negro Riddance Act." *Social Work Today* 1:1 (March 1934): 13–14.

Ricord, F. W. *History of Union County, N.J.* Newark: East Jersey History Co., Newark, 1897.

Rogerson, Idonia Elizabeth, comp. *Historical Synopsis of the Woman's Home and Foreign Mission Society, African Methodist Episcopal Zion Church*. Charlotte, N.C. : AME Zion Publishing House, 1967.

Sackett, William Edgar. *Modern Battles of Trenton, Being a History of New Jersey's Politics and Legislation from the Year 1868 to the Year 1894*. Trenton, N.J.: John L. Murphy, 1895.

Scott, Emmett J. *Negro Migration during the War*. New York: Oxford University Press, 1920. Reprint, New York: Arno Press, 1969.

——, ed. *Scott's Official History of the American Negro in the World War*. Chicago: [Homewood Press], 1919. Reprint, New York: Arno Press, 1969.

Stafford, Paul Tutt. *Government and the Needy: A Study of Public Assistance in New Jersey*. Princeton, N.J.: Princeton University Press, 1942.

Stoddard, Lothrop. *Clashing Tides of Color*. New York: Charles Scribner's Sons, 1935.

——. *The Rising Tide of Color against White World-Supremacy*. New York: Charles Scribner's Sons, 1921; reprint Westport, Conn.: Negro Universities Press, 1971.

Summit, New Jersey: An Ideal Suburban Home Town. Newark, N.J.: Civic Publicity Co., 1909.

Terrell, Mary Church. *A Colored Woman in a White World*. Washington: Ransdell Publishing, 1940.

Walters, Alexander. *My Life and Work*. New York: Fleming H. Revell Company, 1917.

Washington, Booker T. *The Booker T. Washington Papers*. Edited by Louis R. Harlan. Urbana: University of Illinois Press, 1972.

White, Alma. *Heroes of the Fiery Cross*. Zarepath, N.J.: Good Citizen, 1928.

Unpublished Manuscripts

Adams, B. "African American Baptist Identity and the Idea of Missions to Africa, 1880–1900." MS, in author's possession, Summit, N. J.

Libby, Maria C. "Women's Activities during World War I." MS, Summit Historical Society, Summit, N.J.

"Town Improvement Association of Summit April 1913 to April 1922. A Paper for the Occasion of the Twenty-Fifth Anniversary." MS, Summit Historical Society.

SECONDARY SOURCES

Abrams, Charles. *Forbidden Neighbors: A Study of Prejudice in Housing*. New York: Harper, 1955.

Adams, Betty Livingston. "'The Best Hotel on the Boardwalk': Church Women, Negro Art, and the Construction of Interracial Space in the Interwar Years." In *Sensational Religion: Sensory Cultures in Material Practice*. Edited by Sally Promey. New Haven, Conn.: Yale University Press, 2014, 275–296.

Allen, Robert. *Reluctant Reformers: Racism and Social Reform Movements in the United States*. Washington: Howard University Press, 1983.

Andersen, Kristi. *After Suffrage: Women and Partisan and Electoral Politics before the New Deal*. Chicago: University of Chicago Press, 1996.

———. *The Creation of a Democratic Majority, 1928–36*. Chicago: University of Chicago Press, 1979.

———. "Women and Citizenship in the 1920s." In *Women, Politics and Change*. Edited by Louise A. Tilly and Patricia Gurin. New York: Russell Sage Foundation, 1990, 177–198.

Anderson, Benedict. *Imagined Communities: Reflections on the Origin and Spread of Nationalism*. London: Verso, 1991.

Anderson, Karen. "The Great Depression and World War II." In *A Companion to American Women's History*. Edited by Nancy A. Hewitt. Malden, Mass.: Blackwell, 2002, 366–381.

———. "Last Hired, First Fired: Black Women Workers during World War II." *Journal of American History* 69 (June 1982): 82–99.

———. *Wartime Women: Sex Roles, Family Relations, and the Status of Women during World War II*. Westport, Conn.: Greenwood Press, 1981.

Armstead, Myra B. Young. *"Lord, Please Don't Take Me in August": African Americans in Newport and Saratoga Springs, 1870–1930*. Chicago: University of Illinois Press, 1999.

Baker, Paula. "'She Is the Best Man on the Ward Committee': Women in Grassroots Party Organizations, 1930s–1950s." In *We Have Come to Stay: American Women and Political Parties, 1880–1960*. Edited by Melanie Gustafson, Kristie Miller, and Elisabeth I. Perry. Albuquerque: University of New Mexico Press, 1999, 151–160.

Bates, Beth Tompkins. *Pullman Porters and the Rise of Protest Rallies in Black America, 1925–1945*. Chapel Hill: University of North Carolina Press, 2001.

Bauman, John F. *Public Housing, Race, and Renewal: Urban Planning in Philadelphia, 1920–1974*. Philadelphia: Temple University Press, 1987.

Baxnall, Rosalyn, and Elizabeth Ewen. *Picture Windows: How the Suburbs Happened*. New York: Basic Books, 2000.

Bay, Mia. *To Tell the Truth Freely: The Life of Ida B. Wells*. New York: Hill and Wang, 2009.

Bayor, Ronald H. *Race and the Shaping of Twentieth-Century Atlanta*. Chapel Hill: University of North Carolina Press, 1996.

———. "Urban Renewal, Public Housing and the Racial Shaping of Atlanta." In *Depression, War and the New Migration, 1930–1960*. Edited by Kenneth L. Kusmer. New York: Garland, 1991, 235–255.

Bederman, Gail. *Manliness and Civilization: A Cultural History of Gender and Race in the United States, 1880–1917*. Chicago: University of Chicago Press, 1995.

———. "'The Women Have Had Charge of the Church Work Long Enough': The Men and Religion Forward Movement of 1911–1912 and the Masculinization of Middle-Class Protestantism." *American Quarterly* 41 (September 1989): 432–465.

Bennett, James B. *Religion and the Rise of Jim Crow in New Orleans*. Princeton, N.J.: Princeton University Press, 2005.

Birkner, Michael J. *A Country Place No More: The Transformation of Bergenfield, New Jersey, 1894–1994*. Rutherford, N.J.: Fairleigh Dickinson University Press, 1994.

Blackwelder, Julia Kirk. *Women of the Depression: Caste and Culture in San Antonio, 1939–1949*. College Station: Texas A&M Press, 1984.

Blee, Kathleen M. *Women of the Klan: Racism and Gender in the 1920s*. Berkeley: University of California Press, 1991.

Blum, Edward J. *Reforging the White Republic: Race, Religion, and American Nationalism, 1865–1898*. Baton Rouge: Louisiana State University Press, 2005.

Bordin, Ruth. *Women and Temperance: The Quest for Power and Liberty 1873–1900*. Philadelphia: Temple University Press, 1981.

Boyle, Kevin. *Arc of Justice: A Saga of Race, Civil Rights, and Murder in the Jazz Age*. New York: Henry Holt, 2004.

Brandt, Allan M. *No Magic Bullet: A Social History of Venereal Disease in the United States since 1880*. New York: Oxford University Press, 1985.

Breen, William J. "Black Women and the Great War: Mobilization and Reform in the South." *Journal of Southern History* 44 (August 1978): 421–440.

Bristow, Nancy K. *Making Men Moral: Social Engineering during the Great War*. New York: NYU Press, 1996.

Brophy, Alfred L. *Reconstructing the Dreamland: The Tulsa Riot of 1921: Race, Reparations and Reconciliation*. New York: Oxford University Press, 2002.

Brown, Elsa Barkley. "Negotiating and Transforming the Public Square: African American Political Life in the Transition from Slavery to Freedom." *Public Culture* 7 (1994): 107–146.

Brown, Mary Jane. *Eradicating Evil: Women in the American Anti-Lynching Movement, 1892–1940*. New York: Garland, 2000.

Brown, Nikki. *Private Politics and Public Voices: Black Women's Activism from World War I to the New Deal*. Bloomington: Indiana University Press, 2006.

Buenker, John D. "Urban, New-Stock Liberalism and Progressive Reform in New Jersey." *New Jersey History* 87 (Summer 1969): 79–104.

Butler, Anthea D. "'Only a Woman Would Do': Black Reading and African American Women's Organizing Work." In *Women and Religion in the African Diaspora: Knowledge, Power, and Performance*. Edited by R. Marie Griffith and Barbara Dianne Savage. Baltimore, Md.: Johns Hopkins University Press, 2006, 155–178.

———. *Women in the Church of God in Christ: Making a Sanctified World*. Chapel Hill: University of North Carolina Press, 2007.

Butler, Jon. *Awash in a Sea of Faith: Christianizing the American People*. Cambridge: Harvard University Press, 1992.

Carby, Hazel V. "Policing the Black Woman's Body." *Critical Inquiry* 18 (Summer 1992): 738–744.

———. *Reconstructing Womanhood: The Emergence of the Afro-American Woman Novelist*. New York: Oxford University Press, 1987.

Carter, Paul Allen. *The Decline and Revival of the Social Gospel: Social and Political Liberalism in American Protestant Churches, 1920–1940*. Ithaca, N.Y.: Cornell University Press, 1954.

Cash, Floris Bennett. *African American Women and Social Action: The Clubwomen and Volunteerism from Jim Crow to the New Deal, 1896–1936*. Westport, Conn.: Greenwood Press, 2001.

Chalmers, David M. *Hooded Americanism: The History of the Ku Klux Klan, 1865–1965*. Garden City, N.Y.: Doubleday, 1965.

Clark-Lewis, Elizabeth. *Living In, Living Out: African American Domestics and the Great Migration*. New York: Kodansha International, 1996.

Clemens, Elisabeth S. "Securing Political Returns to Social Capital: Women's Associations in the United States, 1880s–1920s." *Journal of Interdisciplinary History* 29 (Spring 1999): 613–638.

Clement, Rufus E. "Alexander Walters." *Phylon* 7 (1st Qtr. 1946): 15–19.

Collier-Thomas, Bettye. *Daughters of Thunder: Black Women Preachers and Their Sermons*. San Francisco: Jossey-Bass, 1998.

———. "Frances Ellen Watkins Harper: Abolitionist and Feminist Reformer, 1825–1911." In *African American Women and the Vote, 1837–1965*. Edited by Ann D. Gordon, with Bettye Collier-Thomas, John H. Bracey, Arlene Voski Avakina, Joyce Averech Beakman. Amherst: University of Massachusetts Press, 1997, 41–65.

———. *Jesus, Jobs, and Justice: African American Women and Religion*. New York: Alfred A. Knopf, 2010.

———. "Minister and Feminist Reformer: The Life of Florence Spearing Randolph." In *This Far by Faith: Readings in African-American Women's Religious Biography*. Edited by Judith Weisenfeld and Richard Newman. New York: Routledge, 1996, 177–185.

Cott, Nancy F. "Across the Great Divide: Women in Politics before and after 1920." In *Women, Politics, and Change*. Edited by Louise A. Tilly and Patricia Gurin. New York: Russell Sage Foundation, 1990, 153–176.

———. "Feminist Politics in the 1920s: The National Woman's Party." *Journal of American History* 71 (June 1984): 43–68.

———. *The Grounding of Modern Feminism*. New Haven, Conn.: Yale University Press, 1987.

Crocco, Margaret Smith. "Women of New Jersey: Charting a Path to Full Citizenship, 1870–1920." *New Jersey History* 115 (Fall/Winter 1997): 37–59.

Danbom, David B. *"The World of Hope": Progressives and the Struggle for an Ethical Public Life.* Philadelphia: Temple University Press, 1987.

Davis, Morris L. *The Methodist Unification: Christianity and the Politics of Race in the Jim Crow Era.* New York: NYU Press, 2008.

Deutsch, Sarah. *Women and the City: Gender, Space, and Power in Boston, 1870–1940.* New York: Oxford University Press, 2000.

Dickerson, Dennis C. "Walter G. Alexander: A Physician in Civil Rights and Public Service." *New Jersey History* 101 (Fall/Winter 1983): 37–59.

Difenthaler, Jon. "America's Democratic Society and the Authority of the Church." *Currents in Theology and Mission* 7 (August 1980): 230–238.

Dill, Bonnie. *Across the Boundaries of Race and Class: An Exploration of Work and Family among Black Female Domestic Servants.* New York: Garland, 1994.

Dodson, Julyanne E. *Engendering Church: Women, Power, and the A.M.E. Church.* Lanham, Md: Rowman & Littlefield, 2002.

———. "Nineteenth-Century A.M.E. Preaching Women." In *Women in New Worlds,* Volume 1. Edited by Hilah G. Thomas and Rosemary Skinner Keller. Nashville, Tenn.: Abingdon Press, 1981, 276–289.

Dolce, Philip C., ed. *Suburbia: The American Dream and Dilemma.* Garden City, N.Y.: Anchor Books/Doubleday, 1976.

Dowden-White, Priscilla A. "To See Past the Difference to the Fundamentals: Racial Coalition within the League of Women Voters of St. Louis, 1920–1946." In *Women Shaping the South: Creating and Confronting Change.* Edited by Angela Boswell and Judith N. McArthur. Columbia: University of Missouri Press, 2006, 174–203.

Easter, Opal V. *Nannie Helen Burroughs.* New York: Garland, 1995.

Ebner, Michael H. "Mrs. Miller and 'The Paterson Show': A 1911 Defeat for Racial Discrimination." *New Jersey History* 86 (Summer 1968): 88–91.

Eget, Patricia Hampson. "Challenging Containment: African Americans and Racial Politics in Montclair, New Jersey, 1920–1940." *New Jersey History* 126:1 (2011): 1–17.

Ellis, Mark. "'Closing Ranks' and 'Seeking Honors': W. E. B. Du Bois in World War I." *Journal of American History* 79 (June 1992): 96–124.

———. *Race, War, and Surveillance: African Americans and the United States Government during World War I.* Bloomington: Indiana University Press, 2001.

———. "W. E. B. Du Bois and the Formation of Black Opinion in World War I: A Commentary on 'The Damnable Dilemma.'" *Journal of American History* 81 (March 1995): 1584–1590.

Ellsworth, Scott. *Death in a Promised Land: The Tulsa Race Riot of 1921.* Baton Rouge: Louisiana State University Press, 1982.

Enstad, Nan. "Urban Spaces and Popular Cultures, 1890–1930." In *A Companion to American Women's History.* Edited by Nancy A. Hewitt. Malden, Mass.: Blackwell, 2002, 295–311.

Fishman, Robert. *Bourgeois Utopias: The Rise and Fall of Suburbia.* New York: Basic Books, 1987.

Fitts, Leroy. *A History of Black Baptists.* Nashville, Tenn.: Broadman Press, 1985.

Fitzpatrick, Ellen. *Endless Crusade: Women Social Scientists and Progressive Reform.* New York: Oxford University Press, 1990.

Fleming, Thomas. *New Jersey: A Bicentennial History.* New York: W. W. Norton, 1977.

Foley, Barbara. *Spectres of 1919: Class and Nation in the Making of the New Negro.* Urbana: University of Illinois Press, 2003.

Foster, Gaines M. *Moral Reconstruction: Christian Lobbyists and the Federal Legislation of Morality, 1865–1920.* Chapel Hill: University of North Carolina Press, 2002.

Fox, Richard Wightman. *Reinhold Niebuhr, a Biography.* New York: Pantheon Books, 1985.

Fraser, Steve. "The 'Labor Question.'" In *The Rise and Fall of the New Deal Order, 1930–1980.* Edited by Steve Fraser and Gary Gerstle. Princeton, N.J.: Princeton University Press, 1989, 55–84.

Frederickson, Mary E. "'Each One Is Dependent on the Other': Southern Church-women, Racial Reform, and the Process of Transformation, 1880–1940." In *Visible Women: New Essays on American Activism.* Edited by Nancy A. Hewitt and Suzanne Lebsock. Urbana: University of Illinois Press, 1993, 296–324.

Freedman, Estelle B. "Separatism as Strategy: Female Institution Building and American Feminism, 1870–1930." *Feminism Studies* 5 (Fall 1979): 512–529.

———. "'Uncontrollable Desires': The Response to the Sexual Psychopath, 1920–1960." *Journal of American History* 74 (June 1987): 83–106.

Freund, David M. *Colored Property: State Policy and White Racial Politics in Suburban America.* Chicago: University of Chicago Press, 2007.

———. "Marketing the Free Market: State Intervention and the Politics of Prosperity in Metropolitan America." In *The New Suburban History.* Edited by Kevin M. Kruse and Thomas J. Sugrue. Chicago: University of Chicago Press, 2006, 11–32.

Gaines, Kevin K. *Uplifting the Race: Black Leadership, Politics, and Culture in the Twentieth Century.* Chapel Hill: University of North Carolina Press, 1996.

Gatewood, Willard B., Jr. *Aristocrats of Color: The Black Elite, 1880–1920.* Bloomington: Indiana University Press, 1990.

———, ed. *"Smoked Yankees" and the Struggle for Empire: Letters from Negro Soldiers, 1898–1902.* Champaign: University of Illinois Press, 1971.

Giddings, Paula J. *Ida: A Sword among Lions: Ida B. Wells and the Campaign against Lynching.* New York: Amistad, 2008.

Giele, Janet Zollinger. *Two Paths to Women's Equality: Temperance, Suffrage, and the Origins of Modern Feminism.* New York: Twayne, 1995.

Gifford, Carolyn DeSwarte. "Frances W. Willard and the Woman's Christian Temperance Union's Conversion to Woman's Suffrage." In *One Woman, One Vote: Rediscovering the Woman Suffrage Movement.* Edited by Marjorie Spruill Wheeler. Troutdale, Oreg.: New Sage Press, 1996, 117–133.

Gilkes, Cheryl Townsend. "Exploring the Religious Connection: Black Women Community Workers, Religious Agency and the Force of Faith." In *Women and Religion in the African Diaspora: Knowledge, Power, and Performance.* Edited by R. Marie Griffith and Barbara Dianne Savage. Baltimore: Johns Hopkins University Press, 2006, 179–196.

———. *If It Weren't for the Women: Black Women's Experience and Womanist Culture in Church and Community.* Maryknoll, N.Y.: Orbis Books, 2001.

Gilmore, Glenda Elizabeth. *Defying Dixie: The Radical Roots of Civil Rights, 1919–1950.* New York: W. W. Norton, 2008.

———. "False Friends and Avowed Enemies: Southern African Americans and Party Allegiances in the 1920s." In *Jumpin' Jim Crow: Southern Politics from Civil War to Civil Rights.* Edited by Jane Dailey, Glenda Elizabeth Gilmore, and Bryant Simon. Princeton, N.J.: Princeton University Press, 2000, 219–238.

———. *Gender and Jim Crow: Women and the Politics of White Supremacy in North Carolina, 1896–1920.* Chapel Hill: University of North Carolina Press, 1996.

Glaude, Eddie S. Jr. *Exodus! Religion, Race, and Nation in Early Nineteenth-Century Black America.* Chicago: University of Chicago Press, 2000.

Goings, Kenneth W. *"The NAACP Comes of Age": The Defeat of Judge John J. Parker.* Bloomington: Indiana University Press, 1990.

Goodstein, Anita Shafer. "A Rare Alliance: African American and White Women in Tennessee Elections of 1919 and 1920." *Journal of Southern History* 64 (May 1998): 219–246.

Gordon, Felice D. *After Winning: The Legacy of New Jersey Suffragists, 1920–1947.* New Brunswick: Rutgers University Press, 1986.

———. "After Winning: The New Jersey Suffragists in the Political Parties, 1920–30." *New Jersey History* 101 (Fall/Winter 1983): 13–35.

Gordon, Linda. "Black and White Visions of Welfare: Women's Welfare Activism, 1890–1945." *Journal of American History* 70 (September 1991): 559–590.

———. *Pitied but Not Entitled: Single Mothers and the History of Welfare, 1890–1953.* New York: Maxwell Macmillan International, 1994.

Gorrell, Donald K. *The Age of Social Responsibility: The Social Gospel in the Progressive Era, 1900–1920.* Macon: Mercer University Press, 1988.

Gravely, William. *Gilbert Haven Methodist Abolitionist: A Study in Race, Religion, and Reform, 1850–1880.* Nashville: Abingdon Press, 1973.

Green, Elna C. *Southern Strategies: Southern Women and the Woman Suffrage Question.* Chapel Hill: University of North Carolina Press, 1997.

Greenwald, Maurine Weiner. *Women, War, and Work: The Impact of World War I on Women Workers in the United States.* Westport, Conn.: Greenwood Press, 1980.

Gustafson, Melanie Susan. *Women and the Republican Party, 1854–1924.* Urbana: University of Illinois Press, 2001.

Guy-Sheftall, Beverly. *Daughters of Sorrow: Attitudes toward Black Women, 1880–1920.* Brooklyn, N.Y.: Carlson Publishing, 1990.

Hackett, David G. "Gender and Religion in American Culture, 1870–1930." *Religion and American Culture* 5 (Summer 1995): 125–157.

Hahn, Harlan. "Ethnic Minorities: Politics and the Family in Suburbia." In *The Urbanization of the Suburbs.* Edited by Louis Masotti and Jeffrey K. Hadden. Beverly Hills: Sage Publications, 1973, 135–205.

Hall, Jacquelyn Dowd. "The Long Civil Rights March and the Political Use of the Past." *Journal of American History* 91 (March 2005): 1233–1263.

———. *Revolt against Chivalry: Jessie Daniel Ames and the Women's Campaign against Lynching*. New York: Columbia University Press, 1979.

Handen, Ella. "Social Service Stations: New Jersey Settlement Houses Founded in the Progressive Era." *New Jersey History* 108 (Spring/Summer 1990): 1–29.

Hanley, Mark Y. "Revolution at Home and Abroad: Radical Implications of the Protestant Call to Missions, 1825–1870." In *The Foreign Missionary Enterprise at Home: Explorations in North American Cultural History*. Edited by Daniel H. Bays and Grant Wacker. Tuscaloosa: University of Alabama Press, 2003, 44–59.

Harley, Sharon. "For the Good of the Family and Race: Gender, Work and Domestic Roles in the Black Community, 1890–1930." *Signs* 15:2 (Winter 1990): 336–349.

———. "Nannie Helen Burroughs: 'The Black Goddess of Liberty.'" *Journal of Negro History* 81 (Spring, Summer, Winter 1996): 62–71.

———. "When Your Work Is Not Who You Are: The Development of a Working-Class Consciousness among Afro-American Women." In *Gender, Class, Race, and Reform in the Progressive Era*. Edited by Noralee Frankel and Nancy S. Dye. Lexington: University Press of Kentucky, 1991, 42–55.

Hayden, Dolores. *Redesigning the American Dream: The Future of Housing, Work, and Family Life*. New York: W. W. Norton, 1984.

Hendricks, Wanda A. "African American Women as Political Constituents in Chicago, 1913–1915." In *We Have Come to Stay: American Women and Political Parties, 1880–1960*. Edited by Melanie Gustafson, Kristie Miller, and Elisabeth I. Perry. Albuquerque: University of New Mexico Press, 1999, 55–64.

———. *Gender, Race, and Politics in the Midwest: Black Club Women in Illinois*. Bloomington: Indiana University Press, 1998.

———. "Ida B. Wells-Barnett and the Alpha Suffrage Club of Chicago." In *One Woman, One Vote: Rediscovering the Woman Suffrage Movement*. Edited by Marjorie Spruill Wheeler. Troutdale, Oreg.: New Sage Press, 1996, 263–275.

Hewitt, Nancy A. "From Seneca Falls to Suffrage? Reimagining a "Master" Narrative in U. S. Women's History." In *No Permanent Waves: Recasting Histories of U. S. Feminism*. Edited by Nancy A. Hewitt. New Brunswick, N.J.: Rutgers University Press, 2010, 15–38.

Hickel, K. Walter. "War, Region, and Social Welfare: Federal Aid to Servicemen's Dependents in the South, 1917–1921." *Journal of American History* 87 (March 2001): 1362–1391.

Hicks, Cheryl D. *Talk with You Like a Woman: African American Women, Justice, and Reform in New York, 1890–1935*. Chapel Hill: University of North Carolina Press, 2010.

Higginbotham, Evelyn Brooks. "Clubwomen and Electoral Politics in the 1920s." In *African American Women and the Vote, 1837–1967*. Edited by Ann D. Gordon with Bettye Collier-Thomas, John H. Bracey, Arlene Voski Avakian, and Joyce Avrech Berkman. Amherst: University of Massachusetts Press, 1997, 134–155.

———. "In Politics to Stay: Black Women Leaders and Party Politics in the 1920s." In *Women, Politics, and Change*. Edited by Louise Tilly and Patricia Gurin. New York: Russell Sage Foundation, 1990, 199–220.

————. "Religion, Politics, and Gender: The Leadership of Nannie Helen Burroughs." In *This Far by Faith: Readings in African-American Women's Religious Biography*. Edited by Judith Weisenfeld and Richard Newman. New York: Routledge, 1996, 147–157.

————. "Rethinking Vernacular Culture: Black Religion and Race Records in the 1920s and 1930s." In *The House That Race Built: Black Americans, U.S. Terrain*. Edited by Lubiano Wahneema. New York: Pantheon Books, 1997, 157–177.

————. *Righteous Discontent: The Women's Movement in the Black Baptist Church, 1880–1920*. Cambridge: Harvard University Press, 1993.

Hine, Darlene Clark. "Rape and the Inner Lives of Black Women in the Middle West." *Signs* 14 (Summer 1989): 912–920.

Hirsch, Arnold R. "'Containment' on the Home Front: Race and Federal Housing Policy from the New Deal to the Cold War." *Journal of Urban History* 26 (January 2000): 158–190.

————. "Less than *Plessy*: The Inner City, Suburbs, and the State-Sanctioned Residential Segregation in the Age of *Brown*." In *The New Suburban History*. Edited by Kevin M. Kruse and Thomas J. Sugrue. Chicago: University of Chicago Press, 2006), 33–56.

————. *Making the Second Ghetto: Race and Housing in Chicago, 1940–1960*. New York: Cambridge University Press, 1983.

Howe, Daniel Walker. "The Evangelical Movement and Political Culture in the North during the Second Party System." *Journal of American History* 77 (March 1991): 1216–1239.

Hunter, Tera W. *To 'Joy My Freedom: Southern Black Women's Lives and Labor after the Civil War*. Cambridge: Harvard University Press, 2002.

Hutchinson, William R. *Errand to the World: American Protestant Thought and Foreign Missions*. Chicago: University of Chicago Press, 1993.

Jackson, Kenneth T. *Crabgrass Frontier: The Suburbanization of the United States*. New York: Oxford University Press, 1985.

————. *The Ku Klux Klan in the City 1915–1930*. New York: Oxford University Press, 1967.

Jackson, Kenneth T., and Barbara B. Jackson. "The Black Experience in Newark: The Growth of the Ghetto, 1870–1970." In *New Jersey since 1860: New Findings and Interpretations*. Edited by William C. Wright. Papers Presented at the Third Annual New Jersey History Symposium, December 4, 1971. Trenton: New Jersey Historical Commission, 1972, 36–59.

Jacobson, Matthew Frye. *Whiteness of a Different Color: European Immigrants and the Alchemy of Race*. Cambridge: Harvard University Press, 2001.

Johnson, Kenneth R. "White Racial Attitudes as a Factor in the Arguments against the Nineteenth Amendment." *Phylon* 31 (Spring 1970): 31–37.

Jones, Adrienne Lash. "Struggle among Saints: African American Women and the YWCA, 1870–1920." In *Men and Women Adrift: The YMCA and the YWCA in the City*. Edited by Nina Mjagkij and Margaret Spratt. New York: NYU Press, 1997, 160–187.

Jones, Jacqueline. *Labor of Love, Labor of Sorrow: Black Women, Work, and the Family from Slavery to the Present*. New York: Vintage Books, 1986.

Jones, Martha S. *All Bound Up Together: The Woman Question in African American Public Culture, 1830–1900*. Chapel Hill: University of North Carolina Press, 2007.

Judson, Sarah Mercer. "'Solving the Girl Problem': Race, Womanhood, and Leisure in Atlanta during World War I." In *Women Shaping the South: Creating and Confronting Change*. Edited by Angela Boswell and Judith N. McArthur. Columbia: University of Missouri Press, 2006, 152–173.

Katzman, David M. *Seven Days a Week: Women and Domestic Service in Industrializing America*. New York: Oxford University Press, 1978.

Katznelson, Ira. *When Affirmative Action Was White: An Untold History of Racial Inequality*. New York: W. W. Norton, 2005.

Kennedy, David M. *Freedom from Fear: The American People in Depression and War, 1929–1945*. New York: Oxford University Press, 1999.

———. *Over Here: The First World War and American Society*. New York: Oxford University Press, 1980.

Kirby, John B. *Black Americans in the Roosevelt Era: Liberalism and Race*. Knoxville: University of Tennessee Press, 1980.

Kornweibel, Theodore, Jr. *"Seeing Red": Federal Campaigns against Black Militancy, 1919–1925*. Bloomington: Indiana University Press, 1998.

Kramer, Steve. "Uplifting Our 'Downtrodden Sisterhood': Victoria Earle Matthews and New York City's White Rose Mission, 1897–1907." *Journal of African American History* 91 (Summer 2006): 243–266.

Kruse, Kevin M., and Thomas J. Sugrue, ed. *The New Suburban History*. Chicago: University of Chicago Press, 2006.

Ladd-Taylor, Molly. *Mother-Work: Women, Child Welfare, and the State, 1890–1930*. Urbana: University of Illinois Press, 1994.

Lasch-Quinn, Elisabeth. *Black Neighbors: Race and the Limits of Reform in the American Settlement House Movement, 1890–1945*. Chapel Hill: University of North Carolina Press, 1993.

Lay, Shawn. *Hooded Knights on the Niagara: The Ku Klux Klan in Buffalo, New York*. New York: NYU Press, 1995.

Leiby, James. *Charity and Corrections in New Jersey: A History of State Welfare Institutions*. New Brunswick: Rutgers University Press, 1967.

Lemert, Charles, and Esme Bhan, ed. *The Voice of Anna Julia Cooper: Including a Voice from the South and Other Important Essays, Papers, and Letters*. Lanham, Md.: Rowman & Littlefield, 1998.

Lemons, J. Stanley. "The Sheppard-Towner Act: Progressivism in the 1920s." *Journal of American History* 55 (March 1969): 776–786.

Lentz-Smith, Adriane. *Freedom Struggles: African Americans and World War I*. Cambridge, Mass.: Harvard University Press, 2009.

Lewis, David Levering. *W. E. B. Du Bois: Biography of a Race, 1868–1919*. New York: Henry Holt, 1993.

———. *W. E. B. Du Bois: The Fight for Equality and the American Century, 1919–1963*. New York: Henry Holt, 2000.

Lichtman, Allan J. *Prejudice and the Old Order: The Presidential Election of 1928.* Chapel Hill: University of North Carolina Press, 1979.

Link, Arthur S. *Woodrow Wilson and the Progressive Era, 1900–1920.* New York: Harper & Row, 1954; Harper Torchbooks, 1963.

Lorini, Alessandra. *Rituals of Race: American Public Culture and the Search for Racial Democracy.* Charlottesville: University of Virginia Press, 1999.

Lynn, Susan. *Progressive Women in Conservative Times: Racial Justice, Peace, and Feminism, 1945 to the 1960s.* New Brunswick, N.J.: Rutgers University Press, 1992.

MacLean, Nancy. *Behind the Mask of Chivalry: The Making of the Second Ku Klux Klan.* New York: Oxford University Press, 1994.

———. "White Women, Klan Violence in the 1920s: Agency, Complicity, and the Politics of Women's History." *Gender and History* 3 (1991): 285–303.

Maffly-Kipp, Laurie F. *Setting Down the Sacred Past: African-American Race Histories.* Cambridge: Belknap Press of Harvard University Press, 2010.

Mahoney, Joseph F. "Woman Suffrage and the Urban Masses." *New Jersey History* 87 (Autumn 1969): 151–172.

Maring, Norman H. *Baptists in New Jersey: A Study in Transition.* Valley Forge: Judson Press, 1964.

Marsh, Margaret. "From Separation to Togetherness: The Social Construction of Domestic Space in American Suburbs, 1840–1915." *Journal of American History* 76 (September 1989): 506–526.

———. *Suburban Lives.* New Brunswick: Rutgers University Press, 1990.

Marshall, Susan E. *Splintered Sisterhood: Gender and Class in the Campaign against Woman Suffrage.* Madison: University of Wisconsin Press, 1997.

Martin, Sandy Dwayne. *Black Baptists and African Missions: The Origins of a Movement, 1880–1915.* Macon, Ga.: Mercer University Press, 1989.

Materson, Lisa G. *For the Freedom of Her Race: Black Women and Electoral Politics in Illinois, 1877–1932.* Chapel Hill: University of North Carolina Press, 2009.

Mattingly, Carol. *Well-Tempered Women: Nineteenth-Century Temperance Rhetoric.* Carbondale: Southern Illinois University Press, 1998.

Mattingly, Paul H. *Suburban Landscapes: Culture and Politics in a New York Metropolitan Community.* Baltimore: Johns Hopkins University Press, 2001.

May, Vanessa H. *Unprotected Labor: Household Workers, Politics, and Middle Class Reform in New York, 1870–1940.* Chapel Hill: University of North Carolina Press, 2011.

Mettler, Suzanne. *Dividing Citizens: Gender and Federalism in New Deal Public Policy.* Ithaca, N.Y.: Cornell University Press, 1998.

Meyer, Stephen Grant. *As Long as They Don't Move Next Door: Segregation and Racial Conflict in American Neighborhoods.* Lanham, Md.: Rowman & Littlefield, 2000.

Meyerowitz, Joanne J. *Women Adrift: Independent Wage-Earners in Chicago, 1880–1930.* Chicago: University of Chicago Press, 1988.

Milkman, Ruth. *Gender at Work: The Dynamics of Job Segregation by Sex during World War II.* Urbana: University of Illinois Press, 1987.

Miller, Robert Moats. *American Protestantism and Social Issues, 1919–1939*. Chapel Hill: University of North Carolina Press, 1958.

———. "The Attitude of American Protestantism toward the Negro, 1919–1939." *Journal of Negro History* 41 (July 1956): 215–240.

———. "A Footnote to the Role of the Protestant Churches in the Election of 1928." *Church History* 25 (June 1956): 145–159.

Mink, Gwendolyn. *The Wages of Motherhood: Inequality in the Welfare State, 1917–1942*. Ithaca, N.Y.: Cornell University Press, 1995.

Mjagkij, Nina. *Light in the Darkness: African Americans and the YMCA, 1852–1946*. Lexington: University Press of Kentucky, 1994.

Mobley, Kendal P. "The Ecumenical Woman's Missionary Movement: Helen Barrett Montgomery and *The Baptist*, 1920–30." In *Gender and the Social Gospel*. Edited by Wendy J. Deichmann Edwards and Carolyn DeSwarte Gifford. Urbana: University of Illinois Press, 2003, 167–181.

Molina, Natalia. *Fit to Be Citizens? Public Health and Race in Los Angeles, 1879–1939*. Berkeley: University of California Press, 2006.

Moore, Edmund A. *A Catholic Runs for President: The Campaign of 1928*. New York: Ronald Press Company, 1956.

Moore, Shirley Ann Wilson. *To Place Our Deeds: The African American Community in Richmond, California, 1910–1963*. Berkley: University of California Press, 2000.

Morgan, David. *The Sacred Gaze: Religious Visual Culture in Theory and Practice*. Berkeley: University of California Press, 2005.

Mumford, Kevin. *Newark: A History of Race, Rights, and Riots in America*. New York: NYU Press, 2007.

Muncy, Robyn. *Creating a Female Reform Dominion in American Reform, 1890–1935*. New York: Oxford University Press, 1991.

Murphy, Paul. "Sources and Natures of Intolerance in the 1920's," *Journal of American History* 51(June 1964): 60–76.

Murray, Robert K. *Red Scare: A Study of National Hysteria, 1919–1920*. New York: McGraw-Hill, 1955.

McBride, David. *From TB to AIDS: Epidemics among Urban Blacks since 1900*. Albany: SUNY Press, 1991.

McClymer, John F. *War and Welfare: Social Engineering in America, 1890–1925*. Westport, Conn.: Greenwood Press, 1980.

McCormick, Richard P., and Katheryne C. McCormick. *Equality Deferred: Women Candidates for the New Jersey Assembly, 1920–1993*. New Brunswick, N.J.: Rutgers University Press, 1994.

McGerr, Michael. "Political Style and Women's Power, 1830–1900." *Journal of American History* 77 (December 1990): 864–885.

McGuire, Danielle L. "'It Was Like All of Us Had Been Raped': Sexual Violence, Community Mobilization, and the African American Freedom Struggle." *Journal of American History* 91 (December 2004): 906–931.

Newman, Louise M. *White Women's Rights: The Racial Origins of Feminism in the United States*. New York: Oxford University Press, 1999.

Nicolaides, Becky M. *My Blue Heaven: Life and Politics in the Working-Class Suburbs of Los Angeles, 1920–1965*. Chicago: University of Chicago Press, 2002.

Nielsen, Kim E. *Un-American Womanhood: Antiradicalism, Antifeminism, and the First Red Scare*. Columbus: Ohio State University Press, 2001.

North, Eric M. "William Ingraham Haven." In *The Encyclopedia of World Methodism*, Vol. I. Nashville: United Methodist Publishing House, 1974, 1094–1095.

Olcott, Edward S. *20th Century Summit, 1899–1999*. Summit, N.J.: Howell & Williams, 1998.

Orsi, Robert A. "The Religious Boundaries of an In-Between People: Street *Feste* and the Problem of the Dark-Skinned Other in Italian Harlem, 1920–1990." In *Gods of the City: Religion and the Urban American Landscape*. Edited by Robert A. Orsi. Bloomington: Indiana University Press, 1999, 257–288.

Palmer, Phyllis M. *Domesticity and Dirt: Housewives and Domestic Servants in the United States, 1920–1945*. Philadelphia: Temple University Press, 1989.

Paulsson, Martin. *The Social Anxieties of Progressive Reform: Atlantic City, 1854–1920*. New York: NYU Press, 1994.

Peiss, Kathy Lee. *Cheap Amusements: Working Women and Leisure in New York*. Philadelphia: Temple University Press, 1986.

Phillips, Kimberley L. *Alabama North: African-American Migrants, Community, and Working-Class Activism in Cleveland, 1915–1945*. Chicago: University of Illinois Press, 1999.

Piper, John F. *The American Churches in World War I*. Athens: Ohio University Press, 1985.

Poirier, Suzanne. *Chicago's War on Syphilis, 1937–1940: The Times, the Trib, and the Clap Doctor*. Urbana: University of Illinois Press, 1995.

Poole, Mary. *The Segregated Origins of Social Security: African Americans and the Welfare State*. Chapel Hill: University of North Carolina Press, 2006.

Price, Clement. "The Beleaguered City as Promised Land: Blacks in Newark, 1917–1947." In *Urban New Jersey since 1870. Papers at the Sixth Annual New Jersey History Symposium*. Edited by William C. Wright. Trenton: New Jersey Historical Society, 1975, 10–45.

Promey, Sally. "Taste Cultures: The Visual Practice of Liberal Protestantism, 1940–1965." In *Practicing Protestants: Histories of Christian Life in America, 1630–1965*. Edited by Laurie Maffly-Kipp, Leigh E. Schmidt, and Mark Valeri. Baltimore: Johns Hopkins University Press, 2006, 250–293.

Reed, Christopher Robert. "Black Chicago Political Realignment during the Great Depression and New Deal." In *Depression, War, and the New Migration, 1930–1960*. Edited by Kenneth L. Kusmer. New York: General Publishing, 1991, 82–96.

Reimers, David M. *White Protestantism and the Negro*. New York: Oxford University Press, 1963.

Reynolds, John F. *Testing Democracy: Electoral Behavior and Progressive Reform in New Jersey, 1880–1920.* Chapel Hill: University of North Carolina Press, 1988.

Ritzdorf, Marsha. "Sex, Lies, and Urban Life: How Municipal Planning Marginalizes African American Women and Their Families." In *Gendering the City: Women, Boundaries, and Visions of Urban Life.* Edited by Kristina B. Miranne and Alma H. Young. Lanham, Md.: Rowman & Littlefield, 2000, 169–181.

Robertson, Nancy Marie. *Christian Sisterhood, Race Relations and the YWCA, 1906–46.* Urbana: University of Illinois Press, 2007.

Rollins, Judith. *Between Women: Domestics and Their Employers.* Philadelphia: Temple University Press, 1985.

Rouse, Jacqueline Anne. *Lugenia Burns Hope: Black Southern Reformer.* Athens: University of Georgia Press, 1989.

Rudwick, Elliot M. *Race Riot in East Saint Louis July 2, 1917.* Cleveland: World Publishing Company, 1970.

Salem, Dorothy C. *To Better Our World: Black Women in Organized Reform, 1890–1920.* Brooklyn, N.Y.: Carlson Publishing, 1990.

Sassi, Jonathan D. *A Republic of Righteousness: The Public Christianity of the Post-Revolutionary New England Clergy.* Oxford: Oxford University Press, 2001.

Scharf, Lois. *To Work and to Wed: Female Employment, Feminism, and the Great Depression.* Westport, Conn.: Greenwood Press, 1980.

Schechter, Patricia A. *Ida B. Wells-Barnett and American Reform, 1880–1930.* Chapel Hill: University of North Carolina Press, 2001.

Scheiber, Jane L., and Harry N. Scheiber. "The Wilson Administration and the Wartime Mobilization of Black Americans, 1917–18." *Labor History* X (Summer 1969): 433–458.

Schneider, Mark R. *"We Return Fighting": The Civil Rights Movement in the Jazz Age.* Boston: Northeastern University Press, 2002.

Schuyler, Lorraine Gates. *The Weight of Their Votes: Southern Women and Political Leverage in the 1920s.* Chapel Hill: University of North Carolina Press, 2006.

Scott, Anne Firor. "Most Invisible of All: Black Women's Voluntary Associations." *Journal of Southern History* 56 (1990): 3–22.

Scott, James C. *Domination and the Arts of Resistance: Hidden Transcripts.* New Haven, Conn.: Yale University Press, 1990.

Sernett, Milton. *Bound for the Promised Land: African American Religion and the Great Migration.* Durham: Duke University Press, 1997.

Shaw, Stephanie J. *What a Woman Ought to Be and to Do: Black Professional Women Workers during the Jim Crow Era.* Chicago: University of Chicago Press, 1996.

Sherman, Richard B. "The Harding Administration and the Negro: An Opportunity Lost." *Journal of Negro History* 49 (July 1964): 151–168.

———. *The Republican Party and Black America from McKinley to Hoover, 1896–1933.* Charlottesville: University Press of Virginia, 1973.

Silva, Ruth C. *Rum, Religion, and Votes: 1928 Re-Examined.* University Park: Pennsylvania State University Press, 1962.

Sitkoff, Harvard. *A New Deal for Blacks: The Emergence of Civil Rights as a National Issue: The Depression Decade.* Oxford: Oxford University Press, 1978.

Smith, Susan L. *Sick and Tired of Being Sick and Tired: Black Women's Health Activism in America, 1890–1950.* Philadelphia: University of Pennsylvania Press, 1995.

Southern, Eileen. *The Music of Black Americans: A History*, 2nd ed. New York: W. W. Norton, 1983.

Spruill, Marjorie Julian. "Race, Reform, and Reaction at the Turn of the Century: Southern Suffragists, the NAWSA, and the 'Southern Strategy' in Context." In *Votes for Women: The Struggle for Suffrage Revisited.* Edited by Jean H. Baker. New York: Oxford University Press, 2002, 102–117.

Stellhorn, Paul A. "Boom, Bust and Boosterisms: Attitudes, Residency and the Newark Chamber of Commerce, 1920–1941." In *Urban New Jersey since 1870, Papers Presented at the Sixth Annual New Jersey Historical Symposium.* Edited by William C. Wright. Trenton: New Jersey Historical Commission, 1975, 46–77.

Stickle, Warren E., III. "The Applejack Campaign of 1919: 'As "Wet" as the Atlantic Ocean." *New Jersey History* 89 (Spring 1971): 5–22.

———. "Edward I. Edwards and the Urban Coalition of 1919." *New Jersey History* 90 (Summer 1972): 83–96.

Stilgoe, John R. *Borderland: Origins of the American Suburb, 1820–1939.* New Haven: Yale University Press, 1988.

Strauss, Sylvia. "The Passage of Woman Suffrage in New Jersey, 1911–1920." *New Jersey History* 111 (Fall/Winter 1993): 18–39.

Strong, Douglas M. *Perfectionist Politics: Abolitionism and the Religious Tensions of American Democracy.* Syracuse, N.Y.: Syracuse University Press, 1999.

Sugrue, Thomas J. "Crabgrass-Roots Politics: Race, Rights and the Reaction against Liberalism in the Urban North, 1940–1964." *Journal of American History* 82 (September 1995): 551–578.

———. *The Origins of the Urban Crisis: Race and Inequality in Postwar Detroit.* Princeton, N.J.: Princeton University Press, 1996.

———. *Sweet Land of Liberty: The Forgotten Struggle for Civil Rights in the North.* New York: Random House, 2008.

Sullivan, Patricia. *Days of Hope: Race and Democracy in the New Deal Era.* Chapel Hill: University of North Carolina Press, 1996.

Summers, Martin. *Manliness and Its Discontents: The Black Middle Class and the Transformation of Masculinity, 1900–1930.* Chapel Hill: University of North Carolina Press, 2004.

Sutherland, Daniel. *Americans and Their Servants: Domestic Service in the United States from 1800–1920.* Baton Rouge: Louisiana State University Press, 1985.

Szymanski, Ann-Marie. *Pathways to Prohibition: Radicals, Moderates, and Social Movement Outcomes.* Durham: Duke University Press, 2003.

Taylor, Henry Louis. "Creating the Metropolis in Black and White: Black Suburbanization and the Planning Movement in Cincinnati, 1900–1950." In *Historical*

Roots of the Urban Crisis: African Americans in the Industrial City, 1900–1950. Edited by Henry Louis Taylor, Jr., and Walter Hill. New York: Garland, 2000, 51–71.

Terborg-Penn, Rosalyn. *African American Women in the Struggle for the Vote, 1850– 1920.* Bloomington: Indiana University Press, 1998.

———. "African American Women and the Woman Suffrage Movement." In *One Woman, One Vote: Rediscovering the Woman Suffrage Movement.* Edited by Marjorie Spruill Wheeler. Troutdale, Oreg.: New Sage Press, 1996, 135–155.

———. "African American Women's Networks in the Anti-Lynching Crusade." In *Gender, Class, Race, Reform in the Progressive Era.* Edited by Noralee Frankel and Nancy S. Dye. Lexington: University of Kentucky Press, 1991, 148–161.

———. "Discontented Black Feminists: Prelude and Postscript to the Passage of the Nineteenth Amendment." In *Decades of Discontent: The Women's Movement, 1920–1940.* Edited by Lois Scharf and Joan M. Jensen. Westport, Conn.: Greenwood Press, 1983, 261–278.

Thomas, William B. "Schooling as a Political Instrument of Social Control: School Responses to Black Migrant Youth in Buffalo, New York, 1917–1940." In *The Great Migration and After, 1917–1930.* Edited by Kenneth L. Kusmer. New York : Garland, 1991, 217–230.

Thompson, Dorothy, ed. *The Essential E. P. Thompson.* New York: New Press, 2001.

Tilly, Louise A., and Patricia Gurin, ed. *Women, Politics, and Change.* New York: Russell Sage Foundation, 1990.

Tucker, Susan. *Southern Women: Domestic Workers and Their Employers in the Segregated South.* New York: Schocken Books, 1988.

Tuttle, William B. *Race Riot: Chicago in the Red Summer of 1919.* New York: Atheneum, 1970.

Tweed, Thomas A. ed. *Retelling U.S. Religious History.* Berkeley: University of California Press, 1997.

Vecoli, Rudolph J. *The People of New Jersey.* Princeton, N.J.: D. Van Nostrand Inc., 1965.

Vose, Clement. *Caucasians Only: The Supreme Court, the NAACP, and the Restrictive Covenant Cases.* Berkeley: University of California Press, 1973.

Wall, Wendy L. *Inventing the "American Way": The Politics of Consensus from the New Deal to the Civil Rights Movement.* Oxford: Oxford University Press, 2008.

Walls, William J. *The African Methodist Episcopal Zion Church: Reality of the Black Church.* Charlotte: A. M. E. Zion Publishing House, 1974.

Ware, Susan. *Beyond Suffrage: Women in the New Deal.* Cambridge, Mass.: Harvard University Press, 1981.

Washington, James M. *Frustrated Fellowship: The Black Baptist Quest for Social Power.* Macon, Ga.: Mercer University Press, 1990.

———, ed. *Essential Writings and Speeches of Martin Luther King, Jr.* New York: HarperSanFrancisco, 1986.

Watson, Richard L. "The Defeat of Judge Parker: A Study in Pressure Groups and Politics." *Mississippi Valley Historical Review* 50 (September 1963): 213–234.

Weisenfeld, Judith. *African American Women and Christian Activism: New York's Black YWCA, 1905–1945*. Cambridge, Mass.: Harvard University Press, 1997.

Weiss, Nancy J. *Farewell to the Party of Lincoln: Black Politics in the Age of FDR*. Princeton, N.J.: Princeton University Press, 1983.

———. *The National Urban League, 1910–1940*. New York: Oxford University Press, 1974.

———. "The Negro and the New Freedom: Fighting Wilsonian Segregation." *Political Science Quarterly* 84 (March 1969): 67–79.

Whalen, Mark. *The Great War and the Culture of the New Negro*. Gainesville: University Press of Florida, 2008.

White, Deborah Gray. *Ar'n't I a Woman? Female Slaves in the Plantation South*. New York: W. W. Norton, 1987.

———. "The Cost of Club Work, the Price of Black Feminism." In *Visible Women: New Essays on American Activism*. Edited by Nancy Hewitt and Suzanne Lebsock. Urbana: University of Illinois Press, 1993, 247–269.

———. *Too Heavy a Load: Black Women in Defense of Themselves,1894–1994*. New York: W. W. Norton, 1999.

White, Ronald C., Jr. *Liberty and Justice for All: Racial Reform and the Social Gospel (1877–1925)*. San Francisco: Harper & Row, 1990.

Wiese, Andrew. *Places of Their Own: African American Suburbanization in the Twentieth Century*. Chicago: University of Chicago Press, 2005.

Williams, Heather. *Self-Taught: African American Education in Slavery and Freedom*. Chapel Hill: University of North Carolina Press, 2005.

Williams, Walter L. *Black Americans and the Evangelization of Africa, 1877–1900*. Madison: University of Wisconsin Press, 1982.

Wills, David W., and Richard Newman, ed. *Black Apostles at Home and Abroad: Afro-Americans and the Christian Mission from the Revolution to Reconstruction*. Boston: G. K. Hall, 1982.

Wilson, Jan Doolittle. *The Women's Joint Congressional Committee and the Politics in Illinois, 1877–1932*. Chapel Hill: University of North Carolina Press, 2009.

Wolcott, Victoria W. "'Bible, Bath, and Broom': Nannie Helen Burrough's National Training School and African-American Racial Uplift." *Journal of Women's History* 9 (Spring 1997): 88–110.

———. *Remaking Respectability: African American Women in Interwar Detroit*. Chapel Hill: University of North Carolina Press, 2001.

Woodruff, Nan Elizabeth. "The New Negro in the American Congo: World War I and the Elaine, Arkansas Massacre of 1919." In *Time Longer than Rope: A Century of African American Activism, 1850–1950*. Edited by Charles M. Payne and Adam Green. New York: NYU Press, 2003, 150–178.

Woodward, C. Vann. *Origins of the New South, 1877–1913*. Baton Rouge: Louisiana University Press, 1990.

Wright, Giles R. *Afro-Americans in New Jersey: A Short History*. Trenton: New Jersey Historical Commission, 1988.

Wright, Marion Thompson. *The Education of Negroes in New Jersey*. New York: Bureau of Publications: Teachers College, 1941. Reprint AMS Press, 1972.

———. "Extending Civil Rights in New Jersey through the Division against Discrimination." *Journal of Negro History* 38 (January 1953): 91–107.

Wye, Christopher. "The New Deal and the Negro Community: Toward a Broader Conceptualization." *Journal of American History* 59 (December 1972): 621–639.

Zangrando, Robert L. *The NAACP Crusade against Lynching, 1909–1950*. Philadelphia: Temple University Press, 1980.

Dissertations

Denomme, Janine Marie. "'To End This Day of Strife': Churchwomen and the Campaign for Integration, 1920–1970." Ph.D. diss., University of Pennsylvania, 2001.

Dodyk, Delight W. "Education and Agitation: The Woman Suffrage Movement in New Jersey," Ph.D. diss., Rutgers University, 1977.

Hamilton, Tullia Kay Brown. "The National Association of Colored Women, 1896–1920." Ph.D. diss., Emory University, 1978.

Nimmons, Julius F. "Social Reform and Moral Uplift in the Black Community, 1890–1910: Social Settlements, Temperance and Social Purity." Ph.D. diss., Harvard University, 1981.

Wilson, Leslie. "Dark Spaces: An Account of Afro-American Suburbanization, 1890–1950." Ph.D. diss., City University of New York, 1991.

INDEX

A. Harry Moore Colored League, 120

Ader, Lulu Hawthorne: Glenwood Place controversy, 144–145; Summit public health nurse, 134–135, 205n35; surveys black families, 135, 206n37; WPA funds and "social evil," 134–135

African American population, 6, 7, 17, 36, 59, 127, 129, 130, 178n2, 195n90

African Methodist Episcopal (AME) Church, 47, 48, 49, 50

African Methodist Episcopal Zion (AME Zion) Church, 2, 33, 49, 52, 60, 97, 100, 131, 151, 194n78; WH& FM, 33, 61, 151. *See also* Randolph, Florence Spearing; Woman's Home and Foreign Mission Society, AME Zion

Afro-American Baptists of New Jersey, 42

agency, 2, 5, 15, 39, 54, 64, 125, 155, 178n71, 202n109

Alexander, Walter, 77, 108, 111–112, 113

alterity, strategy of, 32

American Society of Friends. *See* Quaker

American Baptist Home Missionary Society (ABHMS), 7, 18, 20; schools and seminaries, 20, 34; Woman's Home Mission as model of Christian womanhood, 38. *See also* Northern Baptists

American Red Cross. *See* Red Cross

Ames, Jessie Daniel, 193n63

Anderson, Marian, 150

Anthony, Susan B., 87

anti-lynching bill, 86, 88, 90, 110, 157. *See also* Dyer Anti-Lynching Bill

Anti-Lynching Crusade, 13, 83, 87–89, 91, 110; white women's organizations decline to endorse, 88, 91

Anti-Lynching Crusaders, 88–89

Association Opposed to Woman's Suffrage, 74; 184n81

Association of Southern Women for the Prevention of Lynching (ASWPL), 193n63

Baird, David: votes against woman suffrage vote, 74, 184n82; Burroughs and NAACP oppose, 119–120, 201n88; CWRC and Johnson support, 119–121; white women oppose, 201n79

Baptist Woman's Convention. *See* Woman's Convention

Baptists, New Jersey (white), respond to racial violence, 92, 99

Bassett, Mrs. Carroll (Margaret K.), 74, 184n81

Batson, Flora, "Double-Voiced Queen of Song," 26, 168n44

Bederman, Gail, 92

"Better Homes in America" campaign, 79–80, 186n105

Bible Bands, 38, 40–43; opposed by clergy, 41, 173n17. *See also* "woman's work"

Biddle, Eli George, 60

ABOUT THE AUTHOR

Betty Livingston Adams is Research Fellow and Adjunct Faculty in the Department of History and Associate Fellow at the Rutgers Center for Historical Analysis at Rutgers University, New Brunswick, New Jersey. Her scholarship explores the intersection of race, class, and gender in African American/American religious and social history. An associate minister in suburban New Jersey, she returned to academia following a successful corporate career.

Made in the USA
Middletown, DE
18 May 2023